THE MESSENGER

THE MESSENGER

SHIV MALIK

First published by Guardian Faber in 2019
Guardian Faber is an imprint of Faber & Faber Ltd,
Bloomsbury House, 74–77 Great Russell Street,
London WC1B 3DA

First published in the USA in 2019

Guardian is a registered trade mark of
Guardian News & Media Ltd,
Kings Place, 90 York Way, London N1 9GU

Typeset by seagulls.net
Printed and bound by CPI Group (UK) Ltd, Croydon CR0 4YY

A CIP record for this book
is available from the British Library

ISBN 978-1-783-35045-2

2 4 6 8 10 9 7 5 3 1

To F.D.B. and E.V. Crowe

'Neither a man nor a crowd nor a nation can be trusted to act humanely or to think sanely under the influence of a great fear'

Bertrand Russell

'War is deception'

The Prophet Muhammad

PROLOGUE

I put it to you that it has always been like this. A sudden, horrific event occurs – a volcano erupts, a plague breaks out, an economy collapses – and we become overwhelmed by fear. But the event is not what we are afraid of. As soon as it occurs, it becomes the past. It is over. What we fear most is the future; the idea that out of nowhere disaster might befall us again.

In these moments we force ourselves to hunt for an explanation, a pattern, lines of cause and effect. We must know why these events have happened to us because we must reclaim a sense that tomorrow can again be made predictable. Our psychological survival depends on it.

Just imagine even the simplest human interaction being undertaken in a world where we were completely unable to foretell whether the sun will rise in the morning or the air will remain breathable hour by hour. Our minds would not endure more than one day.

The explanations we find for these horrific events do not necessarily have to be correct or true. They just have to serve their purpose – the story must make us feel the world is certain again. And as history shows us, if the facts do not comfort, a fiction will work just as well.

Our readiness in these instances to accept the reassuring fiction over the uncomforting fact has been the source of some of mankind's most inhumane deeds. The volcano erupts because the gods are unhappy with us and so we make a human sacrifice. Disease abounds because the devil has made mischief through his servants and so we hunt for witches. The German economy collapses because traitors are at work and so Jews are rounded up in their millions.

And yet, however inhumane the results, we are quietly grateful for these stories because they allow us to cope. They let us believe that the solution to averting future disaster is within our control. And those who tell us the stories – the shaman, the church, the dictator – are granted impressive powers over us.

This is also how terrorism works.

First the tactician, the military trainers, the explosive experts, the cell leaders, and the suicide bomber band together to induce fear by creating apparently random destruction involving as many people as possible. The more arbitrary the target – the train, the bar, the sporting event, the office block – the more we fear because the harder it becomes for us to predict what tomorrow will hold for us.

The person who follows this is the messenger. He has two further roles which are just as essential to the overall process. His first task is to threaten more of the same. He makes it clear that the future – both immediate and distant – will continue to be ambushed by bloody violence. This is the easy part – these words can be spoken by any thug. It's the second task that requires the oratorical skill.

Competing against other narratives, the messenger must somehow persuade us to do what he wants – leave his lands, hand over political power, give him money, convert to his religion. He does this by convincing us that we are the ones to blame for the destruction which has just been wreaked; that it is our actions that have brought about these consequences.

At first this may seem an unpromising strategy, but the messenger tells us this because he knows that his narrative holds a particular charm to our ears; if we are the cause of such events, then we must also hold the key to our own security. Who better to bring normality back to our lives than ourselves?

Like this, the messenger's speech suddenly becomes a comfort. His words become a siren's song. We want to do as he asks because he promises that life will go back to normal. But unless we resist the temptation, we will find ourselves ruined and sold out by the lowest of our mind's conceits: fear.

However, like volcanoes, plagues and war, the mechanics of terrorism have proven far more complex than our frightened minds have permitted us to believe. I should know. For the messenger is never all he seems.

AN INTRODUCTION

1

There it was. The bus. Its sidings peeled apart like the petals of a wilted red lily. The roof lying crumpled on the road somewhere up ahead. The blood of its passengers splashed so indelicately across the front of the faded grey, Portland-stone building beside it.

It was dark now, some twelve hours after the horror of the explosion. But the emergency services' halogen lamps illuminated far too much detail for a person to stomach.

Reflecting off the white sheeting, which was erected to box off the scene from the public, the light bounced right into the top deck. Blown from their bolts but still attached to the bus's shell, the seats appeared frozen mid-frame, as if caught in a desperate act of escape.

The victims, still nameless and unknown at this point, had been removed. Their limbs and lives had been ripped apart while undertaking the most prosaic of daily activities: riding the number 30.

We had been warned there would be an attack on London. The security services, the politicians, the British jihadis had all been right. And when it came it was nothing less than a series of suicide bombings. This one, the bus bombing, had been committed by a plump teenager from Yorkshire.

As a freelance journalist specialising in British radicalism, I knew I'd be commissioned to be part of the media effort to explain why this had happened, and who was responsible. What did the terrorists want? What would their demands be? And if they were British, how had they come to turn on their fellow citizens? That's why I felt compelled to come see the end point of their journey – their bloody achievement – with my own eyes.

That 7 July morning I'd been in Scotland like many other reporters, watching police beat back protestors from the fences surrounding the grounds of the Gleneagles Hotel, where world leaders had gathered for the G8 summit. When the news broke of a suspected attack I hurriedly drove down an emptied motorway back to London. Packed into vans, their sirens blazing, were hundreds upon hundreds of Metropolitan police officers – London's Praetorian Guard. Deployed to man the lines against anti-globalisation demonstrators far from their parish, you could see the guilty anguish on their faces through the van windows; they'd abandoned their posts and were desperate to return to their besieged capital.

The city's centre was uncomfortably silent without the usual drone of traffic. Lacking functioning public transport, tens of thousands of workers had migrated through the streets on foot to return home. Those who remained coalesced outside of pubs, part shocked, part curious, but still chatting almost casually without any obvious sign of panic on this balmy summer's evening. I could hear their voices as I stood inside the cordon, staring at this everyday object, now disfigured, parked by brute force about forty yards in front of me. I couldn't help but find myself fascinated – its new topography traced the instance of violence inflicted upon it. And yet I also felt physically repulsed by its abnormality and knowing what it now represented: not safe passage through the streets of the metropolis, but murder.

'Sir,' said the female officer beside me. I jolted. 'Sir, you need to step back and return to your hotel.'

'Oh yes,' I said, and turned away. But I was not a guest at the hotel next to the scene – it was a lie used to gain entry past police lines. I lived a mile from where I now stood.

I stooped to tie my shoelaces. Then, checking the officer was no longer looking at me, I quietly made my way into a side street and slipped back beyond the cordon.

'If he's so desperate to martyr himself, then why hasn't he done it already?'

A resigned murmur issued around the BBC meeting room. It was a good question. Then someone else piped up. 'Do we actually know that he was involved in terrorism?'

They were talking about someone called Hassan Butt, a well-known Manchester radical. It had been proposed that I go and interview him. But the people in the meeting room were unsure about who he was. How could someone so outspoken and obviously dangerous not have been locked up already if they were the real deal? They were looking at me, the twenty-four-year-old newly appointed researcher, to somehow give them an answer.

A couple of months after the 7/7 bombings, a senior BBC journalist called Jim Booth asked me to work on a project. Booth was a brilliant reporter. He was a salt-of-the-earth, Mancunian bruiser who could drink with the best of them. But in an instant he could become a distrusting cynic, quietly employing his Cambridge intellect to dig out whatever information he required.

Booth had seen my previous work and asked if I would spend three months in Beeston – the hilltop suburb in Leeds where three of the 7/7 bombers had grown up – to research their lives for a primetime drama documentary that would be aired on the first anniversary of the tragedy. The whole project, including filming with the actors, was to take nine months, so time was precious. But several weeks in, we'd hit a wall. No one wanted to talk.

Booth and I both knew that every other journalist who had trekked to Beeston's cluster of red-brick, terraced streets to try and piece together what had happened had left with nothing. Perhaps we were being naive, but we remained hopeful we'd land the story because we thought we had an edge over the scores of other reporters. Our research was being fed into a script for a 'true-life' drama documentary. So unlike most newsmen, we weren't there to find out who was to blame. Our scriptwriter wanted to know about the chronology and details of people's lives. We wouldn't be asking anyone to point the finger. We thought that might make people more amenable to speaking.

A second advantage was that we didn't have to sit anyone in front of a camera to be interviewed, as they would be for a normal TV documentary, because 'fictional' characters on screen would be retelling their stories. Once all their information had been blended into the script, their identities could be kept secret. Everything was off the record.

At first, this chance to talk tempted people. Young boys and old men wanted to explain what had gone on – or at least to make Booth and me understand that not everyone in Beeston thought that Islam was about killing infidels.

We'd hear brief whispers about drugs and rebellions against forced marriages. But then, on the eve of these interviews, people would suddenly back out and withdraw without any honest explanation. After six weeks of this, Booth and I had nothing – except of course a growing list of demands from our bosses for more information.

Some commentators said the people of Beeston refused to talk because they were fed up with outsiders intruding into their lives, or that they were scared of police involvement, or that the right questions weren't being asked. There was some truth in these theories. But there was something in the way people avoided looking us in the eye, the desperation to hurry away at the first opportunity, the nerves, the strained conversations late at night in the backs of unlit cars, that told us something much darker had descended upon that place.

Only many months later and after an incredibly lucky break did Booth and I manage to piece together some semblance of how Mohammed Sidique Khan, or 'Sid', was radicalised. I discovered that Mohammed had an older brother who was a taxi driver. He plied the night shift at Leeds station. One night, I hovered at the front of the queue until his cab appeared and then I got in. Though he was always reticent, over nine months of interviews (almost all of which took place in his cab) Mohammed's brother gave me enough information to detail how 'Sid' had come to blow himself up. His actions on 7 July were not some simple act of rage at western foreign policy, nor were they the (un)holy act of a disciple of Bin Laden's version of Islam. Sid's involvement in radical Islam grew organically out of Beeston's own politics over several years. A member of the 'Mullah Boys', Khan had sought to rid his poverty-stricken neighbourhood of drugs. His gang kidnapped and then forced

Muslim drug addicts to go cold turkey in the name of Islam. These acts were done with the consent of the families, who were often at the end of their tether and unable to seek help within the community because of the shame their addict sons had brought on their family. The Mullah Boys became local heroes for their efforts. Their pious ways attracted acclaim from the elders, who were more often used to watching their young turn to western culture, rather than east towards Mecca.

However, armed with purist theology imbibed from newly arrived, English-speaking Wahhabi imams, the Mullah Boys were also rejecting the ways of their fathers and the spiritualised version of Islam that appeared to have no time for the problems of the real world. Instead of offering up a batch of what they saw as pointless prayers, Khan and the rest of the gang used their faith to physically put right the wrongs emanating from their neighbourhood.

The issue of marriage was no different. The Boys refused to be betrothed to the spouses – usually their own cousins – that their parents picked for them. They were independent, and in love with those they had met in college or at work. Where in Islam did it say they must marry their cousin from a village in Pakistan, who knew nothing of western life? After failing to win over their parents with their arguments, they began conducting their own ad hoc marriages to Bangladeshis and white converts in a religious bookstore just off of Beeston's main thoroughfare. They felt assured that as long as both parties were Muslim, the scriptures backed them.

Nothing split Beeston apart more than this act of cultural defiance in the name of religion. The Boys were made pariahs, and the isolation served to harden their theological views in the battle against their parents. In Khan's case his views became so extreme that he ended up going down a route from which he never returned.

Khan's story explained why the people of Beeston kept silent: they *were* afraid, but not of the police, as we'd previously suspected; they were afraid of something much more complex. Afraid of explaining that until Sid had murdered a dozen people, he had once been regarded as a pillar of local life. They were afraid of explaining how the elders of Beeston had tried to force Khan and his peers into marrying their cousins in Pakistan. They were afraid to describe how Khan and his friends had stubbornly asserted their freedom to choose their wives. They were afraid to talk about how the elders had then branded Khan and his peers as troublemakers, and shut them out of the community forever; that they wouldn't allow him to ruin their traditions and diminish their power. They were afraid to expose how they were in part responsible for sending Khan and his two Beeston acolytes on their journey to London.

Overriding all of this, they were afraid to speak because they feared their neighbours would find out they'd talked; they were afraid of bringing shame on themselves; they were afraid of being excluded from the community just like Khan and the Boys had been. The honest truth was that the people of Beeston were utterly afraid of each other.

In the end, faced with this impenetrable conspiracy of silence, journalists of all shades had buckled. Deadlines and desperation forced them to turn their cameras and Dictaphones towards those who were most willing to talk: the leaders of British Islamic radicalism, the propagandists and their apprentices, who had learned like their masters to recite al-Qaeda's message to perfection. These people were more than happy to stand in front of the British public and explain why such destruction had occurred.

Foremost on this roll call of propagandists was Hassan Butt. In dozens of interviews with the press and on television, he had helped to create the archetype of the young, angry Muslim. A member of the soon-to-be-outlawed al-Muhajiroun, Hassan was the very embodiment of the hot-headed British youth empowered by the ideology of Islam: a spectacle who'd smile while explaining that he wanted to kill you.

And yet what made Hassan Butt so appealing as an interview subject was that unlike his foreign tutors, with their flowing robes, long beards and hook hands, he dressed like us, used our mannerisms and spoke our language. Like the 7/7 bombers, he had grown up watching the same television programmes, he had been educated in our schools and universities, supported our football teams and been treated in our hospitals. He was born in Britain and this was where he lived. And still he had turned against us.

Like Mohammed Sidique Khan, Hassan Butt portrayed himself as the enemy within, the familiar turned fearsome, and this betrayal was simultaneously captivating and frightening. That was why, in that BBC meeting room, we were discussing whether we should talk to him or not. If the ordinary people of Beeston weren't going to explain the situation to us, then perhaps Hassan Butt – who lived in north Manchester, not so far from where the bombers grew up – would be able to give us the insight we needed into the life and mind of a British jihadi.

The first time I saw Hassan's face and heard his voice was a week before the BBC meeting. Booth had handed me a recording of a TV programme called *Britain's Suicide Bombers*, a film he'd helped to make just after the devastating Madrid train bombings in 2004, which killed 191 and injured more than 1,800 others. Booth had reached out to Hassan and he'd ended up featuring prominently in the documentary presented by the journalist Paul Kenyon. Some time later I drafted a lengthy and detailed description of the main interview with Hassan:

Hassan is dressed in a mixture of Islamic, Pakistani and British clothing. There's a white-latticed cotton prayer cap, a royal-blue cotton *salwar kameez* [tunic and free-flowing trousers] and a pair of beige Caterpillar boots. Over the tunic, he's wearing a sturdy, navy-coloured coat with big easy-fasten duffle buttons. It looks like it might be leftover from his school days.

After shaking hands, the interview moves to the interior of the car. It looks cramped.

Kenyon's first question is direct and to the point: 'Do you admire the Madrid bombers?'

From outside the driver's window – and over Kenyon's shoulder – the camera is focused on the passenger seat, where Hassan is sitting. Hassan has twisted his body to face Kenyon and the camera. His face fills up most of the screen.

Hassan's nose is a thick, solid, isosceles triangle. His eyebrows are also thick. But the feature that sticks out the most is his well-shaped, but thin and wiry, black beard. It sprouts out three inches from his chin and jaw. However, the oval of hair around his lips has been trimmed right down to stubble. It makes it seem as if his beard isn't fully integrated into his face – more like a separate appendage, something stuck on.

In that first moment on screen, Hassan looks far older than his twenty-four years. But as he begins to reply to Kenyon's question, and the camera continues to hold his face in shot, his other features – a small, delicate mouth; fair, unblemished skin; almond-shaped eyes; long, bovine eyelashes – suggest that a softer, younger, and more feminine form has been covered over. He speaks:

'*If* they were Muslims,' Hassan tells Kenyon, 'and they did it for the sake of Allah and they did it in accordance with Islamic injunction, I have no reason to condemn them. Absolutely not.'

Hassan's accent reveals little of his Manchester upbringing. It isn't the characteristic nasal twang of his hometown, nor is it the Lancashire–Pakistani patois that's so typical of first- and even second-generation immigrants from the north of England – across the Pennines in Leeds they call it 'Yorkshirestani'. Instead, Hassan takes care to enunciate every word. (Hassan later tells me that his family and his 'brothers' rib him for speaking like a southerner. He hates the Mancunian accent: it sounds 'lazy', 'uneducated'. He says he prefers to 'speak properly', at least for the sake of his nephews and nieces. 'I admire people when they take that effort to speak correctly.' But there are a few words like 'guilty', which he pronounces *gil-ee* and 'cool', pronounced *koo-al*, which betray him.)

His replies to Kenyon are concise enough for TV and Hassan talks fluidly, without pauses, or *um*s and *er*s, but as the interview progresses, it quickly becomes clear that he isn't a pro. Like a child, or an adult with an overdeveloped sense of emotional honesty, Hassan wears his thoughts on his face.

As he gives his answer, Hassan gazes out of the car's windscreen to aid his concentration. He needs to think carefully so he doesn't forget to include all of the necessary caveats before launching into an affirmative answer.

Kenyon puts his question to Hassan again: 'Do you admire them?' He wants a straight answer this time.

'Absolutely,' Hassan replies, and then fires off a quick glimmer of a smile. He knows that he is about to up the ante.

Looking out of the windscreen for a half-second of reassurance, Hassan turns to face Kenyon. '*Envy*, I think, would probably be a better word.'

As Hassan says the word 'envy', he closes his eyes. To emphasise the word 'better' Hassan nudges his head towards Kenyon, like he's just headed 'better' into the back of some nearby goal. Without being prompted, Hassan repeats himself to make sure that what he is saying is clear:

'Envy these people. Absolutely.'

Hassan is now visibly enjoying this and his smile is now a smirk – the kind of expression that teenagers make when they get away with talking back to teacher. Making sure that he has this one in the bag, Kenyon asks a new version of the question in full:

'Do you envy the people who carried out the Madrid attack?'

Again, Hassan stares out of the car, as if to once more check the legal, political and theological implications of his answer. He wants to make sure that he can say what he is about to say to Kenyon. And then he does.

'The Madrid attacks, 9/11 … absolutely. These people, as far as I'm concerned, they've stayed true to their covenant with Allah. They've fulfilled and sacrificed their life, which is the greatest thing that anybody can sacrifice for their creator.'

On 'sacrifice' the screen fades to shots of dead bodies on a train platform and a man with a bloodied face – footage from

Madrid. Then, responding to another of Kenyon's questions, Hassan unleashes his crowning statement:

'It is my hope that by the age of forty that I am a martyr. And if I haven't I would probably feel a bit dejected in not being among the martyrs of Islam.'

Kenyon adds, 'And taking other lives with you?'

'And taking other lives with me. Absolutely,' Hassan replies.

A week after watching that documentary, I was now being asked to assess whether Hassan Butt was actually involved in terrorism or was guilty of spouting empty threats. Perhaps I'd paused for too long before answering the senior executives in the room because Booth shot me a slightly irritated glance, but I wanted to order the facts in my head before launching into anything authoritative. There's not much worse you can do as a journalist than getting your facts wrong.

I told them that a source of mine who'd been part of the Leeds radical scene had filled me in on Hassan's early days. Before joining al-Muhajiroun, Hassan had been a member of Hizb ut-Tahrir, the Party of Liberation – or 'HT', as it was sometimes referred to. The group was known as something between a dangerous, potentially violent cult and a harmless talking shop for middle-class Muslims. I'd profiled the group in a long feature article for the *New Statesman* as my very first piece of paid journalism.

My source had told me that when Hassan was part of the group in the mid-90s, he was no lay member. For years he had recruited fellow college students, raised funds, given speeches and generally caused trouble. In 1999, when he was eighteen years old, he was kicked out of HT for insubordination and ended up joining the group's more violent offshoot, al-Muhajiroun.

Not long after this, Hassan moved to Pakistan, where he became al-Muhajiroun's spokesperson around the time of 9/11. Their office in Islamabad acted as a first port of call for British radicals wanting to fight in Afghanistan for the Taliban. As the conflict raged, western jihadis would show up looking for safe lodgings and for someone to point the way to the battlefield, where they could kill soldiers from their own country. Many of the al-Muhajiroun alumni returned to the UK only to be arrested for acts of terrorism. No one doubted that Hassan Butt was working at al-Muhajiroun's Islamabad office at this time because he'd given scores of interviews on camera from just outside its doors.

Searching through the archives of press cuttings, it became apparent that Hassan had been threatening terror for years. As an al-Muhajiroun spokesperson, his first job was confirming the names of the British Muslims in Afghanistan who had died fighting for the Taliban. It didn't take long before he was providing reporters with his personal observations. Talking to the *Daily Mail* in late October 2001, he said: 'For every one British Muslim killed, there are a dozen waiting to take their place and become martyrs as well. We are almost having to turn them away because we cannot cope with the number of enquiries.'

Asked by the reporter whether fighting against British soldiers should be regarded as treason, Hassan replied: 'We do not recognise British or any man-made laws so Muslims will not be afraid of being charged with treason. But if they started charging people, they could open a whole new war within Britain. There could well be attacks on political institutions like Downing Street and Whitehall and on military personnel. British Muslims are only observing their religious obligations to their brothers and sisters.'

Hassan's remarks drew instant condemnation from politicians and media alike, and he was soon being described as a public enemy. The day after the *Mail*'s interview went to press, the defence secretary Geoff Hoon warned that people who went to Afghanistan to fight against UK troops could be liable for prosecution. A fortnight later, when Hassan told the *Sunday Mirror* that he wanted to emulate the actions of the 9/11 hijackers – 'I wish the same happens to me, for it is every Muslim's dream to die a martyr and go to heaven' – the paper ran an editorial which began: 'Hassan Butt is a dealer in death. He is a British traitor.' It went on: 'Butt, 22, only left Britain a year ago. Until then he was quite prepared to enjoy the benefits of a country, and its education system, which he now apparently despises.'

When he eventually returned he was arrested, taken to Paddington Green high security police station and questioned under anti-terror laws. But even despite a series of subsequent arrests and raids on his home, he was never charged with an offence, let alone prosecuted as the newspapers had demanded.

These were the pieces of information that I was certain about. What wasn't known was with whom Hassan was now affiliated. He'd told reporters he'd left al-Muhajiroun, and so it wasn't clear who was now giving him orders. Perhaps he was working alone. I told the BBC executives that I didn't know.

As the room digested my summary, Booth decided to raise a further concern: 'I spoke to Hassan, and he's told me that if we want an interview, we'll have to pay him … He's asking for a few hundred pounds.'

The suggestion of handing over money caused another heated round of anxious discussion. The request wasn't unusual in itself

– I'd often been asked for payment in return for a story. Sources know journalism is a business and if they're giving you information and their time, sometimes they ask for something in return. More often than not the demand is a bad omen.

It took one of the executives to put a stop to it. 'If he *is* a terrorist then we couldn't possibly pay him and if he *isn't* a terrorist then he doesn't deserve to get paid.'

Booth presented a plan, which in hindsight I think he may have been sitting on for a while. As a new face, I could ring Hassan on the pretext of starting up a fresh dialogue. I could make my checks, ask basic questions and have him answer straightforward queries. Hopefully, before Hassan began demanding money, he'd reveal his thoughts on what drove young British Muslims to become suicide bombers. My colleagues and I would then evaluate what he said. If our plan worked, then I'd have something to give to the scriptwriter. If it didn't wash, then we'd never need to speak to him again and wouldn't have to worry about handing over any money. I told Booth that I'd give it a go. What did we have to lose? What harm could possibly be done?

I spent a couple of days running opening lines through my head. Should I start with 'hello' or 'salaam'? Was it best to just go straight for arranging a face-to-face meeting without really explaining why I wanted to meet, or lay everything out upfront? (It's easier to put the phone down on someone than to throw them out of your house.) Should I try and be commanding and assure him that I knew what I was talking about, or feign ignorance so he could feel useful by filling in the gaps? I also wondered whether, as we spoke, he would view me as journalist who wanted to engage in conversation or as his enemy who deserved to die. Though I was nervous, it was less out of concern for my own safety (what could he do from the other end of a telephone?) than that I would mess up our last lead and let Booth and the rest of the team down.

In the end, no one approach seemed better than any other, so on the evening of 14 November 2005, while I waited on a station platform for a connecting train to London, still completely unsure as to how to engage with a proto-suicide bomber, I decided to dial the number Booth had given me.

For a first conversation it lasted a long time: forty-five minutes in all. I began by introducing myself – 'I'm working with Jim at the BBC' – and then I explained a little about what we were doing. Hassan listened without reacting and I started to worry that I was going to lose him. Only when I told him about the time I'd spent profiling Hizb ut-Tahrir did he perk up. Suddenly enthused, he wanted to know how much I knew. I obliged, keen to show him how deep my interests lay, and we began to parry with obscure bits of knowledge about the group. Had I got a list of all the party's literature? Yes. Did he know about HT's internal coup to get rid of their leader in 1997? Of course he did. He'd lived through it. Did I know about the two counter-coups after that? Yes, of course. But had I heard about the US branch? No – I had to admit that I hadn't.

Feeling that he'd won our trivia skirmish, Hassan began to explain everything he knew about the US faction. In itself the information was irrelevant to what Booth had asked me to do, but I didn't want to interrupt his flow now that he was talking. It wasn't until he had exhausted his story some ten minutes later that I asked him about himself.

'Why did you leave?'

'Leave? HT you mean? Oh, they're a joke. Too bureaucratic. Those guys don't even read the Quran. There was this one guy for example – a full member, not a *shabab*' – Hassan explained that a *shabab* was an ordinary party youth who had yet to finish his education and graduate to official member status – 'and they reprimanded him for reciting a few extra lines of the evening prayer. Can you believe that? They were like, "Sorry brother, these extra prayers are not part of the party's mandated scripture, so you can't say them."'

I told Hassan about how the group had complained to my editor from the *New Statesman* about a line that I'd written to describe how they were little more than a talking shop: 'HT don't do elbow grease.'

'I bet they hated that,' Hassan replied. 'That's their worst fear, that people think they're all talk and whatnot. But they are! They don't come up to our part of Manchester anymore 'cos they know they're not welcome.'

A freight train carrying coal was approaching the platform and I asked him to wait a minute because it was too loud to talk. 'Okey-dokey,' he replied. (He liked that phrase, 'okey-dokey', and I'd hear it a lot over the next three years.)

After the final freight car moved off into the distance, I got to the point and asked Hassan why violent Islamic radicalism was taking hold over a generation of Muslims. The reason why the 'British jihadi network', as he termed it, was gaining so much support, he said, was because they kept on winning religious debates against the traditional scholars. The network offered the strongest theological argument about how Islam should be practised, and because of this they had managed to recruit the most intelligent young Muslims in Britain.

'You see,' Hassan continued, 'this is what the west doesn't understand.' He explained that instead of engaging with radical scholars and pointing out their shortcomings in open debate, the British government was now locking them up without charge. This had only widened the gulf between the radicals and the west, because the scholars were the only ones who had the authority to tell the hotheads on the ground that something was right or wrong. Now that they were imprisoned, the west had closed off its last route to a solution.

His confidence that his assertion was undeniably correct jarred with me. I didn't want to be lectured by someone who'd professed to a desire to kill innocent civilians, but I wasn't going to argue back for fear of ruining my chances of a meeting. It wouldn't take me long to learn that, in fact, he loved nothing more than debating his point, even if he lost.

As I boarded my train we agreed that it would be best to carry on our discussion in person at his house in Cheetham Hill in a day or two. But before I hung up, he wanted to say one last thing: unlike other radicals, his group and his emir (his leader) had recently decided that it was worth starting a dialogue between jihadis and the west. They wanted to reach out. Slightly thrown, I was about to ask him to explain more, but before I could reply, the train passed into a tunnel and we got cut off.

Typing up our conversation as I travelled back to London, it was that last remark that stuck in my head. From his public record, Hassan seemed pretty mindless – a thug with an overin-flated sense of his own importance. But his suggestion that he wanted dialogue shifted the ground somewhat. If Hassan really was part of a radical terrorist network and he was genuine about interaction, then perhaps he no longer thought that martyrdom was the ultimate goal, as he'd professed not so long before. At the end of my notes I wrote: 'Butt is an Islamist of the first order. However, he isn't psychologically lost or confused. He's very knowledgeable and he's also rational. He is certainly worth talking to. Personally, I think we got on very well.'

It's been a decade since I wrote that passage, but I can say with absolute certainty that I've yet to write another five sentences where each and every conclusion turned out to be so completely and devastatingly wrong.

2

As you travel north out of central Manchester, one of the rougher areas you pass is Cheetham Hill. The place has a long history – its foundation predates the Domesday Book and its name is thought to mean 'village near the wood'. In the eighteenth century it became a favoured haunt of the highwayman Dick Turpin, but Cheetham Hill's heyday didn't arrive until the late-Victorian era, when wealthy merchants and bankers began building houses there to escape the squalor and stench of Manchester's newly industrialised town centre.

Driving along the main street to visit Hassan it was plain to see that the fruits of that wealth – Cheetham Hill's civic institutions – had rotted away. The library, with its high ceilings and grand façade, replete with celebratory reliefs of Dickens and Shakespeare, was boarded up. The town hall was now an Indian restaurant. The original 1930s interior of the Green Hill Cinema had been gutted and converted into a grubby vegetable market. The old Barclays bank, with its Greek columns and neo-classical marble interior, had become 'Household Bargains', which sold second-hand white goods and sofas that spilled out onto the street and blocked up the pavement.

In fact the high street was populated by a whole host of stores with 'bargain' or 'discount' in the name: Bargain Brands, Big

Discount, International Bargain, First Stop Discount, Buy Save Store, and the more upmarket Poundstretcher. The one shop with any hint of glamour or pretence of economic aspirations was the yellow-and-black Cash Converters pawnbrokers, the front window of which was decorated with the jewellery that Cheetham Hill's residents could no longer afford to own.

The only institutions that remained were the religious ones, and they were posted like sentries at either end of the high street. At the end closest to the town centre was the UK Islamic Mission. Housed in an old church, it was one of three mosques that served the large Pakistani community who'd settled in the area in the 1960s, predominantly to find work in the textile trade.

Leaving Cheetham, the very last building on the high street was the Higher Crumpsall Synagogue. It marked the transition into the well-maintained suburb of Prestwich – home to Manchester's Jewish community, who'd come to the area at the turn of the twentieth century.

Off the main street, a few mid-century Brutalist tower blocks dotted the skyline, but most of the area was dominated by low-level, purpose-built council housing constructed from the kind of characterless modern red brick that refuses to pit or fade over time. It was in one of these houses, located at the end of a cul-de-sac just off the high street and looking onto a little mound of wasteland, which local youths used for burning rubbish and launching fireworks at passers-by, that I found Hassan's home.

When he opened the door, Hassan looked entirely different from his appearance on *Britain's Suicide Bombers*. He had taken an electric shaver to his beard, he was dressed casually – tracksuit bottoms and a T-shirt – and he looked far stockier: at least a couple of stone heavier. The first thing he did was apologise – he was running late with his training schedule. He told me he had to maintain a strict gym routine of ninety minutes every day, and suggested that we talk while he trained. I didn't feel like watching him lift weights on our first encounter. It seemed like a terrible way to conduct a conversation, so I politely told him that I'd prefer to wait, and sat down on the sofa in his living room. While he carried on with his exercises in the next room, I started jotting down some observations about his home in between reading over some old notes.

Inside, the house was clean and tidy but pretty basic – less a home than a lodging. There were no ornaments or decorations; no paintings, posters or photographs. Apart from the gym, and the world map tacked to a wall in the living room, there were almost no personal touches. The furniture in the living room was cheap landlord fare: imitation leather sofa, pine bookcase, laminated wood chip coffee table, green-and-black-patterned curtains covering the patio door to the twelve-by-fourteen-foot garden, and of course a TV. The kitchen was big enough for two people to stand in but no more: MDF faux-granite worktops, stainless-steel sink, little in the way of food or signs of cooking. It was as if no one really lived there.

Despite the fact that the house was like a generic, sanitised, strip-lit student hall of residence, over the coming months I picked up clues that gave some insight into Hassan's life. The small bookcase in the corner was largely empty, but on that first visit there was a copy of *The Sword of Jihad* on the shelf. The book was an exhortation to violence, written by a Scottish convert to Islam, and I knew it to be a staple amongst committed British radicals.

Visiting a few weeks later, I spotted a DVD of the *Manchurian Candidate* remake lying beside the TV. Hassan saw me glancing at it, and without any prompting he volunteered an explanation. He said that he never went to the cinema – the mixed-sex environment was considered to be haram – but he had watched the film because one of his jihadi brothers recommended it. (The premise of the film is that a multinational corporation is trying to take over the US presidency by getting a brainwashed war veteran to stand for election.) The film, said Hassan, had really opened his eyes to how depraved western governments could be in their desire to twist democracy for their own uses. The fact that Hassan's interaction with western culture had been reduced to viewing films confirming his own prejudices irked me less than his apparent inability to differentiate between fact and obvious fantasy.

On a few occasions, Hassan left a Sony Playstation games console on the floor beside the TV. Again, without prompting, he offered an explanation to conceal his embarrassment. He denied ever playing it, saying instead that it wasn't his. It belonged to the other brothers who came around. They were 'always at it'.

Perhaps the most interesting item of all was a Monopoly board, which I once saw neatly placed on the coffee table. I was startled to find that in the midst of this most devout of jihadi households, people were enjoying playing a game so capitalistic in its nature that it had been banned throughout the Soviet Union. Embarrassed once again, Hassan brushed off this seeming incoherence as just another part of the complexity of being a violent radical. 'Oh God, *yaar*, these guys just love playing Monopoly ... The world still has much to learn about jihadi life!'

For such a small house, the gym was kitted out well. Laid out in a room most houses would have used as the dining area, the equipment had been placed in a convenient circuit. Nearest the door was the back-extension machine. Placed up against the side wall were a collection of free weights. Next to them was a rowing machine, and as you moved towards the garden door there was the 'cage', which included a bench press, a shoulder press, a lateral-extension machine, and something for helping with squats.

Hassan was proud of his gym, and I was to discover that his fitness routine was deeply woven into his worldview. Training was not just a matter of personal choice. 'You have to keep yourself ready when you're off the battlefield,' he explained. During the first year of our relationship, his schedule also helped me to diagnose his mental health. Whenever he slipped into melancholy or depression he would stop training, thinking it pointless. He would then bemoan his sluggishness and cranky mood. It usually wouldn't take much to buoy him up but I'd only know that he was truly feeling more upbeat about life when he started lifting weights and training again.

His home gym, Hassan told me, also served as a meeting place for fellow 'brothers' from around Manchester. He could adopt an open-door policy because unlike most radicals, who were married or resided with their parents, there were no females living at his house. When brothers turned up unannounced, there wasn't the inconvenience of having to herd women to the privacy of upstairs. The fact that the gym was free and open all hours made it popular with all types, not just jihadis, and so it also became a place to recruit and 'educate' new young males. As they trained, Hassan bonded with these potential recruits over discussions about politics and faith, and slowly he would culture their minds to think like his own.

All this activity gave the house a buzz, and so unsurprisingly Hassan was eager to keep hold of it. However, his landlord was less than pleased. While I sat in the lounge waiting for Hassan to finish his circuit I listened in on a discussion between him and his housemate – a chubby junior dentist whom Hassan regularly bossed about. His flatmate was worried. The landlord had been disturbed by Hassan's well-publicised radical activities and the periodic police raids that went with them, and he didn't want any more trouble. He was threatening to throw them out. Hassan suggested that the six months' advance on the rent he'd just handed over would calm the landlord down. Then Hassan poked his head around the door and asked if I wanted a glass of orange squash.

'Yes,' I said.

'Okey-dokey,' he responded as he went into the kitchen.

I thought that it would be best to have a conversation rather than give the impression that I was here to interview him about the who, what and why. I didn't want him to start thinking of our relationship as a transaction, which would be a sure way of reminding him about his demands for money. Instead, I tried a different approach: I asked about religion.

God was a radical's bread and butter, and I had found that extremists rarely passed up a chance to showcase their knowledge in response to a genuine question. I started by asking Hassan about that infamous piece of Islamic theology: cutting off the hands of thieves. Many modernising Muslims argued that religious laws like this were about the underlying principle of justice more than the literal chopping off of limbs. Hadn't the world put more value in the sanctity of human rights since the time of the Prophet 1,400 years ago? And weren't there better ways of stopping theft than hacking away at a criminal's chances of earning a decent living?

Of course there was room for interpretation, Hassan replied, but in the Quran seven or eight things had been mandated forever as haram. This was to ensure that these specific practices, such as drinking and adultery, did not become socially acceptable over the passage of time. He said that in the west, for example during the prohibition era in the US, drinking had once been seen as an evil. Now it was everywhere. Unmarried sex had, until very recently, also been frowned upon. Now it wasn't a problem. Again, drug use had also been liberalised. What if, one day, paedophilia was no longer viewed as a crime? This is why God had eternally mandated certain punishments for certain crimes because, unlike the Almighty, people were fickle, changeable and liable to be led by their baser instincts.

However, Hassan added, it was also not up to him to enforce the punishment of chopping off a thief's hand. Such acts could not be carried out by individuals. They had to be managed by the proper Islamic authorities.

'So what about slavery?' I asked. I thought I had caught him here. The Quran made it perfectly clear that a Muslim was permitted to own slaves, yet surely he didn't agree with keeping another human in perpetual bondage? And if he didn't agree, wouldn't that mean that he was deviating from the literal word of God?

Hassan had – like all my other questions – heard this one before. 'Yes, slavery is permitted, but the Quran also says it is better to unshackle than to shackle a slave,' he replied. The moral compass was pointed towards freedom. But even then, the debate about slaves was pointless unless you had a state that was willing to enforce the laws of God. 'That's why the network is fighting for an Islamic government.' The network he was referring to was the global jihadi network: what the rest of the world called al-Qaeda.

'So,' I said, 'killing isn't about revenge. It's a means to this end.'

Hassan replied a little wearily, as if the answer was obvious: 'Yes.'

If I wanted to know more, I should try – as he had done – to speak to the cleric Abu Qatada, the Jordanian preacher branded 'al-Qaeda's spiritual leader in Europe', whom various home secretaries had attempted to deport back to Jordan to face trial for terrorism charges (a goal finally achieved in 2013). Hassan told me that while Abu Qatada had been released from prison and placed under house arrest, Hassan had gone to speak with the preacher about theology. Then he told me that the government would never solve terrorism unless they started taking these radical scholars seriously. These scholars had valid Islamic opinions and they should be heard.

It was the same argument he'd used before. I'd kept my mouth shut that time, fearing he'd stop talking to me, but now I challenged him. 'Why should the government start a dialogue with these people?' I asked. Weren't preachers like Abu Qatada the very same people who had radicalised much of the British Muslim youth in the first place? Why not just ban all these groups and lock up all dangerous radicals, so they couldn't cause any more trouble?

'Yes,' he replied, this was 'one option', but it would fail.

He pointed to the front door. Outside, he said, when everyone was asleep in their beds, there was another world that was just getting started. Young kids in gangs, drug addicts, the homeless. Hassan knew these people. He played football with them, let them use his gym. He regularly helped drug addicts to try and kick their habit. He worked with gang members to try and resolve disputes. It was easy to talk to them because he was from the same area. That's how he recruited people.

On the other hand the government, with all its resources, shut its youth centres at six in the evening, when 'these guys are just getting up ... They never meet these people, so how do they expect to win hearts and minds? It's a battle of ideas but the government can't even find the battleground. So do you think that locking up a few scholars is going to help?' The ideas were already out there, he said, and it wasn't only him doing this work. 'Personally, I know a hundred people like me, all doing the same thing, out there every time of night or day.' As long as Britain had a dark heart of poverty and alienation, the radicals would be there, manipulating its beat to their own ends.

Then, casually, he said: 'You know, I once met Mohammad.'

I knew straight away he meant Mohammad Sidique Khan, but I hesitated to respond because we'd just stumbled into very dangerous legal territory. The BBC's lawyers had already warned me that under Schedule 19 of the Terrorism Act 2000, anyone who had reasonable grounds for suspecting that a person has committed a terrorism offence could be sent to jail for up to five years if they did not inform the authorities. Such a rule didn't apply to any other types of crime, such as assault, theft, robbery, paedophilia or murder. Just terrorism. Since the ordinary public were unlikely to know terrorists, the law affected few people. However, it did affect families and associates of terrorists. Those were meant to be the law's intended targets. But it also affected journalists; creating all sorts of concerns about journalists being turned into informants for the state. By telling me about his specific association with Khan, Hassan could land both of us in jail. I chose not to say anything in response, I just let Hassan carry on talking.

He said he'd been introduced to Khan in 2002 at Hassan's flat in Pakistan. He didn't know him too well – their meeting had only been brief, more or less in passing. He remembered him as serious and quiet, not the kind of person to mess around, boast of his own importance, or 'blow his mouth off' like many other British jihadis. He was intelligent, polite and considerate. He had good manners – Hassan had heard that whenever brothers went out to eat with him, Khan would offer to pay for the entire meal.

During their short conversation, Hassan brought up the question of how Khan had come back to his religion. Khan said that his marriage to an Indian Muslim had caused a rift in his family. He also spoke about his resentment at being 'Anglicised' at school, and how his parents hadn't stopped this. At sixth-form college, confronted by drunken students, Khan had started to wonder about Islam and began to think differently. This was as much as Hassan knew.

I was too busy fretting over the legality of all this to feel excited about what Hassan was telling me. (In the end it was felt that simply meeting Khan wasn't a terrorist offence.) I also had no way of knowing whether what he was saying was true, or how I would demonstrate that it might be. On one hand such an episode was easy enough to invent – Hassan hadn't said anything that hadn't already been reported in the papers. But

Hassan had also characterised his meeting as something in passing. There was little that was profound or shocking about it. In that respect, what was there to disbelieve?

One bit of partial proof he offered was that someone called Junaid Babar had made the introduction. Babar had been one of the most remarkable figures in the western jihadi movement. A bespectacled dumpy figure, who looked like he belonged on a sofa watching daytime TV instead of in a combat zone, Babar was from Queens in New York. He'd flown to Pakistan a week after 9/11 despite the fact that his mother, who worked for the Bank of America on the ninth floor of the Twin Towers, had only just escaped with her life that day.

By spring 2004 he was back in the US, trying to start a new life as a taxi driver, and was detained a few weeks later walking along the street outside his home. Babar was eventually charged for running a terrorist training camp for westerners in the mountains of Pakistan. To reduce his prison time Babar turned state's witness and in 2007 he would testify in court against his fellow terrorists, including several ex-members of al-Muhajiroun who had been caught trying to make a fertiliser bomb in order to blow up a shopping centre. Later, British security services disclosed that one of the dozen or so Brits at Babar's mountain terror training camp was Mohammed Sidique Khan. Hassan Butt and Junaid Babar knew each other well enough. The evidence was there on film: on several occasions during 2001 and early 2002, reporters had interviewed them alongside each other, talking about killing western soldiers.

I asked Hassan what he thought the reason for the London attacks had been. Why pick July 2005 to murder dozens of innocent civilians? The spark, Hassan believed – he admitted that he had no direct knowledge – hadn't been the invasion of Iraq per se, but the re-election of Tony Blair. Hassan himself had questioned his emir about the reasoning, in relation to the Madrid bombings a year earlier. He said he had been told that people in Spain and Britain were different. There had, for example, been many more marches in the UK against the Iraq War, and that is why Britain hadn't been attacked earlier. But after the prime minister's re-election in May it was clear that, as Hassan put it, the British people 'valued their own comforts above Muslim lives'. Although Hassan had felt that the bombings needed to be combined with negotiations about Muslim grievances, 7 July was intended as a wake-up call to the public.

What, I asked, about the people who hadn't voted for Blair, or hadn't voted at all? Why did they deserve to die? 'If you accept the democratic process then you accept the person who wins,' he said. Then, with a touch of relish, he added, 'Even Michael Howard [the then leader of the Tory opposition] acknowledges that Blair is his prime minister. As far as we're concerned, you're just as guilty as Blair.'

So what about the deaths of fellow Muslims who were travelling, unaware, on public transport that day? There had been five in all. How had Khan squared the possibility of killing Muslims to avenge the death of Muslims, before setting out from his home that morning?

In terms of strategy, Hassan told me he disagreed with the bombings. Back-pedalling from his previous aims of martyrdom and striking at the heart of the British establishment, Hassan said he thought it had been a bad move to unsettle things in the UK because it had been such a good base for supporting operations throughout the rest of the world.

He also conceded that the fallout from the bombings would cause suffering to British Muslims – but this was what Khan had wanted. In an environment of increased hostility, believers would be forced to choose between Muslim and non-Muslim, Islam and the west, Bin Laden and Bush. They would have to get involved in the struggle because, by killing his co-religionists, Khan was reminding them there would be no safety for them on the sidelines. Despite Hassan's reservations about the bombings, he said that ultimately Khan and his group had done 'a great thing', which would not be easily emulated again. 'For a long time no one will be able to do what he has done.'

3

My full-time contract with the BBC ended a month later, on 16 December 2005, but I agreed with Booth that I would carry on talking to Hassan on an ad hoc basis. No one at the BBC had any way of knowing if what Hassan was saying about Mohammad Sidique Khan was true. But everyone agreed that as long as we didn't have to pay him, the conversations should continue. It was better to have some information to keep the 7/7 project afloat than nothing at all. So after the New Year, Hassan and I held a series of meetings at a restaurant called Sanam to talk more about the history of the British jihadi network and how it had come to materialise.

Going to dinner with Hassan was often an inconvenient experience. Most times he politely refused to eat. I took this to be something of a snub. Both of us were Asian, so we knew the importance that sharing food held for us. When we did go out to eat, he was obstinate about making sure that his meal was fresh and Islamic – and, most importantly, that the restaurant was one where he could feel assured of a warm reception. He once persuaded me to travel across London so I could sample the menu at a place he said was 'really good. The best!' After driving for an hour and a half, we finally arrived at a chicken shack on a busy main road – no different to fifty other takeaway

chicken shops we had passed, except that Hassan knew the pro-
prietors and that the cook's deep-fried chicken was apparently
free range.

The cuisine at Sanam was nothing special. It was located
right in the middle of Manchester's curry mile – a Las Vegas-
like, neon-lit parade dedicated to selling dishes from the sub-
continent. To avoid the hydrogenated oil, I tended to stick to
lamb mixed with rice or vegetables. On the rare occasion he ate,
Hassan would have chicken and naan, nothing too spicy. But
more often than not, he would say that he wasn't hungry and
order a starter and let it get cold in front of him.

Sanam was one of the few restaurants in Manchester that
refused to serve alcohol and that, Hassan said, was the main reason he preferred eating there. The staff welcomed him whenever
we turned up – shaking hands, touching their hands to their hearts
as a symbol of friendship. Another journalist who had been taken
to the same place a few years before noted: 'We went to Sanam …
Everyone there knew him and greeted him like a celebrity.'

From the rough details that Hassan was giving me, it seemed
that the invasion of Afghanistan in 2001 had been a central
episode in the formation of what Hassan grandly termed the
'worldwide jihadi network' – a sprawling series of groups of
violent Islamists connected in some way by previous affiliation
or reputation. When the Afghan war began, many of the most
fervent British radicals, who had spent years organising themselves for the coming Islamic revolution, seized the moment and
travelled to Pakistan.

Unlike making a journey to Chechnya, Bosnia or the Middle
East, for almost all of these young men Pakistan was a second

home where they could speak the language and live with family if they got stuck. From this base, it was easy to smuggle themselves over the highly porous, 1500-mile-long border with Afghanistan in order to take up arms for the Taliban. Unskilled and naive in the ways of fighting an actual war, many volunteers also brought thousands of pounds with them in order to pay for weapons training. Unsurprisingly, pro-Taliban Pakistani terrorist groups were more than willing to receive both men and money.

Some were killed, some survived, most seemed to arrive too late to join in the action. But after the war, a rag-tag group of ideologically like-minded people, bonded by shared experiences and determined to wreak havoc, were left behind. Hassan explained that what developed over the next few years was an organic machine without much hierarchy: membership was loosely acknowledged and depended upon introduction; there were no set targets or goals – initiative for planning terrorist actions came from individual cells at grass roots – but things seemed to get done when the right connections were made.

Hassan said the main reason he was so well connected was that he had been in Pakistan, working for al-Muhajiroun, a number of months before 9/11. And it seemed that he was still in contact with a wide range of people. Our conversations would often be interrupted by phone calls from his friends. (Hassan always had two, sometimes three mobile phones with him at all times, which he never had any problem managing.)

They would call about their troubles, and whatever they needed – legal advice, mediation in some dispute, spiritual guidance or, curiously, dream interpretations (supposedly a speciality of his) – Hassan always liked to help. During one conversation, Hassan listened for a couple of minutes and then told the person on the end of the line, 'No, it sounds serious. I'll have to think about it. Let me call you back.'

'What was that about?' I asked.

'Oh just one of the brothers. He had a dream about decapitating a prisoner in Iraq. He wants to know what it meant.'

The last of these meetings in Sanam was held on 19 January 2006. We finished another long evening meal and a discussion about the network, and I thought about how good Hassan was at recounting moments in his life. He peppered his stories with humorous asides and details about fellow radicals who were now behind bars, like Junaid Babar (a 'fat' and 'lazy' American, Hassan said, but one of his best friends), and the Crawley bombers (who he described as 'arrogant' and hopelessly 'incompetent southerners'). I'd laughed over the fact that many of the stereotypes that existed in the regular world had been imported wholesale into jihadi life.

He was witty too – one of my favourite of Hassan's jokes was one he told me while trying to explain the nature of Pakistani corruption. He kept telling me how awful it was, when I interjected saying that they had plenty of corruption in India, too; wasn't corruption a universal problem? Hassan said no, this was different. Corruption in Pakistan was so endemic that it was grinding the country to a halt. And then he explained his point with a joke about a General Khan from Pakistan who goes to visit a General Singh in India on an army exchange.

When Khan arrives at Singh's house he stares at his abode wondering how he can afford such a huge house with several luxury cars, servants and manicured gardens on his pay? General Singh guides General Khan over to the window and says 'see that newly built bridge over there in the distance?' 'Yes' says Khan. '10 per cent kickback,' says Singh, giving Khan a quick wink.

The next month, Singh goes over to visit Khan and he is the one to be amazed. Khan's house is a mansion with two dozen luxury cars, a whole host of servants and acres of land. 'General Khan, if you don't mind me asking, how on earth do you afford this on your pay?' Khan takes Singh over to the window and asks, 'See that bridge in the distance?' 'No,' says Singh, straining his eyes. 'Exactly', says Khan.

I'd enjoyed our lively conversations and noticed that he was also generous. When we finished our meals he would insist on paying, and often did. And, without fail, he'd go out of his way to give me a lift back to the station, never accepting no for an answer. At first I put this down to his family's roots in Kashmir, a place where showing hospitality towards strangers is a matter of pride. But it soon became apparent that, for Hassan, it was something more than a learned trait. It genuinely pleased him to share, to be amongst others, to make them happy and to be liked in return.

During one of our trips back to the station, I asked him whether he shook women's hands. Much to the annoyance of fellow jihadis – who would never touch any woman they weren't married or directly related to – Hassan said that he did. Personally, he felt that things like refusing to shake hands with a woman stopped Muslims from engaging with other people, so it was better to do so. Then he told me about a job in Manchester where he'd worked with a homosexual man. Though he disagreed with the man's sexual practices, 'we got on *really* well,' he said. 'I like to think that I get on with everybody.'

Something else from our early meetings stuck with me. At the restaurant one evening he ran out of water and began drinking from my glass, which was mostly full. He didn't ask, he just picked it up and took a sip while continuing to talk. With anyone else, I wouldn't have been bothered. I could have accepted the gesture as a sign of trust and familiarity. But with Hassan, the more I grew to enjoy his company, the more I listened to his stories and was made privy to insights into his world, the more I found the entire situation uncomfortable. He was my enemy in this war on terrorism. It was one thing to attempt to understand him and his cause and what it stood for. That was in the public interest. But to *want* to spend time with him, to laugh at his jokes, to treat him like a friend, to let him drink from my glass, this was dangerous fraternisation in the ongoing battle against violent extremists. Yet as our meetings continued, signs emerged that even this exacting division might be made malleable.

Ever since the first mention of it over the phone, Hassan had continued to express how he wanted the jihadis who were close to him to open up a dialogue with the west. If people were better informed, he said, then perhaps better decisions would be made by policymakers. (It bugged me how he bandied that term 'the west' around, employing it as a catch-all term whether he was talking about the government, the security services, Americans or the regular British public. I guessed that at one point in the past, his imprecision had been a deliberate affect – everything which was not 'Islamic' was to be set apart in an amorphous mass. But now I think he no longer knew what he meant when he used the phrase.)

Hassan had an idea he wanted to put into motion: to film a documentary that would show what it meant to be a jihadi. More ambitiously, he said that he would try to get permission from his leaders to tour the Pakistani training camps and allow journalists to interview those who'd been behind the 7/7 attacks. He wanted them to explain their actions to the world on camera.

He was eager for the project to get started and I promised to see what I could do. It was a fair trade for all that he'd done to help me with my work. After that, without fail, any time we would meet or talk over the phone he would ask whether I had got any further with getting the programme commissioned at my end.

Television commissioners loved the initial idea but ultimately the proposal was rejected. It was fraught with practical and ethical dilemmas. How could safety be guaranteed? How would a team working on the documentary be able to corroborate whom they were talking to? And most of the work would fall foul of the law – if journalists did manage to interview those in command of the 7 July atrocities, they could face prosecution.

On top of all that, would it really be possible to engage critically with those in the Pakistani training camps? Would programme makers be free to ask them the questions they wanted? And if that couldn't be done, then wouldn't the channel be guilty of helping to produce a piece of al-Qaeda propaganda?

At the end of January, I called Hassan to tell him that none of the main television stations I'd spoken to wanted to go for it. It wasn't going to get commissioned. That did not seem to deter him. He just complained that he was also having problems persuading his emir to take the idea seriously, but he was steadfast in believing that another broadcaster would be found. Or perhaps he would record the documentary himself and sell the film afterwards.

It was time to bring our relationship to an end. The BBC were pleased with the progress that Booth and I had been making on the drama. I'd struck up a relationship with the taxi-driving brother of Mohammad Sidique Khan and was now interviewing him in the back of his cab on a regular basis. I no longer needed to stay in contact with Hassan; he had confessed himself that he knew little about Khan directly, and so was a secondary source. In return I'd fulfilled any sense of obligation vis-à-vis trying to get his documentary commissioned, and I was now increasingly bothered about getting too close to a source like him.

Sure, Hassan had been friendly and genial and he'd surprised me with his willingness to enter into debate and lengthy conversation. He was, without doubt, an interesting character with a fascinating personal story and he could probably tell me more, but as he began to ask things from me, I realised that I felt uncomfortable with doing him favours. I'd done all I could pushing his film and I wanted to get on with the rest of my work. Over the phone I wished him the best of luck with the documentary and said that I'd keep him posted if I heard anything more about it. So when Hassan dropped out of contact altogether, it just seemed like the natural order of things.

4

On 5 February 2006, around the time that the Danish cartoons controversy was becoming a global event and people were being killed in the related protests, I was at a university reunion when a number with the dialling code for Dubai flashed up on the screen of my phone. I was certain that it was Hassan so I let it ring out. I didn't have the energy to get into a discussion about his film aspirations.

A few days before, he'd sent me a vague email. Blind to obvious failure, he'd again asked for an update on the documentary. He'd also mentioned that he hadn't been able to get in contact for the past few weeks because he'd left the country. It was, he wrote, the first time he had been outside of Europe for years, and he'd left because he needed some time and space to get his head together.

A minute later my phone began ringing again. Reluctantly, this time I answered because I knew he would keep calling until I did.

'Salaam, Shiv.'

'Wa-alaikum salaam,' I replied.

'Did you get my email?'

'No,' I lied. 'I haven't checked my email for a few days. Sorry, I'll check it as soon as I can. What's up? Are you okay?'

Hassan told me that things with his visit had gone a little awry – he'd tell me more when he could – but that I should check my email. The next morning I wrote to Hassan to confirm that I'd got his message and then on the 7th I received his reply:

Hope u receive this email in the best of health. What am abt to tell u i pray stays between you and I. I had to leave as i have been asking many many questions that my sheikhs did not like or could not answer. Which one it was i dont know. As a result i was asked to take a break to get my mind clear. Its not that am having doubts in what i believe, far from it. Rather i am having doubts once again in the ppl that i have taken as my ameers (leaders). The exact nature of my concerns i cant really get into, except to say that we have been clashing on ideas and roles for what we are supposed to be doing in the west. My concerns are very deep. Over the past 2 weeks that i have been away, i have met with more senior ppl that i have in Europe. Even though they agree with me, our structure is so rigid that they can't do much to help me. Now my only option is to leave under my current leadership and go it alone.

However as u can imagine am very reluctant to do this as i rely on them for more then just answers. Basically am asking for your help. In order for me to go alone i need a sound financial base. This means getting a job. Now i dont want to be a normal 9–5 call centre position. I have much to offer in the world of journalism and thought. I want your help to get a job in a think tank or as a consultant for ppl who are concerned to work towards building bridges into my world. I have many ideas and plans as how we can begin to build bridges. But in order for me to work freely and unhindered i need to be able to have the freedom of being my own ameer. And in order to do that i need a sound financial basis. I hope this is not too much to ask for?

My funds have already been cut off as i think ppl dont trust me as they once did. Things are ok at the moment financially, but i need to know something can be done b4 i breakaway. Again let me stress i dont have any doubts in what i believe and my vision for the future, however i just have ppl above me who do not share this vision and will hinder me until i conform. I guess i can tell u this now, as b4 i was bound by my oath, however now they themselves have not asked me to do anything, hence i think my oath is over. Neway please let me know if you can help. Until then take care.

At first I felt apprehensive about offering my aid. It seemed that Hassan was about to burden me with all of his financial problems and, even if I could, I had no desire to help him in that way. If he wanted help finding a job I couldn't see him fitting into a think tank. He wasn't really the report writing type. But as I continued to mull over his email, a potential solution to his problems began to present itself. Just six months before, I had encouraged another radical who'd quit Hizb ut-Tahrir to start writing about the group. His articles had helped expose not only how people fell into radicalism and the methods used to recruit them but also how dominating and cult-like HT were behind closed doors. Once published, the truth put a stop to invitations to community events from politicians and police officers who thought HT represented mainstream Muslims. It also helped to dissuade other young Muslims from joining and becoming trapped in the group's anti-Semitic and anti-democratic worldview.

Perhaps, I thought, if Hassan wrote about his experiences, maybe even a book, he could also effect change and forge a new life in the process?

For the moment he wasn't recanting his extremist views, so I couldn't see book publishers biting without serious reservations. But he sounded like he was having doubts. Maybe in time he would change completely. At the very least, the basic story of how he'd come to be radicalised would be of great interest at a time when the public were completely confused about why their own citizens were attacking them. After sleeping on it, I wrote my reply the next day:

> Though your email suggests troubled times I hope that you are otherwise good in health. I apologise for the delay in getting this to you but I felt that I needed to put some thought into the situation. I hope you can forgive me for that.
>
> I think the best plan of action will probably be this. If you want to get into the role of a consultant or be able to operate in the world of journalism you will first need credibility.
>
> Unlike law or medicine, the field of journalism doesn't really have any professional qualifications. So what people use to reference others is trust and past record. The best way I think for you to be able to gain this trust is to write a book about your experiences.

I then explained that a book would be a good exercise in focusing his mind and, if he wanted, I could help him structure and edit his story and serve as his agent to help get the book commissioned. I then signed off 'my sincerest regards and please keep safe, Shiv'.

Within a few hours he had replied; he was interested but he had a number of questions: 'When u talk abt a book abt myself or my experiences what exactly do u mean?' he asked. He made it clear that there were 'many things' he couldn't write about. Then he updated me about his physical health. I hadn't really asked for details but he proffered them nonetheless. He told me his exercise regime has stalled because the hotel he was staying at had no gym. As a result, he said he felt 'very lazy' adding, 'Let's see what develops over the next 2–3 weeks.' As for now he said he was no longer part of any organisation. 'Who knows for the future,' he wrote somewhat cryptically.

Sometime that week I told Booth what had transpired with Hassan. The idea of writing a book about his life was certainly interesting, Booth said, but he was concerned for me. 'Do you trust Hassan?' he asked.

Ever since making the documentary, *Britain's Suicide Bombers,* Booth had long had this nagging sense that Hassan wasn't all he seemed. These questions over Hassan's credibility had been there from the moment people had started writing about him. I'd been over them once with the BBC executives but looking over the newspaper clippings again, it became clearer that others shared those doubts. Buried in the very first article about Hassan, back in October 2001, a *Manchester Evening News* journalist had written that 'many of those who knew him in the UK say that nothing he says should be believed'. Even more damning, a few months later, the prime minister's spokesman had branded him an 'attention-seeker'.

I told Booth that these people had an interest in writing Hassan off. Calling him a liar was one of the easiest ways to dismiss all of the uncomfortable things he brought to their attention as an example of a young British jihadi. It was much simpler to call him an 'attention-seeker' or a liar than for the government or the Muslim community to admit they had a problem with radicals in their midst. And none of these doubts had stopped those from the BBC, or a panoply of other journalists, from quoting him at length whenever they needed to.

But this wasn't what Booth was getting at. What was worrying him was that Hassan was talking at all. 'What if ...' he said. He then paused for a few seconds. 'This is probably not very likely, but what if Hassan is working for the security services? For MI5?' Confused, but not wanting to let on that I didn't understand at all, I asked him quite plainly why he thought that might be the case. He replied that this was just a hypothesis, but perhaps Hassan's real job was to fake the role of a jihadi in order to supply stories to journalists, to keep them 'informed' about terrorism. The security services could not only keep reporters out of the ambit of the real terrorists who they were monitoring, but also ensure they wrote up lines they could control. Such tactics, he said, had been used in Northern Ireland many times before.

I didn't know what to tell Booth. Of course it could be true. But as Booth conceded, this was just speculation. He didn't have any proof to back up what he was saying, but he wanted me to stay alert to the possibilities. I told him that I would.

On his return from Dubai, Hassan and I chatted at length about what we could do together and we agreed to write up a lengthy synopsis of his life story to give to publishers to get them interested. In order to begin, I would need to interview Hassan about his past and find out how he had become radicalised. I needed to know about his family, his upbringing, and the inner workings of al-Muhajiroun and HT. He would also have to tell me what he'd got up to in Pakistan. The only free period I had to do this was in late April, so in the meantime Hassan would try to complete a synopsis under his own steam.

On 15 March he sent me what he had written. At twenty three pages – some 12,306 words – *Radical Islam: A Muslim's View* was a first attempt to sketch an outline for the book. It was written without spelling and grammatical errors, and there was a sense of an overall structure – Hassan had obviously put in some time producing it – but it nonetheless read like a Islamist polemic. It was as if Hassan's first reaction to leaving the network was to try and salvage the last ten years of his life from insignificance by reaffirming the rightness of his cause. And, as he had reminded me bluntly whenever we spoke, although he had broken off connections with his former associates, he hadn't stopped being a jihadi; his departure from the network was a change of strategy, not a change of heart. He was bullish about his desire to become some sort of middleman, an interlocutor between 'the west and the Muslims' – his language was still 'we' and 'you', 'them' and 'us' – and all this was reflected in the end of his long introduction:

All along there has been a voice suppressed ... These are people who have not only been through all the radical education courses themselves but have also been involved in every major radical Muslim organisation in Britain and many abroad. They know exactly what the 7/7 and 9/11 bombers felt, thought and were taught spiritually and physically ...

There have been many books and studies done on why young Muslims turn to radical Islam. However, all of these have been done by non-Muslims who have never really lived the life of a radical. I have decided to write this book, not a so-called expert nor an ex-radical, but someone who from the age of 16 has had constant contact with radical Islam …

I myself do not see myself as a radical … nor do the millions of others who follow and believe what I do. Rather we pray to God that he accepts us, that we are amongst the God-fearing Muslims. I do not claim to be a scholar or religious cleric. The purpose of writing this is so that the rest of the world can take the time to understand what motivates us to form our views in which some are even willing to kill and be killed in order for them to find peace. I want to give the world an insight into what ideas and concepts are instilled into our minds.

By doing this I pray that the people of the west, governments and thinkers, open up their eyes and realise that they can never win the hearts and minds of Muslims until they acknowledge that the beliefs and opinions we hold are valid and legitimate, rational, but more importantly, in accordance with Islamic Law. Until the thinkers sit down with us, to devise a plan to end this war, rather than look to exterminate both us and our ideas, I regret to say that more blood will flow on both sides of the river.

There is no power except for that of Allah (SWT).

Hassan Butt
8th Muharram
7th February 2006

After his introduction, the rest of the tract deteriorated in its readability and reeked of the same self-importance that I'd seen saturate his other public statements. As gently as I could, I explained to him that the essay he'd written would be quite likely to put off prospective publishers entirely. What was needed was detail and colour, and a firmer outline of his experiences – not a political pamphlet. I told him to do what he did so well when speaking: tell his story.

At this point he said that since I was the journalist, I knew best and he'd be happy to take my advice. But he didn't think he could do this by himself. Would I help him, he asked, turn his life story into a book? Would I be his ghostwriter?

From the moment I'd read the first few pages of his essay, I knew Hassan would need someone to help him write his book. I had no idea how to approach such a task but I was young and cocksure and believed that if I put my mind to it, I could do this much. As a young freelancer still trying to make a name for myself, it would also be incredibly foolish to pass up the chance to work on a potentially huge story. This might be the most interesting thing I'd ever get involved in. It would be a dereliction of duty as a reporter to let this story slip through my fingers. So without putting any more thought into it, I agreed and said he could leave the writing to me.

Come April, I was making regular trips from London up to Hassan's flat in Manchester to interview him and put together a more digestible proposal. To begin with it was easy work. Hassan's natural sociability and his previous experience with the media meant that he was used to opening up in front of a Dictaphone. I would only have to prompt him with a quick question and he would be able to talk for five or even ten minutes without pause. His skill at telling a good tale carried over into our interviews and he liked to entertain. But his jocular nature – sometimes he told stories like he was holding court over a street gang – didn't mean that he wasn't taking the book seriously. Hassan was eager to help me with whatever I needed because, as he put it, the prospect of writing a book was the only thing keeping him from the drudgery of a nine-to-five job – something he clearly dreaded.

This kept him focused, and on the occasions when he went off on a tangent, pursuing a more amusing facet of his life, he would always – often without pausing for recall – weave his digression back into an answer to my original question.

At the start of the interview process, Hassan believed that I was trying to analyse him. His notion of psychology was that it was all Freudian and he figured that I was after small, buried details about his family, which I would somehow use against him, causing him to lose control over his own story. Because of this, he felt the need to counteract any judgements I might be making. As we trawled through his upbringing, he would fervently deny that events, such as his father 'beating him' as a child, had had any effects on him that he had not already come to terms with. There was nothing I could enquire about that he didn't already have the answers to.

At the same time, Hassan didn't try to steer me towards the obviously big occurrences in his past. 'Oh, did I not tell you about … ' was the usual casual refrain by which Hassan would introduce me, as if by chance, to the most significant moments in his life: his first marriage, the time when the spooks came to visit him in the cells of Paddington Green police station after he fled Pakistan in 2002. He was most enlivened when telling a boy's adventure involving some sort of daring or bravado. These were usually stories that he and his fellow jihadis had told each other dozens of times before, and so they were well rehearsed. There were also plenty of them: fights that he and his brothers had gotten into, training for jihad in the wilds of the north-west of England, evading gangsters in Lahore.

There were also incidents that he fretted about because he realised he could no longer remember the details. 'There are certain things in my head that I've blocked [out] and I find it really difficult to recall,' he told me one evening over the phone. This was a reference to the crimes he said he'd committed in Pakistan and he thought he was unconsciously blocking them out for his own safety. Surprisingly, on more than one occasion he voiced the idea that he should see a psychologist. Perhaps they could unlock his memories? I encouraged him to do just that both for himself and the sake of the book. It would be fascinating to know what a professional thought of him. But in the end he decided against it. He told me he was scared that if he sat with a stranger he'd freeze up and not say anything at all. I didn't think this likely – he'd been opening up in front of strangers all of his adult life – but he wouldn't be persuaded otherwise.

After some discussion about the different possibilities, Hassan and I settled on a structure for the book, which we decided to call *Leaving al-Qaeda*. I would write a long preface about how we'd become acquainted. Drawing upon our interviews, the main section of the book would tell Hassan's life story. As the interviews progressed, I was struck by the similarities between us. I knew many of the themes in his early life first-hand. We both originated from roughly the same part of the world so despite the gulf of difference that religion had produced there was much that we shared. There was the constant parental insistence that the key to success was getting a good education. We both knew what it meant to defend yourself against racists – and how such insults could burn a hole right through your sense of place and belonging. And then, amongst family, how one had to maintain an awareness of the other homeland – that silently solid force, which permeated every aspect of life away from school. Without much trouble I could imagine Hassan's father's village back in Pakistan – I'd seen a hundred of these places as a child travelling through India in the summer holidays. We also both shared a childhood spent in a community that was quietly consumed by the economic and social frustrations of migration.

It was not just these broad themes we had in common, but also a remarkably similar set of incidents centred around our fathers. They had both been somewhat unsuccessful business-men, so Hassan and I knew what it was like to grow up in a family where money came in waves of feast then famine. Both of our fathers had ended up in jail at one point or another – his for insurance fraud, mine for drug dealing. And according to what he'd told me about recent events, both our fathers had cheated on our mothers in later life and then left home. His father Zaid had only recently gone back to Pakistan to live with a second wife, abandoning his mother in Manchester.

We'd taken these experiences, specifically the imprisonments, in different ways. I was much younger than Hassan when my father was incarcerated. For some reason I'd become keenly aware of the need to help my mother through the trauma of the event and ended up feeling overly responsible for everything around me.

Hassan was almost a teenager when the misfortune of prison hit his family. He'd gone off the rails, looking for a replacement for the man whom he'd looked up to with such reverence.

Because of the similarities, we could talk about such intimately personal topics with ease. I didn't usually have to ask him for a hundred clarifications to get him to explain this or that cultural nuance. Instead, I'd interrupt him when I realised that the same thing had happened to me. I'd tell him my own story and we'd chuckle about the stupidity of people's attitudes or about how awful this or that part of our lives had been. The only thing we passed over in relative silence was our fathers' recent affairs with other women – it was too raw a subject for either of us to broach, and I think Hassan still held out hope that his dad might return to Manchester.

In this way it seemed that the more we shared, the more we grew to enjoy each other's company, coming to treat each other like brothers rather than professionals engaged in a project. But as a ghostwriter I was meant to be doing much more than just listening to his story. Even though our interviews often drifted into something that felt less like work and more like reminiscing, my job was to get inside Hassan's head and express his thoughts to the world, to elucidate every facet, twist, moment of sorrow, bad decision and violent reaction he'd had. I had to know his trials, tribulations and intimate secrets for a reason. I had to be an understudy to his life of anger, idealism and violence in order to create a published work. I didn't always do this well. But although it seemed that by telling me his story we were becoming closer, even becoming friends, the truth was that he didn't have to care about the details of my life in quite the same way that I did about his.

His radical religious views had always stood in the way of us becoming friends. But over the eighteen months it took me to get the narrative of his life down on paper, even this became something we could bond over, as his own theological perspective took the most dramatic of turns. My first inkling that his extremist beliefs were shifting was after one of the first interview sessions for the book at his house in Cheetham Hill. Hassan was giving me a lift back to the train station and as we were about to turn the corner at the bottom of his road, I looked over at the pavement. Perched on the seat of a BMX was a young white male dressed in a blue shell-suit. As the car approached, the boy raised his hand and gave Hassan a quick wave of acknowledgement. Hassan returned the gesture as quickly as it had been offered. I thought it was odd. How did they know each other – the jihadi and the white boy in the tracksuit? Hassan's remarks about how he liked to 'get on with everybody' came back to me. Perhaps this was true.

After a moment of silence Hassan spoke. I thought he would explain the incident away like he had done with the board games and films in his living room. But Hassan wasn't worried about justifying himself to me any longer. 'See, this is exactly the kind of person I'm talking about,' he said.

He was referring to the interview we had just finished, and his explanation of one of the pillars of jihadi theology. Anyone, he had told me, who was living in a country that was at war with Islam was also part of that war. It didn't matter whether they were a soldier or civilian. It was a lesson that came directly from the life of the Prophet Muhammad. During times of war, Muhammad had ordered his generals to attack civilians as they carried goods back to enemy soldiers. The implications for the here and now were clear. Though the Quran was absolutely explicit about the wrongs of killing innocent civilians, the jihadis argued that no one in Britain was 'innocent'. The British public were the same as the defenceless men and women transporting supplies through the desert 1,400 years ago, whom the Prophet had ordered to be robbed and slain. By paying taxes or voting their governments back into power, the ordinary people of Britain were helping to support the war against Muslims, and so they could be killed.

But Hassan now had his doubts about this reasoning. 'This guy on his bike doesn't know anything about the wider world, about Palestine, Chechnya, Iraq – so how can he be responsible? He can't vote. He doesn't pay taxes, so how can people like him be guilty of anything?'

After a pause, Hassan made a last remark, perhaps to make a joke of his insight, or perhaps because he meant it: 'And these are the people the west call chavs, right?'

Slowly, after many lengthy, late-night conversations with me and with others – and months of study and questioning – Hassan not only left his extremist views behind him, he transformed himself into a determined and erudite foil to the jihadis. He stood up in public, penned articles and took to the airwaves, using their own theology and beliefs to undermine them.

During this time, he became more than just a subject of study for the purposes of putting together the book. I marvelled at his determination. I was in awe of the personal risks he was prepared to take to stand up and battle with the dangerous radicals he'd once helped create. I truly believed in him and I was willing to give almost anything to see him succeed.

HASSAN'S STORY

5

Hassan's father Zaid Butt didn't care much for Islam. In the days before the extremists began persuading their children to embrace evil deeds, it was money that was at the forefront of everyone's minds. Like many other immigrants in Manchester, Zaid was a businessman who would try to turn a profit out of whatever opportunity arose. What mattered to him was who was getting rich and who was heading for the gutter. Religion, he'd say, was for children and Fridays. But even on a Friday Zaid refused to venture to the mosque. The place, he said, was run by hypocrites; people who'd preach purity and charity but would siphon off the congregation's funds given half a chance. So Hassan and his three brothers stayed at home and received moral instruction of a different kind.

What Zaid disliked the most in his children was physical weakness. He had contracted polio as a child and the disease had left half his body withered. He had dragged himself out of his family's mud brick home in rural Pakistan and made it to England where his sons could have everything they wanted, so he'd be damned if they didn't show the same resilience.

The beatings began from a young age, Hassan said. Most of the time discipline was administered with a wooden spoon. But when his father was really angry, when his pride was at stake,

Hassan alleged that he'd reach out for whatever was closest – slippers, boots, belt – or he'd just use his hand and let rip. One of Hassan's earliest memories was being thrashed by his father after he and his brother came home bruised and bleeding after losing a fight against just one kid on their street. His father flew into a rage, unable to comprehend how the both of them had failed to win when the odds were in their favour. After that day, Hassan said, he couldn't remember another occasion when he didn't give as good as he got. Not because he was driven to triumph over his opponent but because he was too afraid of the consequences of losing.

Such an upbringing made him an overly aggressive child, Hassan admitted. But he loved his father, he said. I don't know whether Hassan was protecting his father's reputation or protecting himself from hard truths but any time he recalled how he was beaten, Hassan would be quick to add that he was grateful for the discipline. On more than one occasion he actually thanked his father for raising him as 'a man rather than a child'. Though his father could be a brute with a belt, Hassan added, Zaid also deeply cared for his sons.

When Hassan was born on 27 April 1980, the family was living in Luton and Zaid was working at the Vauxhall car plant. When recession hit, Zaid was one of the first to get the boot. Using his severance and savings squirrelled away over two decades, Hassan's father moved the family up north and founded a textiles factory with his two brothers called Butt Fashions. ('It wasn't the best of names,' Hassan admitted, but amongst the Pakistani community their surname had status so his uncles kept it.) Zaid's brothers ended up taking most of the responsibility for the day-to-day running of the business and so Zaid ended up with plenty of time to spend with his children. Unlike most Asian men, he'd pick them up from school, drop them off at karate lessons and take them to the factory on weekends to give their mother a break. There, the boys would play hide and seek amongst the fabrics and push the industrial clothes trolleys around the factory like they were bumper cars.

Zaid was a stickler for getting his sons an education in the way that only those who have never been to school can be. Education, he told the boys, would open up all the doors of opportunity that hadn't been available to him, and he pushed them to excel academically. If they worked hard, and got the best grades, they could get anything they wanted. But the simplicity of this instruction was complicated by Zaid's attitude to the English. He told his children that the natives were 'two-faced' and had base morals. They were perpetually getting drunk, had no sense of family, and their women had no shame. In the Butt household, like in many other Asian families, being called '*angraize*' – English – was one of the worst insults you could throw at someone. The English were also innately racist, Zaid warned. It was only a matter of time before they kicked the Asians out of the country. 'They'll send you back,' he'd say, 'so make the most of now before it's too late!'

Zaid's master plan was that once his sons had completed their education they would find work and send their earnings back to their motherland: Pakistan. His patriotism was blind and boundless. The brothers were forever being lectured on the greatness of the country and its founding father, Mohammed Ali Jinnah, who had won Muslims their freedom from the British Empire. In their living room a large, framed photograph of Jinnah loomed ceaselessly over the boys. Pakistan was where they belonged. And one day, when they had made enough money, they would all return home – Hassan's father said – proud, educated, and above all rich.

Hassan rarely had anything interesting to say about his mother Ameenah. During our interviews about his early life, he remained almost entirely focused on Zaid. When I enquired about her, his usual loquaciousness came to a dead stop and I had to bombard him with question after question to get an ounce more detail. At one point he openly stated that he didn't want to talk about her because he was trying to protect his mother from the public glare. When he did describe her to me, he painted a picture of her as the ideal housewife. She was the fastidious homemaker who scrubbed and combed her children before they exited the house. She was the nurse who patched up her kids after every bashing they received. She was the cook who made English, Italian and Greek food as well as she made Asian dishes – 'her shepherd's pie with chilli mincemeat was so popular that my school friends came around just to be fed by her.' And she worked no other job save that of looking after her family.

Married at twenty-two, Ameenah had wanted to work, at least part-time, but her husband put his foot down whenever she broached the topic. He brought in enough money for the family, he said. The only thing she was eventually allowed to leave her homemaking for was to take part-time English courses. When she became fluent enough, Hassan chuckled, the first thing she did was make friends with the Jewish lady next door.

I got the sense that, rather than it being an ideal he'd manu-factured uniquely for her, Hassan's vision of his mother had been constructed by borrowing clichés he'd picked up along the way. It was as if he were regurgitating a poorly worded script about what Asian mothers were supposed to be like and the utter devotion their sons were meant to have for them.

The more I pried, the more I sensed that Hassan didn't have anything original to say about his mother because he wasn't willing to tell me what he really thought about her, which was that she was weak. His mother had been unable to battle with her husband to get what she wanted and she had been unable to stop her own teenage sons from being radicalised. The only thing Hassan said his mother was ever insistent about was that the boys should be able to read out the Quran from beginning to end. She was not a devout follower of religion herself. She said her prayers and fasted on the designated days, but like Zaid she never encouraged her children to attend the mosque. She never wore the hijab until her sons forced it upon her. But even her one request – that her children be able to recite the entire Quran – was not drawn from her own conviction. She just didn't want her neighbours to question whether she had raised her kids properly. That her sons were able to read God's book aloud from start to finish was a matter of social standing. She carried this task out with love and affection, but once it was over she asked nothing more of them.

When Hassan was about ten or eleven, drugs started to flow into Cheetham Hill and gang violence began escalating. Worried that his sons were going to end up entangled in the wrong sort of crowd, their father moved them up the road to a bigger house in Prestwich, a predominantly Jewish area. From a class perspective, it was a significant step up. The new house was far larger, situated on the edge of the sprawling, six-hundred-acre Heaton Park. But the move had long-lasting consequences for Hassan's sense of belonging. Suddenly the family became the only Pakistanis on the road, which strengthened his belief that he was an outsider in the country of his birth.

Hassan began attending the predominately white Prestwich High School. It had a reputation for excellence, and everyone in Prestwich's Asian community was eager to get their children enrolled. But Hassan was bitter about the transfer. Racism was rife, and now that the children of the first wave of Pakistani immigrants were entering the education system en masse, schools were struggling to adapt to the new situation. In the playground kids would shout 'Paki, go home!' and in the classroom it was not uncommon for the teachers themselves to be racist.

The racism wasn't just isolated to school. A few weeks after the family had moved to Prestwich, Hassan's eldest brother Bashar was beaten up by British National Party thugs while he was jogging in the park by their house. You'd only have to walk to the shops, Hassan told me, and gangs of grown men would start up with a chorus of 'Go home, Paki'. The black kids would join with whites in baiting the Asians. Their alliance, Hassan said, had a lot to do with familiarity: black kids celebrated Christmas, went out on dates, and spoke English at home. Asians seemed different in both looks and behaviour. Hassan said his school did nothing. Soon he began to feel his father was right – he would never be accepted in England. Since teachers and other authority figures like the police weren't inclined to help, Asian students began looking to themselves for solutions – banding together and shutting white people out of their circle of friends, Hassan said. They began developing a vigilante mentality and division soon turned into segregation, which then descended into violence.

In one sense Hassan profited from this. The aggression knocked into him by his father helped him and his brother, who'd also joined Prestwich, win fight after fight against the white kids. Soon the other Asian kids came to them with their problems and Hassan was happy to go around enforcing solutions. After his intervention, he said, the Pakistanis at his school felt a little bit more confident.

But then at some point, Hassan was never exactly sure when, the hostilities within Prestwich High spilled out of the school gates and overwhelmed him. Brawls that had started on the playground escalated into long-running feuds within the neighbourhood. A kid whom Hassan, or his second eldest brother Ali, had beaten up would phone his family, and all of a sudden a dozen men would come to give them a kicking when the bell rang at the end of the day. Eventually, after 'taking a battering in tussle after tussle', Ali returned to his old stomping ground of Cheetham Hill to look for protection. There he found a local gang called the CHP.

When it was first formed, 'CHP' had stood for 'Cheetham Hill Posse' and had once been a mixture of blacks, whites and others from the area. But when Cheetham became a predominately Pakistani neighbourhood, the name changed to 'Cheetham Hill Pakis'. To fight the Asian influence, a group calling themselves the NHC popped up, which stood for 'Niggers, Honks and Chinks'. Their slogan was blunt: *No Pakis Allowed*. When Ali joined the CHP, he asked them to protect his fellow Asians at school. In return he got involved in their street fights, which soon became his street fights.

Though there were petty offences and minor drug deals going on, this wasn't organised crime. The gangs around Cheetham were about protecting territory. Kids would get punished for stepping over a certain road or for straying into the wrong estate. Or looking to earn respect, mobs of young boys would roam en masse into a neighbouring area and pummel anyone they could find.

One day, Hassan explained, the CHP got wind that an Irish guy was boasting about robbing a 'Paki' house. According to the rumour, he'd also made a sexual slur about Asian girls. For the CHP, this was all the provocation they needed. When they tracked him down they chased him through a park, cornered him in a store and beat him to a bloody pulp. Then, for good measure, someone smashed his skull with a crowbar.

Ali got caught up in the criminal investigation that followed. He was eventually exonerated, but not in time to prevent his expulsion from school. The headmaster then gave Hassan's father Zaid an ultimatum. Hassan could leave voluntarily, or they'd expel him as well. So, halfway through his two-year GCSE course, Hassan departed for another school. But just as life for the family looked like it might calm down, the police arrived at the door and arrested his parents for fraud.

The factory that Zaid had helped to establish had always been a legitimate operation, but over the course of several years Zaid had been defrauding his insurance company. Whenever he had needed some extra cash, he'd report that all their clothing stock had been stolen from the factory's van. 'Eventually my dad realised that instead of using clothes he could be claiming for jewellery – my mum's jewellery,' Hassan recalled with a smile. But after one too many claims, the law caught up with him. The police turned the entire house over in their search for evidence and then dragged his parents off to the station.

The trial lasted six weeks. The jury cleared his mother but they were not convinced by his father's defence. He was found guilty and sentenced to eighteen months in the notorious Strangeways Prison. At home, no one talked about his father's incarceration. Hassan buried himself in his school work and pretended to be unfazed. Underneath, he was furious at what life had dealt him. His brother had been investigated by the police and expelled. Hassan had himself been thrown out of school. And then just before his sixteenth birthday his father was put in prison.

More than a decade on, he still sounded bitter and traumatised. He abjectly refused to heap any blame upon his father for helping to create this well of rage within him. He still believed his father had ended up in jail for trying to do the right thing. 'There are people who do crime because they are greedy. My father was doing it so he could give to his children. He wasn't squandering [it] on himself,' he said.

When Hassan spoke these words they were delivered with such conviction that I was taken aback. He admired his father's 'screw the system for everything you can get' attitude. Such an outlook appealed to the rebel and contrarian within him. (It reminded me of the time he told me that he'd started supporting Liverpool FC as a kid to stick it to his friends, who were all Manchester United supporters. When I asked him why he'd want to antagonise his peers, he replied that he relished any chance to stand out from the people around him.)

But he wasn't excusing his father for his misdeeds out of admiration for his blasé attitude towards the rules. Hassan viewed his father's reckless criminal undertakings as a symbol of his love for his children, a way he could make sure his kids had everything they needed. If Zaid ended up behind bars, Hassan wouldn't blame him for trying.

Instead, his fury at being forced to live through so much dysfunction, violence and alienation had been directed at the outside world: his teachers, his neighbourhood, white people, and authority in general. It was at this point in his life, when he was at his most vulnerable, that he met Nadeem.

6

After his father was sent to prison, Hassan spent many years looking for a replacement figure. There would be a long line of candidates, but all these relationships would land him in deeper trouble than he'd been in before they were forged. The first of these paternal substitutes was a man called Nadeem, a recruiter for Hizb ut-Tahrir, the Party of Liberation.

Hassan said he could remember vividly the day they met, 17 February 1996, because in the Islamic lunar calendar it was the twenty-seventh night of Ramadan — the night when God revealed the very first verse of the Quran to Muhammad.

Dressed in leather jacket and jeans, Nadeem was a complete contrast to the elders around him. He wasn't an Urdu-only speaking imam or a member of the beard brigade who had sent Hassan and his mates scarpering in the past. He was a hard-working Master's student with a cropped goatee who was brought up in the UK and spoke English. He had a knack for taking Islam's parables and transfiguring them so they would relate to contemporary life. (Talking about the value of asceticism in Islam, he'd reference giving up the urge to own a pair of Nike Airs from the market, or to drive a BMW.) And, Hassan said, Nadeem didn't try to get him onto a prayer mat to beg God for forgiveness, or try to scare him with talk of Judgement

Day. Nadeem reassured him that to be a good Muslim you didn't have to live your life prostrating on the mosque floor – that wasn't the Prophet's example at all. In fact, Muhammad had commanded an army to take over half of the world. Like the Prophet, he told Hassan, Muslims needed to start working together to make themselves strong again. Hassan had never met anyone like Nadeem. Suddenly the religion that he had long ignored became meaningful.

After this first talk, Nadeem invited Hassan to a series of private get-togethers, where he met Muslim men from all over the north-west of England: teenagers, *shabab*, and older adults who'd completed their party education and earned full membership. They'd chat and debate, and eat dates together to break their Ramadan fast.

Some of the conversation was highly charged. He was told about Bosnia, where his Muslim brothers had been slaughtered and his Muslim sisters had been raped by Christians, and all the while the tyrants of the Middle East, so-called Muslims, were too weak to save them.

There were discussions about democracy and whether it applied to Muslims or not – man-made laws, someone explained, were against Islam. Only God could lay down the law. Others reminded him that if Muslims voted in Britain they would be taking part in man-made systems of governance. As the slogan went: 'Democracy is hypocrisy'. People also spoke out against America – their policy of promoting freedom was a conspiracy to smother the true message of submission to the one true God.

Real Muslims, Hassan was told, should work for the establishment of their own Muslim state – a Caliphate that would rule using the system of Islam. This state would then be able to send armies to liberate Muslim brothers and sisters in Bosnia and Chechnya and even Israel. This was the Party's plan and one day soon, when the time was right, it would be enacted.

A few weeks later, Hassan's brother arranged for Nadeem and a few party members to come back to their house for dinner. Bashar had departed for university and their mother, scared of what her younger sons might do while their father was in prison, was only too pleased to find that they were taking an interest in religion and happily fed everyone. The evening remained relaxed until they entered the living room, when Nadeem suddenly turned on them.

'Why do you have a picture of Mohammed Ali Jinnah hanging on your wall?' he asked Hassan. Ali eagerly took the lead in reciting their father's creed: the great leader had created Pakistan, sacrificing everything for the struggle, bravely wresting our land from the British so that Muslims could rule over themselves.

Nadeem waited patiently, and when Ali ran out of steam he quietly replied, 'Do you know Jinnah never spoke a word of Urdu?'

'No,' the brothers replied.

He then asked if they knew that Jinnah had married a non-Muslim? And never bothered with his daily prayers? And smoked and drank alcohol? Hassan was shocked. How did his father not know any of this?

Nadeem went on like this for another hour, explaining that Jinnah was another conspirator working against the true message of Islam. Ali tried to put up a defence, but being so ignorant of the facts he was at a loss, and their father's idol was soon belittled and dismantled.

*

Towards the end of February, Hassan invited Nadeem to his new school, Abraham Moss. Located in Cheetham Hill, the school was ninety per cent Pakistani and Bengali, and in no time Hassan had made plenty of new friends. It was for them that he asked Nadeem to give a talk at the school's exit ramp.

Nadeem stood on a low brick wall and when the final bell rang he began beckoning students to come listen to him, just like a Christian evangelist. He set out to persuade them to renounce gang culture, quit drugs, and start behaving like followers of the Prophet by sticking together, becoming unified. His voice was commanding and the crowd grew and grew. No one had heard anything like this before. Hassan said that by the time Nadeem got into the swing of things, the entire rampway was overflowing with more than 150 people.

It wasn't long before the deputy head decided to put an end to it. Forcing his way into the centre, Mr Simister grabbed Nadeem and dragged him off the premises. The pupils were in uproar. 'We're not having a fight, we're just listening to somebody,' they shouted. But Mr Simister didn't want to know.

That evening, still dressed in their uniforms, a dozen pupils including Hassan returned to school. They worked their way through all the unlocked classrooms they could find, tossing the chairs around, smashing the tables, demolishing the teachers' desks and ripping down blackboards. They graffitied the walls with spray paint. In the morning, when everyone returned, the message was there for all to read: 'Mr Simister hates Muslims'.

7

Hassan met Rabia at his new school, Abraham Moss. He'd been at the school for just a week when a girl turned to him and said, 'You're Hassan Butt, aren't you?' A look of wariness came over his face. Because of the gangs and court case his brother had been involved in, Hassan's name was well known throughout Cheetham Hill. When he arrived at Abraham Moss, people seemed to know his life history well before he even knew any of their names. This had made him guarded. So, without looking at her, he nodded his head in silence.

She said she was Aisha's sister. Hassan remembered Aisha. A few years below him at Prestwich, she had been one of the girls who'd approached him and Ali, looking for help dealing with the boys in her class. She was sweet and kind, and he had treated her as if she were his own sister. When he turned to look at the girl who was speaking to him, Hassan said there was an instant attraction. Her heart-shaped face, framed by shoulder-length, jet-black hair, drew him to soft brown eyes that shone with confidence. Most interestingly for him, instead of wearing trousers and a shirt, she was wearing a *salwar kameez*, one of the only girls at school to do so.

Rabia and Hassan shared classes for science and Urdu, and so they ended up spending a good deal of time together. But they didn't dare sit next to each other. Even though there were some whites at the school, the majority of the students were Pakistani, and it was their parents' values that dominated the school's culture. All the children were on the lookout for impropriety.

Despite the hurdles, they began a relationship of sorts. Their parents would never have approved so they couldn't have met up after school or during the holidays. Instead, almost every break time, they'd walk up and down empty corridors or find private places away from the prying eyes of the lunch hall and the playground, so that they could talk. In college he began driving – illegally, because the 'Party of Liberation' said that insurance was un-Islamic – and he would sometimes pick her up and drop her off in secret, allowing them a few precious moments alone. The discretion did not pay off. Hassan said everyone seemed to know they were a couple, even his favourite teacher.

With the other boys at school, Rabia was often curt, not wanting to give the wrong impression. But with Hassan she was gentle and generous. Their conversations switched between the mundane, like what was on TV, to schoolwork (her marks were always gained through hard toil, and it irritated her that Hassan could achieve decent scores with little effort), right through to plotting out their lives together.

Yet Hassan said they never kissed, held hands or touched, even in private. (After they both joined Hizb ut-Tahrir, their feelings about impropriety became much stronger.) Only when they were married could that be acceptable. So a couple of months into their courtship, Hassan suggested just that.

They were standing in one of the corridors at school, talking about what they wanted to do at university. Rabia had always aspired to being a dentist. Hassan's own ambition was to be a renowned barrister. The lunch bell was about to ring, but he hadn't said everything he wanted to say.

'So I said, "Anyway Rabia, you can either be a dentist who does well for herself and whatnot or you could be a dentist who does well for herself and is the wife of a famous barrister." As the words left my mouth, she went red. She was like, "Hassan, what are you talking about? What are you trying to say?"' Both of them began to laugh.

They knew it was going to be hard for their parents to accept the match. Rabia's family were Pathans, originally from the tribal areas in the north-west of Pakistan – they would never agree to their daughter marrying a Kashmiri. And even if they got past that barrier, it would be impossible to surmount the cruellest twist of fate. At his trial, Hassan's father had requested a court translator. The person who he'd been assigned was Rabia's mother. When they realised this, their hearts sank.

Joining Hizb ut-Tahrir changed the way Rabia and Hassan associated with each other. As party affiliates, their conversations began to revolve around Islam and the 'coming revolution'. Hassan also tried to convince Rabia to cover up and wear a hijab, because that was what the party expected of all its female members. There were only a handful of girls at school who wore the scarf and Rabia was reluctant. She promised Hassan that she'd try it when they went to university.

The party's teachings also affected his own behaviour. Suddenly the cinema, where men and women could mix, was haram. In the classroom, he was encouraged to be political; when sixteen primary school children were shot in Dunblane the school held a minute's silence, but Hassan refused to stay silent. 'I told my form tutor that Muslim kids die all the time — I wouldn't stay quiet for British kids, they weren't any more special.'

Hassan increasingly devoted himself to weekly study sessions, working his way through the party's "adopted" books, in which the philosophy of Hizb ut-Tahrir was outlined in intricate detail. These works were often full of dense intellectual prose that dealt with a range of subjects, from why the party's mission was necessary, to why God must exist.

The books taught Hassan that if they were to remain true Muslims, every single one of their deeds needed to be Islamically justified – based upon evidence from the Quran (the direct word of God) or the Sunnah (the collected sayings and traditions, or Hadiths, of the Prophet). Each adopted text took a year of study to complete, but Hassan did not mind the long and exhausting sessions. It was thrilling to have been selected to be part of the vanguard of a new Islamic generation.

The party, modelled on socialist revolutionary political movements, made other arduous demands on his time. Hassan and his friends were directed to distribute the Party's leaflets outside of their local mosques; they'd flyer door to door, man a stall on the high street, paste posters on billboards in the small hours of the morning. This and Hassan's increasing politicization took a toll on his studies. By the time he, Rabia and most of his friends moved on to study at Bury College Sixth Form in 1996, Hassan's insistence on challenging teachers' authority with Islam became more brazen. Hassan would protest every apparent mistreatment of his fellow Muslim students. The pamphlets became ever more inflammatory. In class he'd spend hours arguing with teachers and disrupting lessons if he didn't agree with what was being said. It wasn't long until he was hauled up in the middle of the library, in front of Rabia and dozens of other pupils, and suspended. To add insult to injury, the school called security to take him away. The suspension, he said, was 'like a smack in my face'. As he was dragged out he could see Rabia crying, but all Hassan could think about was what his father would say. Zaid had only just been released from prison.

After serving around a year of his eighteen-month sentence, Zaid Butt was let out early for good behaviour. While incarcerated he hadn't wanted any of his children to visit him, and so the only contact Hassan had with his father during this time were the rare occasions when Zaid would call his wife and permit her to hand over the phone.

Prison had tempered Zaid's anger. After he was released he shouted and swore less often, and he no longer had such a short fuse. This was in part because he felt guilty about letting his family down. He was taken aback at how well his four boys had survived without him, and this realisation dented his pride. But the changes to his personality were minor in comparison to those of his sons, whose characters had been irreversibly altered over the past year. 'We had become men without him,' Hassan said. Their father could no longer beat them into submission. Once he returned home, they no longer accepted the authority he had once wielded.

That didn't mean that their father wasn't still anxious to maintain an influence over the direction that they were taking. With Bashar now in his early twenties, the issue of marriage became Zaid's means to reassert control. He had always wanted his boys to get married early, and to his mind twenty was already a little late. Only Ali knew about Hassan's intentions concerning Rabia

– he was in the same boat, having also met a girl that he hoped to marry. However, Zaid had other plans.

A few months after his release, he persuaded Bashar to do his bidding and wed one of their cousins in Pakistan. After the ceremony, Hassan and Ali knew their father would move straight on to them. Somehow they had to make him understand that they would never be as obedient.

The cousins that Zaid wanted his sons to marry were from their village in Pakistan. Hassan and Ali had met them many times before, and on a superficial level they got on. But getting betrothed to them was out of the question. The cousins' knowledge about life in Britain was non-existent. More importantly, there was no attraction. They'd all seen relationships like this fail: the girl down the road, forced to marry a relative in Pakistan, ending up going crazy, deserting her children and running off with a white man.

The brothers also resented the fact that the matchmaking was mostly about money. The unions were an easy way of keeping the wealth and property within the family, and the fact that Zaid had four eligible boys in an extended family of young females meant pressure was being put upon him to make sure they were all wedded within the family.

But it was the principle that mattered most to Hassan. When the boys argued that they should be able to choose who they married, their father would invoke their family's honour – if they weren't willing to marry their cousins, what would everyone else think? Or he'd deliver blunt instructions: he'd brought them up and provided them with everything they could see, so he would now choose their wife.

'It was like a bombshell every time we'd tell him that we weren't going to marry into the family,' Hassan told me.

The boys' mentors within Hizb ut-Tahrir supported them. For the party it was un-Islamic to force a couple to marry on the basis of tribal or national affiliations. Such a union meant putting those loyalties above your loyalty to God.

'It was this tussle between Islam and something that is alien from it, that my father was trying to impose – Pakistani culture.' With HT's help the boys were able to quote scripture in their arguments against their father. This made Zaid livid. Hassan said he'd resort to screaming or swearing and that made them feel they'd won the battle. 'He couldn't take our ideas,' Hassan said, still gleeful all these years later. After the verbal abuse, Zaid would stop talking to them for four or five days. And then it would start all over again.

Hassan's suspension from college had made Rabia despondent. She faced similar battles at home whenever she mentioned marrying outside her own extended family. They argued and fought and, on one occasion, Rabia admitted she was fed up with him. 'She said, "Why can't you just be like everyone else? I'm fed up of you trying to be this person who's leading everyone in the Islamic way."'

Hassan said he was hurt by her remarks but he knew Rabia was right. He had let her down. In that second year of college, the party had taken over his entire life. Rabia then told Hassan that her parents were never going to accept them marrying. She'd finally been brave enough to mention him by name and they had gone ballistic. Rabia's mother knew all about Hassan's father and his criminal history. On top of this, their cultural backgrounds were too different to make a good match. Like Zaid had done, Rabia's parents had already picked out a spouse for her, and there was no way they'd suffer the embarrassment of having to renege on their arrangement. But Rabia said to Hassan: 'Why don't we get married anyway?'

Hassan was shocked and wondered whether she was trying to test him, waiting to see how he would react. His first reply was that they should be patient. Even though the whole affair might take years to resolve, they should try their utmost to get their parents' consent. He thought this was the right thing to say. But the next day, after having given it some thought, he changed his tune. He told her that if she was serious they should do it. She was serious; it seemed as if her old spirit was back. That afternoon, Hassan began to plan their wedding.

HT promoted the idea that an Islamic marriage, or *nikah*, could be performed without a trained priest. Nadeem had always advised Hassan that all you needed for an Islamic ceremony – neither of them cared about a state-sanctioned registry wedding – were two male witnesses, someone to read the rites, and a paper contract that the couple had to sign. Unlike those in the Christian Church, clergy in Sunni Islam have never been invested with any special religious powers such as the ability to bless or forgive sins, or the sole authority to create a union between a husband and wife. In fact, Nadeem said that he'd officiated over two weddings himself.

A friend's father was the chairman of a mosque in Radcliffe, just north of the Manchester city limits. On the day of their wedding, this friend appropriated the keys and, with two others acting as witnesses and a third to read the rites of offer and acceptance, Hassan and Rabia were married in the mosque's central chamber. Once the ceremony was over, they stepped into one of the empty offices. There, Hassan said he took her hand and they kissed for the very first time.

As luck would have it, a few weeks after their marriage Rabia's family decided to return to Pakistan for a three-month holiday. As she was in the middle of her A-level revision, Rabia had to stay behind, giving the newlyweds the opportunity to be alone. Every day, Hassan told his mother that he was going to revise at a friend's house. It was, Hassan said, a blissful few months together, dreaming of a time when their relationship would no longer be a secret. Before her family returned, they agreed to a plan. They would tell their respective parents that they loved each other and that they would wed with or without their permission. 'We were hoping our stubbornness would make them realise that they couldn't tell us what to do and impose their will. Hopefully they'd have to give in. And then, only after they'd given in would we tell them what we'd actually done.'

A few days after Rabia's parents returned from Pakistan, Bashar – who had come to hear about Hassan's courtship with Rabia – asked him if he had gone and married her. Caught unawares, Hassan didn't know what to say, so he lied. 'No, why are you asking?' he said to his brother.

Bashar explained he'd just received a phone call from Rabia's uncle telling them to come to their house. Rabia only lived down the road, so the journey didn't take long, but in the car Bashar questioned him again.

'Are you sure you haven't married her?' he asked.

'Don't be stupid,' Hassan replied. 'I think I'd remember if I got married.'

When they arrived, Rabia's uncle and aunt were sitting in the living room. 'So you've married Rabia,' her uncle said. 'She's told us everything.'

Hassan remained calm and came clean. He apologised that her uncle had had to find out this way, but Rabia's uncle interrupted: 'Do you realise what you've done? You've gotten *married* to her. If she was just your girlfriend we would have just given you both a couple of slaps and left it at that. But now what are we supposed to do?'

Having spent the last three years trying to do things 'properly', Hassan now lost his temper. 'So it's alright to date your niece and show her no respect. Yet when I marry her, it's a bad thing? What type of Muslim man are you?' he shouted. Bashar told him to calm down but Hassan couldn't let it go. 'I want to make one thing clear – you've just admitted that you don't have any respect for your niece.'

Rabia's aunt then waded in. 'Do you think we would ever allow Rabia to marry someone like you? We know that your father is that million-pound fraudster. Are you proud of what your father did?'

'Obviously I'm not proud of what my father did but *he*,' Hassan said, now pointing at Rabia's uncle, 'he doesn't mind me dating your niece and doing whatnot with her, as long as we don't get married. What type of people are you?' Hassan had had enough. 'Do you want to know something? I haven't got time for what you people have got to say to me,' he said, before storming out of their house.

The next day Rabia's family called again. This time Hassan's father picked up. Hassan was out, so Bashar rang him and told him to get back home as quickly as possible.

When Hassan returned, his father was in the shower. Hassan sat in the living room trying to fathom his next move – thinking about what he would say and wondering how he would hold his own against his father's inevitable rage. When Zaid came downstairs, he was wearing his good *salwar kameez*. His hair was still glistening – he was on his way to meet with Rabia's parents. Standing in the doorway of the living room, in a very calm voice – Hassan was amazed at how composed he was – he said, 'Just tell me one thing – are you married to that girl?'

'Yes father, I am,' Hassan replied. Remaining utterly calm, his father told him to go upstairs, pack his bags and get out of his house. Hassan pleaded with him, and then with his mother, but neither of them would speak.

Hassan never discovered what arrangement his father had come to with Rabia's parents, but after spending the night with friends, he received another call from Bashar. Rabia's family had requested that he return to their house. He had always assumed that if their secret ever got out, both sets of parents would accept the arrangement or kick them out. In the event of the latter, Hassan planned to leave Manchester with Rabia and start a new life in another city. He was prepared for either outcome when he arrived. He was not prepared for what took place.

The living room was crowded with family from all sides – paternal and maternal uncles and aunts, Rabia's father, Hassan's parents, Bashar and his wife – every interested party except for Rabia and her mother. He was asked to recite their entire story: when they had met, who had initiated their courtship, and how and why they had married. When Hassan came to the end of his story, he wanted to know where Rabia was. Everyone knew about girls who had been beaten, locked up for weeks on end, or mysteriously killed in a 'hit and run' for much less a slight on a family's honour.

Hassan was desperate to know she was safe.

Rabia's uncle – who did all the talking on Rabia's side as he spoke the best English, the families' mutual language – told Hassan that Rabia no longer wanted to remain married to him. Doubtful, Hassan demanded to hear her say it in person. 'When she tells me herself, we'll take it from there.'

He was told he would not be permitted to see her. 'Well then, I'm not going to give her a divorce,' he said. Rabia's relations laughed. Even from Hassan's basic account of their wedding, they could tell that the marriage had been a fraud. Where was the priest? Who had been there to grant parental blessing? Where was the marriage contract?

Hassan had brought their *nikah* with him and promptly showed it to them for inspection. They stared at it for a few seconds before ripping it to shreds.

'You're ripping up a copy,' Hassan snorted. Deliberately trying to offend their cultural sensibilities, he launched into another one of the party's formulaic tirades to prove that the marriage was perfectly legitimate under Islamic law and that they therefore had no choice but to accept it.

Mystified, they asked what was wrong with him. 'Can't you understand,' they said, 'that Rabia doesn't want to be with you anymore?' Hassan informed them that all she had to do was come downstairs and tell him herself.

Hassan recalled hearing the wooden stairs creak with each of her steps, his heart skipping with nerves. Rabia turned into the hallway and walked into the living room. Her head was slightly upturned and Hassan could see her cheeks were blotchy and red from crying. But the only thing he could focus on was that she was uncovered. He couldn't believe it. Rabia was shamelessly standing in the middle of the room, in front of his brother, without a hijab to cover her hair. Loudly, and with conviction, she said: 'Hassan, I don't want to be married to you anymore.'

Many years later, Hassan heard Rabia's side of the story from a mutual friend. Her parents had gone crazy when she told them what she'd done. Trying to calm the situation down, Rabia's uncle and aunt stepped in and told her that they would call him to the house for a meeting. They would 'test' whether he was a suitable husband or not. After a few hours' wait, her father came into her room and told her that Hassan had refused to show his face – the boy she had married was a coward. Rabia broke down. She couldn't understand why Hassan had abandoned her – how he could have let her face the brunt of her parents' anger alone. The betrayal was too much, and so Rabia told her father that she would submit to whatever he wanted. With a simple trick, she had been deceived.

8

University was a new start. Despite poor grades, Hassan believed he might still make it as a 'renowned' barrister, and he won a place at Wolverhampton to read politics and law. He'd be there with five of his closest friends from Hizb ut-Tahrir as well as Ali, who'd arrived the year before. In this new outpost, they started the cycle of recruitment once again.

With seven members all seasoned in the art of recruitment, the party's new Wolverhampton branch grew quickly. Approaching potential recruits, a classic question during that time was: 'What would you do if you saw Salman Rushdie?' If they answered that they would like to see him punished or killed, as various fatwas had decreed, Hassan knew he was on to winner. It was a surprisingly popular stance, he recalled.

Another tactic was to ask how they felt about Palestine or Chechnya. Again, if they voiced concern about the state of affairs, the brothers would stick close – offering lifts in their car, helping with essays, guiding them around the campus. From the moment the potential recruit left his house in the morning to the time he returned late at night, the brothers would be there.

Because of their own background, they knew the people they were recruiting better than anyone else. If Hassan was talking to a Pakistani, he could ask him questions about Jinnah and the partition of India and Pakistan, and was able to judge what kind of household he came from in under a minute – liberal, conservative, highly religious, patriotic. This knowledge gave him power. With a turn of phrase, he could provoke the most unsettling thoughts. 'If you love Pakistan so much, why do you live in Britain?' he'd ask.

Coming from another British Pakistani rather than a white racist, this question would seriously perturb potential recruits. The actual answer was obvious. Like Hassan, they were here by accident of birth. But no one would say such a thing because it wasn't the kind of answer you could be proud of. When they floundered, Hassan would show them that they weren't just Pakistani – they were also Muslim, and a Muslim could be proud of his identity anywhere in the world.

Hassan told me that within a month or so they had twenty additional activists – enough to take control of the university's Islamic society and the delivery of the sermon for the two hundred or so students who attended Friday prayers. On campus they remained as boisterous as ever – gate-crashing the meetings of other Islamic groups to pick holes in their theology. 'They were teaching [that] if you uttered this or that prayer a dozen times you'd be cured of your headache or stomach pain. And we'd say: "Where's your proof that this works?" We'd be met with blank stares.'

As HT members, they'd been shown the logic behind every proposition – every assertion had a proof behind it. 'This made us feel superior,' Hassan said.

But he began to feel that something important was missing. He could condemn other Muslims for being irrational, but it dawned on him that a person's religion needed to be more than just a logical formulation – more than just a collection of reasoned arguments and a 186-point constitution for seizing power. Although they were timid, the Muslims who sat in their prayer meetings, reading mystical poetry and awaiting guidance from the Almighty, had something that he didn't: a relationship with God. While he might be carrying out Allah's will, Hassan couldn't say he felt God's presence in his heart. 'HT never put any emphasis on any spiritualism whatsoever. And that had a big effect. There were big deficiencies in people's character. They'd be talking about Islam but then they'd be watching pornography behind closed doors. Or they'd be smoking because of the lack of spiritualism inside them.'

Until he met al-Muhajiroun's Sheikh Omar Bakri, the solution as to how to fill this gnawing hole in his own system of belief eluded him.

Hassan said he'd first made contact with al-Muhajiroun the previous summer, after walking past one of their posters advertising a conference about the 'return of the Khilafa'. He hadn't realised that anyone else was promoting the return of the Islamic state, and he and the other brothers wanted to find out who this other group were. He rang the 'hotline' number and asked for thirty tickets.

The next day, a man called Sajeel Shahid showed up at his house. A little older than Hassan, Sajeel was dark-skinned and skinny, and had a slight Pakistani accent. His oval glasses were perched on his nose, and lent him an academic look. But he had the unmistakable sign of a devout believer: a big, thick beard. Intrigued by the volume of tickets ordered in one go, Sajeel had come in person to deliver them. Hassan invited him inside.

Over the next weeks and months Sajeel, a student at Manchester University, tried desperately to recruit them to al-Muhajiroun. There weren't many differences in ideology between HT and al-Muhajiroun – both groups used the same books – so it would have been an easy transition for Hassan to make. But Hassan was wary. He and his followers had just broken off from HT because they'd ordered him and his group to cancel the conference they were organising. What Hassan didn't know was that HT's central leadership was in the throes of an internal coup. Members around the world had been instructed to halt all activity. Hassan had refused and quit before he could be thrown out for insubordination. Still raw from the experience, Hassan said he wasn't eager to start taking orders again. It took the charisma of Sheikh Bakri to convince him otherwise.

In mid-January 2000, fifty members of the Islamic society crammed in to get their first view of a real sheikh. A hush descended as soon as Omar Bakri entered the room. Like Sajeel, he had a long beard and flowing, white Arab robes that amply covered his large belly. One by one, he shook hands with everyone, giving them each a blessing in Arabic as he did so. Then he sat down on a chair beside the bay window at the front of the room and began with a prayer of thanks to God. Everyone joined him.

Bakri then asked the boys what they wanted to know. Someone asked him to tell them about how he had become a sheikh and for the next five hours Bakri captivated the room.

Born in Syria in 1958, Bakri was fifteen when he joined the Muslim Brotherhood, an Islamist organisation much like HT but with a stronger line towards using violence. When he was seventeen there was a crackdown on political dissidents of all kinds, so he fled to neighbouring Lebanon, where he signed up with HT. A year or so later he won a place to study at the great Islamic university at Al-Azhar. But, as he was inclined to mention on most occasions, his university tutors could not handle his ideas, so he left to study in the holy city of Mecca in Saudi Arabia.

While he was living in the city, there was a major uprising against the royal family. Militants occupied the Kaaba, Islam's most holy site, holding scores of pilgrims hostage. The siege was only broken when Saudi security forces used tear gas to get them out. Hundreds were left dead.

Bakri said he came to a realisation after this: until the people were educated, such uprisings would be doomed to fail. He created what would be the first incarnation of al-Muhajiroun and built a team of supporters. During the day they studied Islam. At night, they covertly distributed their message. Eventually, the Saudi secret police raided Bakri's house. When they found his literature, he said they imprisoned and tortured him for seven days. Once more, he was forced to flee. He came to Britain and joined an embryonic contingent of Hizb ut-Tahrir members who had arrived in London after fleeing similar persecution around the Middle East.

Bakri was a masterful orator. At times, Hassan said, he acted the buffoon – cracking jokes and borrowing references from popular culture like 'the Spicy Girls'. Other times he was deadly serious. Unlike HT, who didn't believe that you could work for an Islamic revolution in Britain itself, he told his acolytes that it was their duty to see the flag of Islam rise over Downing Street – the UK could become as much a part of the Caliphate as Turkey, Egypt or Pakistan.

As he spoke that night, he filled the air with the classical Arabic of the Quran. Few second-generation Pakistanis could string together more than a handful of words. But Bakri could quote the Quran and all the Hadiths (sayings of the Prophet) in their original form, then translate them into English, all from memory. HT leaders may have known their theology but they didn't *feel* Islam in the way Bakri did, Hassan explained. Talk about deep convictions, logic and rational proof could not cover up their lack of inner belief in the unknowable. Bearded and robed Sheikh Bakri not only looked the part, his life appeared to embody that of a true Muslim. He was the example they could all follow.

'I'd usually fall asleep after a couple of hours of HT's lectures but Omar I could listen to and listen to. He was so charismatic, unbelievably approachable and so clever. You could ring him for guidance at any time of the day and he'd be there for you.'

After Bakri had finished, the brothers asked to be left alone to discuss how to proceed. It didn't take long to decide – there was not one person amongst them who didn't want to swear an oath to the sheikh.

The euphoria of that night didn't last long. There had been another show of hands to decide who would become the new group's supervisor and Hassan was elected leader of Wolverhampton. But, now he was within the inner circle of al-Muhajiroun, he quickly learned how shambolic an organisation it was.

Bakri had put a group of Londoners in charge of running the day-to-day affairs. Ironically dubbed the 'A-Team', they were led by Anjem Choudary, an Afro-Caribbean convert called Trevor Brooks, and a few others who had come to Bakri early on. Most of them lived on the dole and over the years they'd frittered away thousands of pounds of al-Muhajiroun's money because, Hassan said, they'd been happy to indulge in building up their own fiefdoms while the general organisation was left in disarray. They gave themselves ridiculous and unwarranted titles – Anjem had been appointed a 'senior judge' in al-Muhajiroun's shariah court even though he could not speak or read Arabic.

When it came to assisting other members, they'd only lift a finger if Bakri ordered them directly. Then they'd scramble to be first to complete the task, hoping to be the first to receive his praise. 'They were losers, no doubt about it. They were jokers,' Hassan said, still spitting contempt all those years later. Most of them ended up in jail, including Anjem Choudary, who spent years forging a career out of regularly appearing on TV to warn the British public that they were in danger of being attacked by his followers.

Outside of London's A-Team there were people whom Hassan came to respect. Sajeel was one, and the director or *naqeeb* of the north of England, Zaheer Ali – a tall, lanky Pakistani in his early thirties – was another. Zaheer, like many others in al-Muhajiroun, was an ex-member of Hizb ut-Tahrir.

Despite the fact that he hadn't lived up north (he actually lived in north-west London) during his time in HT, Zaheer had planned many of their conferences, and so Bakri trusted him to run the region. In between his duties, Zaheer had to look after his four children, including one who was disabled and required constant care. He was known for always being ready to lend a sympathetic ear and, most importantly, remaining cool in the middle of a dispute – a rare quality amongst so many madcap egos.

On campus, Hassan was emboldened by al-Muhajiroun's marketing strategy: attract as much attention in the crudest possible manner. They'd quote the most offensive, violent passages of the Quran – lines like, 'The last hour will not come until the Muslims fight the Jews and the Muslims kill the Jews' – and regularly vented abuse at homosexuals, or Jews, or anyone who disagreed with their message.

On one occasion, the university authorities accused Hassan of physically threatening a student. Usually happy to admit his misdemeanours, Hassan told me the accusation was a lie. He followed al-Muhajiroun's beliefs to the letter, he explained, which at that time forbade members to use violence to spread their message.

Because of this adherence to al-Muhajiroun's rulings, he also stopped attending lectures entirely. Sheikh Bakri had declared that the mixed environment was akin to that of a cinema, so lectures were haram. The only way to make it permissible to attend was to evangelise about Islam during the class. Hassan quickly gave up trying to do this and, instead, he would borrow notes from his friends and attempt to keep up with the work in the library. But with poor attendance rates and a charge of violent conduct on his record, it wasn't long before the university authorities kicked him out.

Hassan said that up until the turn of the millennium, he'd heard little talk of getting involved in armed struggle – in jihad. The year before, when al-Qaeda had bombed two American embassies in Africa, he'd had to ask HT officials who Osama bin Laden was. He was told that he was an agent of the west – eventually he'd take over the Saudi royal family to give the world the impression that Islam had succeeded in taking back the holy lands of Mecca and Medina. 'The party will have to work against him as well,' he was warned.

Unlike HT, Bakri believed that bin Laden was a 'good and sincere Muslim', but Islamist groups like al-Muhajiroun clashed with jihadis like Osama bin Laden over the correct method to establish an Islamic government.

Within Britain there was little kinship between Bakri and jihadis like the hook-handed Abu Hamza. Hamza and his band of Finsbury Park Mosque followers had the wrong type of mentality, Bakri told him. These people don't have good Islamic knowledge, Hassan was told. They were fighters by nature. The idea, for example, that it was permitted to steal from the *kuffars* – non-Muslims – or to kill them wherever you found them, wasn't Islam, Bakri said; it was 'gangsterism'.

Bakri stood by what he said. He once lectured everyone for an hour on the topic of respecting the individual's right to property. Good Muslims, he said, shouldn't so much as lean on someone else's car – even if it was owned by a *kafir*. Nevertheless, Bakri believed it was an Islamic obligation, in the same category as making the pilgrimage to Mecca, to be trained for jihad. They should prepare themselves for battle in case it should be thrust upon them. There was only one condition: if he was going to introduce them to the British-run Sakina Security Services, then they had to understand that this was nothing to do with official party business.

9

As our interviews continued and Hassan got into the swing of talking about his life, he became more measured and thoughtful in his replies. I could see him working things out as he spoke, pausing every now and then to ponder what he'd just told me.

He sat for a long time contemplating, for example, why the Muslim community failed to spot that their children were being radicalised, or why his father hated English people even though he had English friends, or why he'd been turned off religion as a child – and whether it had made a difference to his attraction to radicals later on in life.

In these moments of thoughtfulness he was never quick to jump to conclusions and he'd hedge his new lines of mental investigation with 'I guess' or 'my personal view is'. He also reflected on his own past behaviour, such as his relationship with Rabia. After several hours of talking about her, he came to the realisation that the heartbreak and his subsequent inability to commit to any woman since had made it easier to become a terrorist because his heart had become 'hard like stone'.

I'd expected that the sense of machismo apparent in his father would make Hassan reluctant to admit past mistakes. So I was quietly surprised when he was openly contrite for how he'd failed Rabia, and for how he'd treated his teachers and his fellow Muslims on campus.

I also thought that since he'd built a reputation – with his recruits and with journalists – for being *the* person in the know, he'd get irritated or hostile if he couldn't respond definitively. Instead, Hassan would become even more enlivened if an answer escaped him. He'd perk up and start putting forward a number of possible theories. Sometimes he would bury himself in the minutiae, believing that the details would crystallise an answer. Often this meant feeding me unwieldy amounts of information that I couldn't readily digest.

But once in a while he would happen upon a story that he'd told many times before, either to his friends or even, I suspected, to other journalists. These were set pieces – rehearsed, as if they were scripted, for their pauses and punchlines. When narrating these stories, there were no breaks for reflection. Hassan would lean in and start to wave his hands around. He'd talk faster and his grammar would become sloppier as he got carried away with the telling. His training with the Sakina Security Services was one such story.

Anticipation built up that February 2001 as they waited for Bakri and Sajeel to organise the Sakina jihad-training weekend in the Lake District. First, Sajeel had to lecture them about the various religious proofs showing why training was an obligation for every male Muslim. There was one Hadith in particular that struck Hassan: 'Whoever dies without having fought in battle, nor having the sincere wish in his heart to fight in battle, dies on a branch of hypocrisy.' By now they were bored with studying; after four years of books, everyone was eager to see some action.

Sajeel informed them that Sakina (Arabic for 'tranquillity') were the 'real deal'. They were ex-members of al-Muhajiroun who were now providing the best training in Britain, including 'Ultimate Jihad Challenge' workshops, and instructions on the 'Islamic Art of War'. For £25, Hassan and the others were getting only the basic course, but they would be taught how to assemble and disassemble a Kalashnikov.

A few weeks before, Sakina sent them a strict list of items that they had to prepare: sleeping bags, boots, coats and combat trousers. Everything else, Hassan was told, would be provided. To keep outside the purview of the law, they decided that all instructions would be passed by word of mouth only. Hassan managed to assemble thirty al-Muhajiroun brothers in the living room of their parents' house at 'twenty-hundred hours' on the dot, as Sajeel had instructed.

But it was now half-past eight, and the people from Sakina Security Services were late. Outside, snow was falling and settling on the ground. Sajeel was giving them some last-minute reminders. This wasn't going to be like the political work or the evangelising, he said. They couldn't talk back. 'When they arrive,' Sajeel explained, 'you'll be joining the army of jihad, so whatever happens, you have to obey.'

At nine o'clock, Hassan became impatient. 'Hassan, it's a Friday and they're coming from London. God willing they'll be here soon,' Sajeel told him. Finally, at eleven o'clock, a car pulled up outside the house and three men dressed in military fatigues entered the living room. Mohammed, a white convert who appeared to be the second in command, stood in the middle of the room and addressed them.

'I was with the British Army and now I'm working with the Mujahideen,' he said. 'I am going to quote you some Hadith.' He began quoting them assorted Hadiths about the obligation to obey your emir during times of jihad and the punishment that would ensue if they disobeyed. As Mohammed spoke, the emir from Sakina reclined on the sofa and remained perfectly silent.

Soon, all thirty of them squeezed into their cars and drove off in convoy to the Lake District. Heading up in the darkness towards the hills, thick drifts of snow had formed on both sides of the road. As they entered the densest part of the blizzard, the emir's vehicle jerked to a halt. Hassan got out to ask Mohammed if something was wrong. Sheepishly, he replied, 'Our car has run out of petrol.' Everyone was called out of their vehicles. Then Mohammed ordered them into formation. Someone asked what he meant by that.

'Right,' Mohammed barked, 'all of you, twenty press-ups.'

They all got down, their hands crunching deep into the snow, and did twenty press-ups. Then Mohammed shouted the order again: 'Everyone, get into formation.'

Now it was Sajeel who spoke. 'Mohammed, we don't know what you mean. You'll have to explain.'

'Twenty more press-ups!'

The snow was halfway up Hassan's arms and his hands were already numb.

'Do any of you have a spare container of petrol?' Mohammed asked.

No one dared answer. In a frustrated tone, Mohammed pointed at three of them. 'You, you and you, go find the nearest petrol station. The rest of you, sign on and sign off.' Of course, no one knew what that meant either.

A hundred press-ups later, the brothers who had been sent to search finally returned and informed Mohammed that there was a petrol station down the road but it was closed until the morning. The silent emir was now lying horizontal on a log with a military balaclava over his face. With the fewest words possible, he advised Mohammed that they should camp where they were for the night. Suddenly, one of the brothers spotted another car and shouted 'Police!'

Mohammed told everyone to stand at ease. He would deal with this. After sending the police car away with an explanation about a waylaid camping trip, he turned and asked who had shouted that the police were coming. Readying himself for praise, the brother who had raised the alarm stood upright. Looking straight at him, Mohammad said, 'Give me a hundred press-ups.'

By now Hassan had realised that Sakina were 'clowns' but, remarkably, it got worse he told me:

So I go to him, 'Where are the tents?' [and] he goes, 'You're supposed to bring them'. I go, 'No, we've got a list here that says what you're going to bring and provide for us and it's got tents on there'.

And he looks at the list and goes, 'Right we haven't got any tents'. I'm thinking oh my goodness, so I ask him, 'Have you got any food?' And he goes, 'No we've not brought nothing'.

And I was so glad that I had packed my own stuff. So I had this tent that was for ten people right, so we get the tent out. And I'd never put a tent up in my entire life. So I go up to the emir and by this time, he's lying on a log and he's got all this state-of-the-art military stuff keeping him really warm.

He didn't need a tent or anything else. He had a balaclava on and everything and I go to him, 'We've got a tent; can you give us a hand?'

And he's laying there, and I'm saying, 'I've got a tent can you give me a hand putting it together?' And then I hear, 'Twenty press-ups'. That's all I heard: 'Twenty press-ups'.

The next day, after they had all recited the morning prayer together in the snow, Hassan told Sajeel that he'd had enough. He was frozen to the bone and was fairly sure that none of them would last another day, so with the exception of a few of the brothers, who were looking forward to seeing the guns, he gathered their belongings and left.

Twelve hours later, the gun-hungry faction returned from the mountains. Asked if they'd fired a Kalashnikov, they said no. The emir had told them to break up some tree branches and hold them against their shoulders. Then, with their 'guns', he ordered them back into formation.

Despite their incompetence, Hassan's faith in al-Muhajiroun's ideas remained strong. In debates with HT up and down the country, they were wiping the floor, he said.

Recruitment work in Wolverhampton was paying dividends, and surrounding cities became energised by their example. Stoke and Sheffield became active again and Hassan and the boys started supporting the Newcastle branch. They also helped found new al-Muhajiroun groups in Dundee and Glasgow.

Bakri had always been eager to establish full-time offices around the world. The dream of an American branch had already been realised a few years before. As in Britain, HT affiliates in

New York had been converted to the cause and by late 2000, one former member, Junaid Babar, was helping Zaheer, Sajeel and Anjem as they travelled to the US to give lectures to this new group of students. Given al-Muhajiroun's sizeable Asian membership, opening an office in Pakistan certainly seemed to be the next logical step.

Between work and spreading al-Muhajiroun's message, Hassan felt he was too busy in Britain to go to Pakistan. But then one night, not long after Sajeel had departed the country, he had a dream that changed everything he told me, which I later wrote up for his autobiography as follows:

I was riding a horse through the mountains with my best friend Habib. With us there was a third man, who was masked to me. I was wearing a *salwar kameez* and on my head was a *keffiyeh*, the Arab headdress, which was blowing around in the breeze. Strapped over my shoulder was a gun.

So we passed out of the mountainous valley and arrived at a sandy desert plain. In the distance I could see a crowd of people, friendly, but they were talking amongst themselves. I could make out the face of just one man standing in that crowd. I approached. Then I realised who I was looking at. It was the Prophet surrounded by his disciples.

For a moment he turns and looks at me and I see his face. I saw the Prophet's face. He smiles and nods as if to say what I was doing was right. I'd always been told that the Prophet speaks through dreams so when I awoke, well, I knew where I needed to be.

10

For all of Sheikh Omar Bakri's talk of the flag of Islam flying over Downing Street, deep down almost everyone in al-Muhajiroun knew their goal of creating an Islamic state could only be realised in a country that was majority Muslim. So for Hassan, packing a few belongings and moving to al-Muhajiroun's Pakistani offices in July 2001 felt like the first act of a true revolutionary. In the months before 9/11, Pakistan appeared ripe for change. The country was the first major nation in the modern era to be founded upon the basis of a religion and not race. Out of the British Empire's greatest possession, Mohammed Ali Jinnah had forged a land for Muslims to the east and west of India. Separated by culture, ethnicity, language and a thousand miles, only their religion would serve to bind East and West Pakistan. Islam was the country's whole reason for being and yet it also became its poison pill.

After its bloody inception, Pakistan soon found itself rocked by coups, wars, military takeovers, foreign interference, tribal conflicts and endemic corruption. Democracy and nationalism had faltered, but Islam too failed to tie the country together. In 1971, a vicious civil war broke out as Bangladeshis in East Pakistan attempted to free themselves from the yoke of Islamabad's rule. But this did not deter the growing followers of the new political

Islamism. During the 1970s and 80s, General Zia ul-Haq seized control and introduced parts of shariah into law. Soon, whole regiments of the army and the country's internal security force – the ISI – came under the sway of pan-Islamic ideology. Their legions of supporters only grew as the ISI trained up tens of thousands of Mujahideen soldiers to fight the Soviet Union following the Soviet invasion of Afghanistan during the 1980s. Then came the Taliban.

One of the most interesting stories of how the Taliban was brought into existence begins after Pakistan's cotton harvest failed in 1994. Ravished by insects, the failure of the crop threatened to put an end to the country's textile industry. The democratically elected prime minister at the time, Benazir Bhutto, sent her husband to oversee the delivery of replacement cotton from central Asia. But there was a problem – every time the trucks made their way through Afghanistan they were attacked and looted. The Bhuttos despatched an up-and-coming army general, Pervez Musharraf, to defend the convoys. For muscle, Musharraf recruited Mullah Mohammad Omar, who banded together a large number of religious students – Talibs – from the madrasas of Pakistan. Guarded by this new militia, the convoys battled their way through. Mullah Omar's small band of fighters was the start of the Taliban and, very soon, this force originally raised to protect cotton convoys was taking over the whole country.

After the destruction of the Twin Towers, Hassan said, the streets around al-Muhajiroun's offices in Lahore were awash with crowds praising those who had hijacked the planes, and shouts of 'The Americans are dogs!' Drivers hooted their horns in celebration, people danced to music and fired their guns into the air.

In contrast Pervez Musharraf, who had recently seized power in a coup d'état and was now president of Pakistan, delivered a message of condolence. 'We share the grief of the American people in their grave national tragedy,' he said. 'We strongly condemn this most brutal and horrible act of terror and violence.' He then added: 'This world must unite to fight against terrorism and root out this modern-day evil.'

In permitting Afghanistan-bound US jets to enter Pakistani airspace, Musharraf overturned years of official policy in a single moment. Backing the Taliban's takeover of Afghanistan had cost the country blood and treasure. Pakistan's security services effectively ruled the unruly nation alongside the one-eyed head of the Talibs, Mullah Omar. No one knew this more than Musharraf – after all, he himself had directed the supply of guns and money to the Taliban.

US planes were now bombing the Taliban into oblivion, and suddenly what was a fragile balance – between Pakistan's different ethnic groupings, the system of pay-offs and backhanders, the locus of political and military power, and the operation of a multitude of Islamic terrorist organisations waging covert wars in India and Afghanistan – was thrown into complete disarray. Overnight, Pakistan was in chaos.

As soon as battle looked imminent, jihadis and radicals from around the world came to Pakistan to join the caravan of war. There were hundreds of them, Hassan said: people who had waited all their young lives for just such a moment to prove themselves on the field. They all needed a place to sleep and a way to get to the frontlines. Those who didn't know how to fire a gun needed to be trained. Those who had donations needed some way to deliver them to the Mujahideen.

The ramshackle al-Muhajiroun office in Lahore became caught up in the chaos. After days of shifting like a feather in the wind, Sheikh Bakri finally wrote out his fatwa. Al-Muhajiroun had never proffered violence as a solution. It had genuinely believed in persuading the Muslim masses to support change through political education. But now Bakri declared that the act of 9/11 was permissible – al-Muhajiroun would stand in solidarity with al-Qaeda. Word soon got around that the Pakistani branch of al-Muhajiroun would offer support to aspiring jihadis, so any Brit who had once had a connection to Bakri came to them looking for assistance.

Having tried to get the office in working order for more than three months, Hassan knew al-Muhajiroun weren't prepared for the influx. For a start, despite the fact that it was located on a residential street in one of the plusher areas of Lahore, al-Muhajiroun's headquarters were practically derelict. The paint and plaster crumbled away from the office walls when touched. The bedrooms where some of the new recruits were living didn't have any mattresses. An array of wildlife was to be found breeding in the overgrown front garden, and without air conditioning the house became intolerably hot in the summer. There was no stove or refrigerator, and the nearest cold drink was a mile-and-a-half walk away. Hassan had tried to make the place habitable but the task had defeated him, so he was grateful that the first to arrive after 9/11 were people who could help al-Muhajiroun get organised.

Zaheer had decided to leave Britain for good and brought his wife and four children to settle in Pakistan. Junaid Babar, the New Yorker, followed. When Hassan heard that Junaid's mother had been inside one of the Twin Towers when they had been attacked, he was amazed Junaid was in Pakistan at all. Remarkably, Junaid had kept faith with al-Muhajiroun and was now helping to support his mother's attackers.

Come October, a flood of jihadis began passing through the office. Sometimes they would stay for just a few hours; sometimes for the night. Others stayed for months and became good friends of Hassan's. There was Kazi Rahman, the thin, clean-shaven East London Bengali plumber in his twenties whom everyone called 'Tipu'. Unlike those who had joined al-Muhajiroun because Sheikh Bakri had charmed them or because of their dedication to theology, Tipu had joined because he had taken the suffering of others to heart. 'He was emotional like that and the other brothers respected him for it. He was one of the few Londoners I got on with,' Hassan said.

But Tipu also had a dark past. When he was still the UK head of Hizb ut-Tahrir, Sheikh Bakri had come to speak at Tipu's college. Four days later, there had been a religious argument between a Christian Nigerian student, Tundi Obanubi, and a group of Muslims. Armed with knives and a hammer, the Muslim boys attacked Tundi and he died on the pavement beside the school gates – stabbed through the heart. Tipu had been charged with Tundi's murder, along with three of his friends. There hadn't been enough evidence to convict him and he was found not guilty. Now, five years later, Tipu was readying himself with an assembled band of other fighters to head into Afghanistan.

Amongst Tipu's group Hassan said, was Imran, a heavy-built, twenty-eight-year-old father from Bradford. Unlike Tipu, Imran talked a lot and fancied himself as a philosopher. But unfortunately he didn't have the intellect to live up to the pretence.

'And he didn't do himself any favours by swearing all the time,' Hassan said.

Hassan told me a story that explained just how difficult it was to travel into Pakistan and join the jihadi cause. Imran wasn't a member of al-Muhajiroun, and so when he arrived in the country he headed to the offices of the biggest and best-known of all the militant groups: Lashkar-e-Taiba (LeT). However, Imran hadn't realised that after 9/11, LeT had decided to betray the jihadi cause and side with Musharraf's government. So when Imran showed up with £20,000 in his pocket asking how to get to the frontlines, they robbed him and locked him in a room with an Australian who'd made the same mistake. Fearing he was going to be sold off to the ISI, who'd in turn hand him in to the Americans, Imran managed to pull himself out of a window and escape to the shelter of al-Muhajiroun's office.

Other groups of young Muslim men arrived from Tipton, Luton, Glasgow and Crawley. Some had fallen out with Bakri in the early days of al-Muhajiroun, but with an impending war they were happy to put their differences behind them.

The most famous of all the British jihadis was Omar Saeed Sheikh. From a well-off family, Sheikh had studied at the London School of Economics but abandoned his life in the UK in the mid-1990s to fight against the Hindu invaders in Kashmir. He was eventually caught by the Indian authorities and imprisoned. But he was so well regarded that in 1999 a group of his fellow militants hijacked an Air India plane, forced it to land at Kandahar Airport in Afghanistan, and threatened to kill all 149 passengers unless they released him and two other extremely high-ranking militants. The Indian authorities capitulated and released Sheikh, and when he returned to Pakistan he quickly rose to the top of the jihadi movement. It was said that his government connections ran so deep that, before 9/11, Omar could have tea with the head of the ISI whenever he desired to do so.

Even within al-Muhajiroun, no one was really sure as to how they'd join the fight. Sajeel put one of the new Pakistani recruits in charge of guiding people to the border and sending them off to get training. Working on his own initiative, Tipu forged a link with Omar Sheikh. With Sheikh's help Tipu and his gang arranged to smuggle themselves into Afghanistan. They were told to meet Sheikh's contacts at the KFC on the busy Murree Road in Rawalpindi – just a few hours' drive from Lahore. After Hassan dropped them off that night, they gained immediate entry to Afghanistan.

11

After the 9/11 attacks, Hassan was given the job of handling the western media who were flocking to the office demanding information and requesting interviews. Until that point, he'd always busied himself with organisational matters, working behind the scenes, which everyone thought he was good at. But now he was tasked with an important public role. He said he was chosen for two reasons. First, Sajeel didn't trust the local members with anything as important as talking to the press. ('That was a kind of arrogance on his behalf,' Hassan explained, as a good number of the Pakistani members were pretty sharp.) The second reason was that Hassan wasn't married – if anything went wrong he could move more readily than anyone else.

At first he was reluctant, but it didn't take long for him to get into the swing of things. He had observed Sheikh Bakri for so long that he was soon able to create a storm of reaction in the UK with a few well-crafted comments. Hassan told reporters: 'We have literally been inundated with British Muslims aged from sixteen to thirty-five coming to our offices, wanting to go on into Afghanistan. We have lawyers, doctors, engineers and other professionals, as well as the unemployed or former drug addicts, wanting to fight alongside the Taliban.'

Or he'd deliver a pithy quote such as: 'For every one British Muslim killed, there are a dozen waiting to take their place and become martyrs as well.' Or his favourite line: 'This is a war the west cannot win because we love death whereas our opposition fears it.'

Hassan would also corral whoever was in the office to give interviews. One of the first was a white convert called Abdullah, and Imran and Tipu were next. For the American news networks they employed Junaid, who told the world how he was rooting for the Taliban even though al-Qaeda had almost killed his mother. Hassan had the stage to himself because in Pakistan, he said, 'we were the only people who were willing to speak to the media'.

Hassan was instructed to ensure that al-Muhajiroun's stance didn't become blurred with that of the jihadis. For example, he told a reporter: 'As a political organisation, al-Muhajiroun does not recruit or train fighters but ... once they arrive in Pakistan, my duty is to feed, shelter and finance my Muslim brothers.'

At first they offered these interviews for free. Then Hassan told me that, since journalists were being paid to work, al-Muhajiroun could be getting their cut too. They began charging £200 for a story. But they quickly realised they couldn't ask for money if they were saying they were terrorists so they began using the euphemism, 'security fee'. This security fee was something the reporters could justify to their editors.

'We were charging £3,000 per interview sometimes. The American TV networks paid the most,' Hassan said. Along with the donations they were receiving from Britain, they had more than enough to run the office and they decided to give the surplus from these fees to the Taliban. No one was sure how to

actually give money to the Taliban, so Hassan just strolled over
to the Afghan embassy – a little house in a residential suburb
of Islamabad – and handed a packet containing ten thousand
pounds to the ambassador.

At the end of October, Zaheer came to Hassan with a press
release he had written. Sheikh Bakri had given him some information and before he put Hassan's name to it, he wanted him
to look over it. Three Brits from Luton and Crawley, it read,
had been killed in Afghanistan in a US bomb attack. They had
passed through the offices. Hassan had remembered seeing them
and was suddenly disturbed at how fine the line was between life
and lifelessness.

As soon as the release went out, Hassan said the office became
an international information centre. He was receiving hundreds
of calls from journalists around the globe, day and night. He
was given three phones for the media to contact him on (the
habit of manning several phones at once must have stuck).

It didn't take long before Hassan was overcome by adrena-
line from the media attention and started overstepping his brief.
Instead of simply reading the lines he'd been given, he began
proffering his own thoughts on the matter. His on-record briefings to the papers about religious duties, the nature of citizen-
ship and whether British government buildings would be subject
to Mujahideen attacks or not got him noticed by the political
establishment back in the UK. They attacked Hassan personally
as a traitor who should be locked up for inciting treason. He
became a notable public enemy, which only increased the number of calls he received from reporters who were desperate for
ever-more inflammatory quotes. As the bombs in Afghanistan
kept falling, Bakri kept sending Hassan the names of the dead to

give to the press, and Hassan was happy to stand in front of the cameras and ramp up the rhetoric. By the end of the bombing campaign, he'd released the names of twenty-five people – all of them British, all of them martyred for their religion.

The speed at which the Taliban lost power took everyone by surprise. By mid-November it was clear that they no longer had control of the country. Tipu and his gang still hadn't returned, and now their families were calling the office every day to see if there was any news. Just as Hassan began to lose hope of seeing them again, two of the missing men stumbled into the office carrying Imran, who was in desperate need of medical attention. Hassan couldn't believe the transformation. When Imran had left he'd been strong and muscular. Six weeks later he was so dehydrated and emaciated that he didn't have the strength to speak. He looked like he was going to die right there and then.

Their story horrified everyone in the office. People had been going to the frontlines, waiting for combat. But as they sat in the trenches, they started to get bombed from the air. There'd been almost no fighting at all; they were continually forced to scatter and flee from the jets overhead. The whole thing was a mess. Then orders had come from the Taliban to retreat, and all foreign fighters were told to go home. Tipu had decided to take his chances and stay at the front in case the Americans did arrive, but the other three left.

Getting back hadn't been easy. The Americans were offering thousands of dollars for captured foreigners and, as the tide of war turned, Taliban commanders would suddenly switch sides and claim their rewards. They hadn't been able to trust anyone and so they'd trekked hundreds of miles by night, mostly on foot, all the way from the far north of Afghanistan to Kandahar in the south. All their money had been extorted from them in bribes, and for weeks they'd eaten nothing. Eventually they'd made it across the border to Peshawar, and finally to Lahore.

Hassan said most Brits who came back had a similar story. The conflict had been too short, too one-sided and badly organised, and no one had been able to put their training to use. Some hadn't even fired their weapons. There had been no grand battle against the British and American soldiers. Around the al-Muhajiroun office, frustration built up and suddenly people began talking about what to do next.

For the six months Hassan had been in Pakistan, he'd tried to live like a local, eating food from the vendors on the street and drinking water straight from the tap. He said he'd developed a crippling ulcer in his stomach. Local doctors told him he needed injections and prescribed him an assortment of drugs, but nothing worked. In the meantime his medical bills kept rising. Hassan decided to go back to Britain for a second opinion.

When he told Sajeel about his plans, he thought Hassan had finally cracked. 'You can't be serious. Your face has been everywhere. They'll arrest you as soon as you get to the airport.' But Hassan was set on going. He was exhausted, mentally and physically. He needed a break.

To Hassan's surprise, he passed through customs without fuss. However, back on home soil he felt strange. The billboards full of nudity, the pubs, even tiny cultural differences seemed alien to him now. For the first time, he felt out of place in the UK. The smell of alcohol made him sick and the sight of so much wealth being enjoyed in such a hedonistic way repulsed him.

The doctors in Manchester advised him that he needed an operation that would take a few weeks to recover from, so he decided to get this done in Pakistan where he could recuperate at ease. With a few days to kill before his flight back, he went to visit Sheikh Bakri. He was hoping to surprise him, but when he arrived Bakri already knew he was in the country. He praised Hassan's work on the media side – 'You are almost as famous as me!' he joked – and asked if he'd give a talk. To a special audience of a few dozen al-Muhajiroun supporters, Hassan described what was taking place in Pakistan.

During the question and answer session, one person asked if they'd personally been involved in any violence. Half jokingly, Hassan replied, 'Oh no, of course not. The only thing we thought about was throwing a petrol bomb at the British consulate.' Everyone laughed except Sheikh Bakri, who looked appalled. He pulled Hassan aside and asked, 'Why are you saying such things?'

Bakri was thoroughly shaken. Hassan had never seen him like this before. 'Don't say those things again,' Bakri said, and advised him to get out of the country as quickly as possible.

On his return to Pakistan at the start of January, Hassan's multiple mobile phones were as busy as ever with calls from journalists. The night before his operation he was still taking requests. The very last of them was what he described as an 'off-the-record' briefing that he gave to a reporter from BBC radio. In remarks that would soon be broadcast to an audience of six million people, including a shocked and infuriated Sheikh Bakri, Hassan said: 'One thing I've always tried to stress is that the Mujahideen that are coming in [to Pakistan] from Britain, should strike at the heart of the enemy, which is within its own country, within Britain.'

When asked to clarify what exactly he thought the Mujahideen should strike, Hassan replied nonchalantly: 'British military and government institutes, as well as British military and government individuals.'

At the end of the three-minute interview, the somewhat stunned reporter asked, 'Don't you feel any guilt about being disloyal to your country and talking of helping to launch attacks on it?' The sardonic tone with which Hassan answered suggested that the question was itself obviously flawed.

'How could I possibly feel guilty for something [to which] I've never had any loyalty?' he said. 'Just because I have a passport doesn't mean that I support that government.'

It took Hassan three weeks to recover from his operation. He spent the last of those days staying with Tipu, who helped nurse him back into shape. Around the start of February, Tipu asked Hassan if he didn't mind him holding a meeting with a few of the other brothers in the next room. A few hours later, people began showing up.

Junaid was one of the first to arrive – an unusual occurrence since he was normally late for everything. Junaid continually shirked his al-Muhajiroun responsibilities, and whenever Hassan came to wake him for morning prayers he'd wave Hassan away and go back to sleep until midday. 'He was one of the most lazy people I'd ever met,' Hassan told me, chortling. When he wasn't napping, Junaid was genial and loquacious, and they soon became friends. Hassan would tease him about how flabby and idle he was, and Junaid would give as good as he got.

If Junaid had a skill, it was that he could speak Pashto. Juanid's family came from the border area between Pakistan and Afghanistan and so, unlike everyone else, he was absolutely fluent. In order to communicate with Afghan jihadis, the ability to speak the language was essential.

When Junaid came through the door, Hassan bid him salaam from his rest bed but wasn't inclined to getting into a lengthy conversation and so fell back to sleep. Perhaps an hour later, Hassan said – once everyone who was meant to be there had arrived – there was another knock at the door. Tipu answered, and in walked Omar Sheikh.

Sheikh had just been implicated in the kidnapping of the *Wall Street Journal* reporter Daniel Pearl in January, and he was well on his way to becoming the most infamous man in Pakistan. Now he was in Tipu's house. As he walked past, he bid Hassan salaam. Hassan was so astounded that he wasn't sure he ever replied. 'I thought, oh my goodness, what the hell is going here?' From what little he could make out from his rest bed, Tipu wanted to buy a cache of weapons and Omar was the man who would help supply them.

Not long after a video of Daniel Pearl's beheading was sent to the US consulate in Karachi, and Sheikh was arrested, Hassan decided to write a leaflet saying that Pearl's beheading wasn't murder. 'I thought he got what he deserved. I thought it was foolish journalism on his [Pearl's] behalf.' When Zaheer read the leaflet he ordered Hassan not to publish it. A lot of the brothers' numbers were on Omar Sheikh's phone and Zaheer was worried that it would help lead the ISI straight to them. Hassan thought he knew better and printed up four thousand copies anyway, distributing them after prayers at the Faisal Mosque – one of the biggest in Islamabad.

The great thing, Hassan said, about distributing pamphlets in Pakistan was that it was a novelty. People weren't accustomed to getting anything for free so, unlike in Britain, they'd eagerly take leaflets from your hands. With such a big pile to give away, a crowd soon gathered.

However, as Hassan was handing them out a police officer tapped him on the shoulder. 'Stop that. Who's given you permission to give these out?'

'No one,' Hassan replied.

'Hand them over,' the policeman barked.

'I don't see any signs telling me to stop.'

Defiant as always, Hassan turned around and began flyering again. In the UK he could be impertinent to the police without thinking about it, but in Pakistan the rules were different. The butt of a gun hit him square in the back and he collapsed on the floor.

Just then, a man on a motorbike pulled him up by the arm and told him to get on. Hassan could see someone arguing with the police officer. He wasn't sure who this stranger was and he stalled.

'Well, you can get on, or you can spend the next few days in jail,' the man said.

As they rode through the city, the biker said he'd recognised Hassan from when he'd been handing out flyers, on his loud-hailer, in the market a week before. He'd been impressed by how vocal he'd been in supporting the jihad. If Hassan was interested, there were some people who'd just come back from Afghanistan who he should meet.

He took Hassan to an office on the fourth floor of a building just off the Murree Road in Rawalpindi. It belonged to Sipah-e-Sahaba, the organisation that was responsible for dozens of killings and bombings of the Shia minority. In the state crackdown on extremist organisations, Sipah had been one of the few groups willing to go to war against Musharraf.

The biker led Hassan into a darkened side room where four men with big beards and ragged *salwar kameezes* sat on the floor. As Hassan entered, they greeted him with a slightly wary salaam. He was shunted towards a guy with broad shoulders and a thick neck. 'This is the brother who gets people into Afghanistan,' the biker said, and then left him there.

Hassan said salaam again and the stocky person on the floor returned the gesture once more. He sat down but he wasn't sure what he was supposed to say, so he asked the first obvious thing that came into his head: 'How is the situation in Afghanistan?'

The stocky man paused for an age before replying.

'It's as Allah wants it to be, brother.'

His words hung in the air. Then he asked Hassan a question.

'What brings you to Pakistan, brother?'

Hassan eagerly told him about al-Muhajiroun, his rambling a contrast to the other man's austere utterances. Being a jihadi, Hassan was expecting him to start some sort of debate about his failure to get involved in the war itself. But he just nodded instead.

'It's a very noble mission that you've come here for.'

Now the man looked straight at Hassan. His eyes were sunk deep into his weathered face but there was an intensity about them that held Hassan's attention for the longest time. Then he spoke again. 'I've seen that many brothers from the west are becoming stronger in their faith.'

Hassan replied that he had some money to give to him for the jihad but the man turned him down.

'There is no need to give now, brother. Return again and then you can learn more about who we are.'

On his way out, Hassan asked the biker who it was he'd just spoken to. He gave Hassan a quizzical look and replied, 'You know, I'm not sure anyone here knows his name.'

Most of the jihadis Hassan had met were hotheads or just too stupid to understand anything about politics. But this *mujahid* (fighter) from Sipah seemed entirely different. The description Hassan gave of him was almost reverential: 'There was an intense look about him when he looked at you, like he was looking right into your heart basically ... It made me very close to him and I felt inspired. No – "inspired" is the wrong word. I felt in awe of him from the very moment I met him.'

A few days later, Hassan returned carrying £1,000 in an envelope. He wanted to prove that al-Muhajiroun was serious and perhaps, he thought, he could even convince the *mujahid* of Sheikh Bakri's reasoning.

They sat in the same side room, but this time there were other jihadis around them. Hassan explained that al-Muhajiroun supported the jihad in Afghanistan because Muslims were repelling an invasion. But Hassan didn't understand why Sipah was in favour of attacks in Pakistan. Killing Musharraf or the people close to him wasn't going to make any difference by itself. Didn't those agitating for an Islamic state need to educate the masses and gather them around, like the Prophet Muhammad had done?

The *mujahid* replied with a question: 'Why are you trying to spread the message of Islam?'

The answer to this was easy – according to the Quran it is an obligation for all Muslims to 'command good and forbid evil'. Wherever Muslims are, they have a duty to make Islam real.

'You do this with words. But can it not also be done with your hand?'

'No,' Hassan replied. 'Only the Islamic state has the authority to punish people with force.'

'But what if there is no Islamic state?'

The *mujahid* gave him an example: say a thief comes into his shop and steals a loaf of bread. What would Hassan do? One could command the thief to be good – he could say 'oh brother stop stealing, this is haram' – but the thief would surely laugh and steal regardless. One would have failed to forbid evil.

'However, you could also grab hold of him. You could stop him with your hand and take your property back. If you do that you will succeed.' Musharraf, he explained, was like a thief stealing their country. 'Words won't stop him anymore.'

Impressed by the *mujahid*'s sincerity, Hassan decided to hand him the bundle of money. 'When I gave it to him I told him I had more. He told me that I should see certain things for myself and that he would contact me when I was ready.'

Before he left, Hassan asked the man his name.

'My name, brother? Amjad. Amjad Farooqi.'

12

Amjad Farooqi was a legendary figure. As a teenager, the story went, he was asked to lead a band of armed fighters to protect the cotton convoys as they crossed from Central Asia to Pakistan – the operation overseen by Mullah Omar and Pervez Musharraf. As this force grew and became the Taliban, Amjad Farooqi then became one of the fighters who not only took control of Kabul, but also went on to raid the UN's compound in the capital. At that time, the compound was giving safe haven to Afghanistan's deposed, communist-backed president – Mohammad Najibullah. Amjad Farooqi's men, it is said, castrated Najibullah, tied him to a truck and dragged him through the streets of the capital. Then they took his broken body and strung it up from a lamppost.

Amjad Farooqi went on to represent the terrorist factions of which he was a part at the meetings of Osama Bin Laden's newly formed International Islamic Front – al-Qaeda and its affiliates. After his supposed involvement in the hijacking of the Air India plane in order to free Omar Sheikh, Farooqi then led hundreds of men to fight US forces in Afghanistan.

At the time Hassan met Amjad Farooqi, however, he knew little of his past or who he was really dealing with. At their next meeting, Amjad was on a motorcycle with sacks of flour and sugar tied to the back. Together they drove from Peshawar, over the border that marked the edge of federally administered Pakistan, and into the tribal areas, towards Afghanistan.

The drive was long; the scenery rapidly changed from the plains of Peshawar to the dry, craggy, unforgiving mountains of the border – the same landscape Hassan could remember from his dream almost a year before. Once over the frontier line he asked Amjad where they were going.

'The money you have given me, it is most needed by the families of the Mujahideen. You will meet them now and if you are happy, I will give your money to them,' Amjad said.

A few hours later he pulled up beside a slope and parked the bike. They each carried one of the sacks up the verge. In the distance Hassan could hear the gentle trickling of a stream. At the top of the slope there was a large windy plateau where around a hundred people were encamped. Their tents were made of tarpaulin and bamboo. Beside a small fire, bone-thin children wrapped in bandages stared up at them. Women in ragged burkas, some without shoes, tended to men who were lying injured on the rocky ground. Some had been hit by shrapnel, and the untreated wounds had become infected and gangrenous. The smell of rotting flesh and faeces was sweet and heavy. Hassan covered his nose but he could still taste it in his mouth as he breathed.

Amjad signalled to Hassan and they carried the two sacks to an old man. He spoke in Pashto, but Amjad interrupted him to tell Hassan that these people were Arabs. They had been hiding in this camp for a week. Dispossessed and on the run from US forces and tribal commanders who'd sell them out for a pretty sum, soon they would be forced to move again. The men who were fit and healthy were bearing arms on the frontlines. Holding Hassan's packet of money in his hands, the old man smiled at him. 'Thank you, by God's mercy anything you can give will help these people.'

Before darkness set in, they drove back into Peshawar. Approaching the city limits, Amjad told Hassan that he wanted to stop at the Graveyard of the Martyrs, where those who had died resisting the Soviet invasion were buried. Following tradition, they knelt down together amongst the headstones and gave prayer. As they did, what he had seen at the camp came back to Hassan and he was suddenly overwhelmed by anger. For the first time, this anger was not directed at the outside world but at himself. The people he'd seen were dying the most wretched of deaths, and all this time he'd believed that he was helping them. But the reality was that his entire life had amounted to nothing but words. While telling me about this, Hassan started to choke up. I'd never seen him cry, but there he was on the verge of weeping, unable to talk. I almost reached over to touch his shoulder as an act of empathy, but I didn't want to interrupt him.

In the graveyard, seeing the tears that had come to Hassan's eyes, Amjad uttered softly, 'My brother, may God always hold you close.'

Before long, Hassan said he swore *Bay'at* – an oath of allegiance – to Amjad, and was sent to be trained for jihad. Since the war, all the Mujahideen's permanent barracks had been bombed, so Amjad took him to a village in Swat, an area in the mountains that was full of alpine forests and fast-running rivers swollen with the melt from that winter's snow. When they arrived, a feast was laid on for him: roasted meat, curried vegetables, lentils and '*jinglie polough*', a rice dish mixed with every sort of ingredient – raisins, bananas and fish – that one could imagine.

In the day, Hassan said he headed up into the mountains with some of the other fighters and received his training. It began with getting him fit. He'd been used to jogging or lifting weights but this was very different. He was ordered to run up the mountainside, and to start with he was utterly hopeless. Women carrying buckets of water travelled up the mountain faster than he could. Having seen lots of city folk fail at this task, those teaching him just laughed, berated him for being fat, and made him try again.

They also showed him how to move on the mountains, which trails were the common paths, and which parts were exposed and best avoided. At the top they built up his courage by making him run down as fast as he could. A few times he fell flat, suffering deep gashes on his arms and legs. But the pain, he said, made him all the more quick-footed.

He also finally learned how to operate a Kalashnikov – how it should be cleaned and maintained, and held when being fired. Though it took a lot of time to get used to, Hassan said he eventually cultivated a decent aim.

In the evenings, under the light of an oil lantern, Amjad and Hassan discussed Islamic history and theology. Amjad told him the story of Khalid ibn al-Walid, the Prophet's military commander who had taken a small Arabian tribe from the edge of the desert and conquered all of the Middle East. Under the Prophet's guidance, he had never lost a battle and was considered to be one of the greatest generals of all time. Amjad also explained the justification for terrorism in Muslim lands.

According to the scholars of Islam, the world was split in to Dar al-Islam (the Land of Islam) and Dar al-Kufr (the Land of

Unbelief). But since there was currently no Islamic state, Amjad explained, everywhere was Dar al-Kufr. Since Muslims had a duty to declare war on unbelief, the whole world was now a battlefield.

At the end of his six weeks of training, Hassan returned to Islamabad, where he learned that, following Omar Sheikh's arrest, Tipu had fallen out with the rest of the group. Junaid had taken on the role of fixer and he was now responsible for negotiating weapons purchases and making contact with al-Qaeda in order to set up a training camp for British Muslims.

As for himself, Hassan said, he was willing to give Junaid money, but he didn't see a reason to get involved because he was already bound to Amjad. He waited eagerly for his first set of instructions; these came in May, when a messenger appeared at his door holding a piece of paper with a phone number on it. Hassan went down to the public telephone and rang the number.

'My brother, can you go to Karachi?' Amjad asked.

'When?'

'Straight away.'

Because of his commitments to al-Muhajiroun, Hassan told Amjad that he couldn't travel immediately, but he said that if Amjad needed money he could give it.

'Can you give £6,000?'

'I've got £3,000 at the moment.'

'Okay, no problem, brother. Whatever you can give. Look out for the news.' And then he hung up.

It was a week later – 8 May 2002 – that the first-ever suicide attack in a Pakistani city took place. A car drove up to the front of the Sheraton Hotel in Karachi and exploded. The target was a group of French naval engineers – eleven of them were killed, as well as two Pakistanis who happened to be nearby.

Whilst telling me all of this, Hassan's voice had dropped to a near whisper, as if he was trying to stop other people from listening in – forgetting that the Dictaphone in front of him would pick everything up precisely and his words would then be turned into a book of his life. But then, pausing to recall something, his voice returned to its normal volume. 'The funny thing was that we had two guys in the Sheraton at that time,' he said. Explaining that there were two people from al-Muhajiroun staying at the hotel at the moment of the explosion, he started to chortle to himself – perhaps out of guilt at the way Amjad and his ilk were so frivolous with life. Or maybe it was just a laugh about the irony of how close he'd come to potentially funding the deaths of his own comrades. Then he stiffened up and added, 'I was shocked'.

Without speaking to Amjad, Hassan couldn't be certain he had helped to finance the operation. Two weeks later the pair met in the North-west Frontier Province – tribal territory – on the outskirts of a town called Kohat. Amjad had brought someone with him called Siraj ud Deen.

'What was the news you wanted me to watch?' Hassan said.

Amjad asked him if he'd seen what had happened to the French. 'We organised it and, thanks be to God, the money you gave us was used for that.'

Now that it was confirmed, the gravity of it all began to sink in he told me:

I go why would you target the French? And he had a reason. He was calm, but I was in shock. He said the government is trying to create stability and we're trying to create instability and by doing this hopefully the contracts that the Pakistani government wants people to fulfil they'll be too scared to fulfil hence we target them.

'And the Muslims who were killed?' Hassan asked.

'My brother, Allah has granted them Paradise.'

Amjad had already explained that the whole world was a battlefield and so, by his reasoning, his actions made sense. Though Hassan was shaken, he did not question what had happened. In fact the words he used were, 'I went with the flow kinda thing, even then.'

Amjad felt that the authorities were catching up with him and he might have to go into hiding. He told Hassan that he should now communicate through Siraj. As a boy, Siraj had fought in the first Afghan war and had carried on fighting for various warlords ever since. The years of conflict had turned him into a remorseless operator and Hassan was disconcerted by his presence. 'He was ruthless and cold-hearted and I got that impression from the onset.'

Just before he departed, Hassan took Amjad aside and asked, 'Can I trust this guy with money and everything else?' Amjad told him that he had nothing to worry about. Then he got on his motorbike and rode away.

As soon as Amjad had departed, Siraj asked Hassan if he could leave for Karachi immediately. He agreed, catching a plane from Islamabad. He met Siraj at a rundown hotel. Karachi, a massive metropolis by the sea, lacked the culture of Lahore or the landscape of Islamabad. Hassan had only been to the one-time capital of the country a handful of times and found the place daunting.

Dressed in western clothes, Siraj took Hassan to Binori Town, where there was a big madrasa known for supporting jihadis. After prayers he introduced Hassan to a few of his acquaintances. Throughout the conversations Hassan would sit quietly, saying little. 'Siraj didn't want people to know they had a British guy amongst them in case it attracted too much attention,' he said.

For the few days Hassan was there, Siraj would leave him in the hotel in the evenings and he never told Hassan whom he was going to meet. But during the day they'd drive around the city together and Siraj would point out this or that hotel or building where he thought Hassan could use his British passport to gain entry. They drove past the American consulate a few times, and Siraj mentioned how badly guarded it was. Hassan simply nodded in agreement.

Hassan said that in retrospect he thought the trip to Karachi was a test – a way of getting him comfortable with certain people and seeing how far he was willing to go. When he flew back to Islamabad, Hassan didn't hear anything from Siraj until five days later, when he phoned asking for more funds and Hassan arranged to have £4,000 sent from Britain. He asked what was going on and was simply told, 'You'll see very soon.' But because they'd driven past it so many times, Hassan had already guessed the next bomb's target: the American consulate in Karachi.

'And I was, I don't know – quite happy, excited and thrilled. And very cautious. I thought, as long as it is an American target and no Muslims die I'm not bothered … It's just the Americans, at the end of the day,' Hassan added.

Hassan was in Lahore when a massive bomb, one of the biggest in Pakistan, went off outside the consulate gates in Karachi. The horror of the deed soon became apparent.

The bomb, reports said, had been hidden inside a female driving instructor's car. It was detonated by remote and when it went off, it instantly killed the four students who were in the car with her. A small Suzuki van carrying a man and his niece had also been obliterated by the blast. They were on their way to pick up money for the niece's wedding. Both of them were killed.

The TV pictures showed the manicured lawns of Mohammed Ali Jinnah Gardens scattered with clumps of hair and human flesh. Twelve people died; all were Pakistanis. Protected behind its thick concrete walls, the consulate remained virtually untouched.

'I found out what happened and … I couldn't understand. I thought surely this is not allowed in Islam?' Hassan said. Siraj then contacted him to ask whether he liked what they did. Hassan was completely startled. 'I was like, "Is he taking the piss?", basically. I was really vexed at that point.' Hassan demanded a meeting as soon as possible and when they were face to face they started arguing. 'You've killed Muslims basically … You put the bomb into a Muslim's woman's car, you can't do that.' Hassan got angrier and says he told him 'That's not what I give you money for.' Siraj told him not to worry about it. They'd be carried by Allah for their good deeds. Hassan replied that you couldn't force someone to be a suicide bomber. 'You go and put a bomb on yourself and blow yourself up if that's what it's about,' he shouted at Siraj.

Anyway it got heated and he said, 'Hassan, why are you being argumentative?' I realised that he didn't give a shit basically… He didn't care what he'd done.

I thought, *we've just killed.* Everything we're supposed to be against, i.e. as *muhajids,* we've just done exactly the same. You know. The British drop bombs and kill Muslims and we're willing to kill Muslims to help our cause. And I couldn't mentally, I just wasn't, it was just something I couldn't understand ... why I had done it, or how stupidly I'd got [involved]. It began to feel like a big burden. And at the same time the burden was mixed with the fact of 'I'm going to be arrested'. I got frustrated because I thought I could end up going to Hell for this.

Back in his flat, Hassan stood by the door looking at the other brothers who were eating quietly on the floor, and his head reeled. He couldn't make sense of anything. He grabbed the handles on the door for support. His chest felt heavy under the pressure of his emotions. He recalled Siraj's words: 'They'll be carried by Allah for their good deeds.' But the fact was that they'd sacrificed the lives of people going about their day. They'd decided when to end other, innocent people's lives. For what? For a good deed? This was murder. And Hassan was responsible for it. He told me he was standing by an open door, and as he got angrier he started shaking. Grabbing hold of the handles from both sides, he started to pull harder and harder.

Suddenly the brothers wrestled him to the ground. He'd gone into a fit and ripped the door from the frame without realising it. They pinned him on the floor until his rage passed, until he submitted, until everything was still again.

LEAVING AL-QAEDA

13

For Hassan, leaving al-Qaeda, its ideology and its people was not brought about by a moment of revelation, some Damascene conversion. It was a slower process filled with backward steps and bouts of depression, disengagement and irrational hope. At least, this is how it appeared to me as we started writing the book together. Following his permanent return from Pakistan in 2003, the network's daily demands had given structure and purpose to Hassan's life. For three years, there had been weekly fundraising meetings to attend, recruitment to organise, and cash to be deposited with associates around the country. This routine had been like a scaffold to Hassan: outwardly supporting his confidence but also masking his inner turmoil and guilt about the consulate bombings. Now, after returning from Dubai in the spring of 2006, with his thoughts no longer taken up by the daily concerns of the network, he began to ruminate on these doubts – and the things that he'd done – and, slowly, he started changing his views.

Hassan sealed his departure from the network by giving back his laptop, his contacts book, a few propaganda videos and the remainder of that month's funding (£600). In a final conversation with his British emir, Hassan made it clear that he wasn't coming back. I asked him who his emir was – who had been giving him orders, provisions and money? After some hesitation, Hassan told me his name: Yassir al-Sirri. I was surprised – al-Sirri was a serious figure. An unassuming and squat man with a sharp, angular nose, his voice was high-pitched and thin, especially when he spoke in English. In the 1990s, al-Sirri had been sentenced to death in absentia for his involvement in the attempted assassination of the Egyptian prime minister. He had also been indicted for terrorism offences by the US, and directly after 9/11 the British police had tried (but failed) to prosecute him for his close links to al-Qaeda. (The judge who released him called him an 'innocent fall guy'.)

I asked Hassan for his phone number and he gave it to me from memory. That detail stuck with me. Hassan had three phones with hundreds of contacts on them and yet, either through habit or by deliberately committing it to memory, this was maybe the only number he knew by heart.

The next day, I dialled the number. When the person on the other end picked up, I recognised the faltering, nasal tone from media interviews al-Sirri had given. He confirmed his name politely. However, when I began to ask him about his activities, he suddenly became riled and asked me where I had got his number from. I told him the truth: 'Hassan Butt'.

A couple of days later Hassan rang me to say that al-Sirri had gone ballistic. He had accused Hassan of giving his details to a journalist and betraying his trust. Hassan told al-Sirri that he was barking up the wrong tree, but now he was ringing me to confirm that I really hadn't told al-Sirri who I had got his number from.

I lied.

'Of course not,' I told Hassan. 'You know a lot of journalists, so given what's just gone on with you leaving, I guess he put two and two together.' I felt bad that I'd lied and got him into trouble, but my actions proved that both parties knew each other.

After word got out that he had left the network and started to reform some of his views, Hassan's friends and associates began to call him. At first they took a 'nicey, nicey' approach, he said. In the past, when others had left the network, they had received the same kind of probing and so this wasn't unexpected. The network wanted to know what Hassan would do next. Would he cause trouble by talking to the media – or, even worse, to the police? Or like everyone else who had left the network, would Hassan get a regular job and quietly fade away?

Hassan said that he'd deal with them all in a consistent manner – polite, courteous, reassuring, vague – but then a friend from his school days accused him of being a flake and a sell-out. That's when he lost his temper and let too much slip. He told the ex-school friend that he was writing a book.

After that, the calls became increasingly hostile, he said. Over the next few weeks, jihadis from around the country advised him to keep his mouth shut – the network wouldn't tolerate him talking. At the end of March, while he was picking up his nieces and nephew from primary school, two men paid him a visit.

The first guy – Hassan said that they didn't give their names – was tall and thin, wearing a T-shirt and jeans. The second man – the one who did all the talking – was shorter, around five foot eight, and chubby. He wore a *salwar kameez* and spoke with the hint of an Arab accent. Standing beside the school gates, he asked Hassan how things were going. Anxiously, Hassan asked 'Brother, do I know you?' He thought that they might know him from the media. The *Sun* newspaper had just done a spread on the five most dangerous Islamic radicals in Britain and Hassan was named as one of them.

The chubby guy suggested that Hassan shouldn't play games. As they were leaving, he stooped down to say hello to Hassan's three-year-old nephew. Then, turning to face Hassan, he said: 'It would be a shame if anything happened to our families – as Muslims we're supposed to do the best for them.'

Hassan said he rang al-Sirri and demanded an explanation. Al-Sirri told him that, although what had happened was unfortunate, the situation had nothing to do with him. If orders were coming from anyone, they must be coming from abroad.

A few weeks later, all the ground-floor windows of his mother's house were smashed in. Not long after, Hassan reported that all the tyres on his brother's car had been slashed. Feeling that enough was enough, Hassan said he decided to drive down to London to pay al-Sirri a personal visit.

As al-Sirri came out of the Walthamstow mosque where he normally prayed, Hassan jumped out and collared him. Hassan explained that the network had nothing to fear from him – engagement with the west didn't have to mean putting people's security at risk. Hassan wasn't a traitor. But if people were going to play dirty, Hassan also knew where people ate, slept and prayed.

For the next few weeks everything was quiet. Hassan thought that his ultimatum must have paid dividends. But in early May, a few days after our first batch of interviews for the book had ended and I had returned to London, Hassan rang me to tell me that something awful had happened. Two men had come from the direction of the waste mound outside his house and shoved him through his front door as he opened it. Ignoring the security alarm that had started counting down as the door opened, one of the men pushed Hassan onto the floor. Pressing his forearm against the back of Hassan's neck, he forced Hassan's face into the steps that led up to the bedroom and pulled his right arm back, almost to breaking point. As Hassan started praying under his breath, the other man took his laptop and, without saying a word, the two intruders left. It was over so quickly that Hassan had time to recover, pick himself up and punch in the alarm code before it went off. 'Honestly, I thought they would put a gun to my head and that would be it,' Hassan told me over the phone.

The attack seemed to leave Hassan totally shaken up. The network, he said, wanted to stop his book from being published and Hassan guessed that that they would come back once they realised they hadn't got what they wanted. (They'd taken a laptop that Hassan had borrowed from one of his brothers to use for email. All the notes and interview transcripts for the book were on my computer.)

Hassan told me that he'd decided to up sticks and leave home for while; for the next few weeks he stayed at various friends' houses in the north of England – Manchester, Stoke, Bradford. But this constant moving to try and stay safe only led him to a larger, more harrowing realisation.

The news of his departure had spread quickly throughout the jihadi network. When he spoke to a friend in Pakistan, Hassan felt he was 'funny and cold'. Even those on the fringes, those whom Hassan had termed his 'sympathisers', had become wary of his presence. A fortnight after leaving his home in Manchester, Hassan was due to spend the whole weekend with one such friend in Birmingham when things came to a head. The friend informed Hassan that it would be difficult for him to stay because his wife was returning. 'The thing with these guys,' Hassan told me, 'is that they always use their wives as an excuse. In the past, he would have cancelled everything for me.' He didn't think anyone knew any of the specifics, but it was more a case of people being told to stay away from Hassan. He decided to stop initiating contact. 'I don't want people to have to choose between me and them so I prefer not to put anyone in that position in the first place.'

Although Hassan couldn't afford it, he told me he had started staying at bed-and-breakfasts. He became annoyed, disappointed and then depressed that friends and acquaintances he had known for years were abandoning him. Hassan had always respected the way al-Muhajiroun and the Pakistani jihadis had been willing to debate ideas. But now, he said, no one was even giving him the chance to explain his reasons for leaving the network. He felt suffocated.

No one comes over to use the gym anymore. And remember how I used to have at least four or five dream interpretations a week? I don't even get those anymore. It's like the world I knew has cut me off.

The change in his routine seemed to be what affected Hassan most. He had been used to following orders. Now, learning how to be the master of his own affairs and making his own decisions was starting to take a toll on his mental health. Everything else in his life had come to a halt, and for that reason the autobiography had become all-important to him. He'd been trying to keep himself busy and get other projects up and running but he felt the book had to be published first, as that would be his 'platform' to get into different fields. In the meantime he was bored, sitting at home doing absolutely nothing besides his weight training.

Trying to get a job to fill his days so that – as he put it – he didn't have to 'think about things too deeply' was proving difficult. Hassan had heard about some serious brawls that had broken out at his old school between the Somali and Pakistani kids, and he wanted to volunteer to do some intervention work to try and stop the violence. He thought he'd be good at it because, as he said, 'that's something I've been through and come out the other end', but he was bluntly informed that with his record he didn't stand a chance of being allowed anywhere near teenagers.

Hassan was finding it hard to do anything at all because, as he discovered, he didn't fit into mainstream society. Apart from the fact that he didn't have any non-Muslim friends, there were other things – small matters – that jarred with him. After years as a radical, he now only felt comfortable in Pakistani clothing or combat trousers, and this made him all the more conspicuous whenever he went out. He knew that he hadn't read the books that 'normal' people had read, nor had he watched regular TV for almost a decade, and of course he'd never been clubbing or inside a pub – the smell of alcohol made him sick. When he had to stay in bed and breakfasts, he found it difficult to sleep on a normal bed. (At home he slept on an unsprung mattress placed on the floor.)

Things came to a head one day when he tried to occupy himself by going to the cinema. Hassan hadn't been to the movies since he'd been instructed that the mixing between the sexes there was un-Islamic. But now he decided that this was bad theology; people mixed as readily in the street as they did in a movie theatre. So he decided to go to a matinee screening. But when he parked outside he found he couldn't shift himself from the seat of his car. He froze – his body simply wouldn't let him move.

I tried to provide him with some solace when he told me things like this, and reminded him that a journey such as his was always going to be difficult and lonely. What he needed to do was to keep an eye on the long game. He'd get through the immediate trauma, and once he'd rebuilt his life and fostered a new circle of friends he could look back without any regrets. But Hassan and I both knew that while I could keep telling him how it would pan out in theory, no one – and certainly not me – knew what leaving the network in such a public fashion entailed in practice. My words sounded formulaic and empty.

I realised there wasn't much I could say that would buoy him, and my inability to help him worried me. What if this got all too much for Hassan? All I could do was encourage him to talk about what was going on. At least that way he might feel a little less isolated.

Following the incident outside the movie theatre, Hassan began to resent his situation. He complained about how slowly the book was taking to commission, blaming the west's 'red tape', 'policies' and 'structures'. He was also worried about what would happen to recordings I had of him confessing to numerous crimes. He sent me a text:

> I am getting very annoyed, even though I may not be showing it, at how long it's taking to arrange this meeting with the [book] agents … I have no idea who these ppl are or how they operate. I feel incredibly paranoid at the moment [about]…where I stand with the tapes u have of me.

In sudden outbursts Hassan would declare that he was 'fed up of causes … I just want to live my own life'. He wanted nothing more than to get married, settle down and raise a family. But at the same time, he desperately missed the network's ability to give him guidance.

'I've never claimed to know all the answers,' he said, 'I just have the questions and I think that one thing the network's structure gave you was, you always had people who you respected and ... who you could go to for answers.'

Soon, Hassan began to regret his decisions. By becoming an Islamic radical he'd always known that he was taking a risk with his future. While his elder brothers had made successes of themselves by going into dentistry and business, Hassan had travelled to Pakistan to spread al-Muhajiroun's message. Now that he'd left al-Qaeda – and become a pariah in everyone's eyes – he realised that the gamble hadn't paid off. He had nothing to show for all those years: no degree, no job, no friends, no money. Sounding despondent, Hassan began to reel off his list of what-ifs: 'If my dad wasn't in prison would I have been involved with these people, would I have concentrated more on my education? If I had concentrated more on my education would I have gone down a different route and never gone through any of this? My whole social scene may have been different.'

Hassan even wondered what would have happened if specific days and hours had been different. What if he hadn't gone to the mosque that day when Nadeem, the recruiter from Hizb ut-Tahrir, had shown up? What if after waking up, he hadn't remembered his dream about the Prophet and the mountains and the desert that had inspired him to quit his life in Britain and go to Pakistan?

'I've not been this low for so, so long,' he told me. 'To be honest with you, I don't remember being this low in my entire life.'

*

It was at this point that one of his oldest friends, a fellow radical and brother who had been there right from the beginning came to his house and sat him down to talk. 'He said, "Hassan what are you doing? You're going to get yourself in trouble. You can't see the whole picture. Why are you breaking that chain of command? What's got into you?"'

The friend asked Hassan if he had been unhappy about the amount of money he had been receiving. 'I told him that it wasn't that – I was thinking I was probably getting more funds than I needed.' (From the £2,800 that was posted through the door monthly by the network, Hassan said he would use £1,000 of that on his personal expenses and the rest would pay for his activities.) The friend asked Hassan what he hoped to achieve by leaving and – when he couldn't give an answer, when he was at his most confused and most despondent – the friend offered an outstretched hand and asked him to come back.

'I just sat there and I said, "no I can't go back in," Hassan told me over the phone. But after his friend left, Hassan said he thought about the isolation.

I thought I really can't hack it, the physical isolation of not being around people. I mean there's one thing being in prison when you're forced. That, I could take. I could sit in a cell all day long and it not really concern me because I know I'm being forced ... And honest to God, I was so tempted to ring him up and say what do I need to do to stop all this?

14

That evening, after his friend had left, Hassan's natural positivity was rejuvenated by what seemed to be the smallest event. Hassan said that he had been surfing the Internet well past midnight when he'd come across an interview with Irshad Manji, a Canadian Muslim author and religious reformist. Manji, who often toured Europe and North America promoting the idea of Islamic reformation, had been praised across the spectrum by press and academia alike. (Harvard University's Adams Professor of Political Leadership and Democratic Values said that Manji was leading the 'most important new movement in several decades'; *Elle* magazine described what she was doing as 'moving' and 'refreshing'.) She had won numerous awards for authorial bravery but, despite all this, Manji was perhaps most known for being both a practising Muslim and openly gay.

During one of our very first theological discussions, Hassan had admonished me for bringing up her (bestselling) book, *The Trouble with Islam Today*, so it was with some curiosity that I found myself listening to how her words were helping to bring him out of his darkest melancholy. Even though he had despised her ideas and had previously disliked her, on hearing her speak on the BBC Hassan said he had been wrong to judge her. Most surprising of all, he recounted a conversation between Manji and

Salman Rushdie that had filled him with hope. Manji had asked Rushdie why she should put her own life in jeopardy to write her book. Rushdie replied that it was worth the risk because once the book was published extremists could take her life, but they'd never be able to take her ideas away from her. Hassan said he found himself wondering if he was being influenced by Salman Rushdie. And then he burst out laughing.

After that night, the outward signs of Hassan's depression quickly disappeared. A few days later I jotted down how he had quoted a biblical verse – 'Blessed are the peacemakers' – to fortify himself for the struggle ahead. Talking to me over the phone he mused that he had regrets, that maybe he could have been an 'average, educated person' with a normal life, but that 'maybe Allah's given me a bigger responsibility to make something [of myself]'.

On 4 July 2006, three days before the first anniversary of the London bombings, I had been asked to participate in a panel discussion about British terrorism for a think tank called the Foreign Policy Centre. The meeting, attended by around forty people, was held at one of the committee rooms in the Houses of Parliament. My talk was going badly. It was a very hot day and the audience were falling asleep but I was grateful to be able to deliver my speech to at least one friendly and attentive face amongst the crowd – Irshad Manji.

Once the seminar was over, and most of the audience had somewhat hastily filed out of the room, I approached Manji and told her about Hassan – how he had left the jihadi network and the night when he had listened to her interview on the BBC. Manji stood nodding her head with interest and then, while we swapped contact details, told me that she was very keen on meeting him. Six days later, Hassan and Manji were sitting at my dinner table.

Whenever Hassan came to my house I became agitated. This was not because I was worried about the increased security risk that his presence might create (though my flatmate often wondered why her safety had to be compromised). My agitation stemmed from the fear that I might not be able to provide the correct Islamic setting, and so would make Hassan uncomfortable.

As well as cleaning my flat each time he visited, something that I would have done for any guest, I also cleared away any traces of alcohol, such as the empty beer cans and wine bottles waiting beside the bins to be recycled. I would tidy away the tobacco pouches and rolling papers that were on top of the coffee table, and empty out and then hide the ashtray that sat on the window ledge. I also made sure to place both my editions of the Quran on the top shelf – placing the Quran on any shelf except the highest is regarded by Muslims as extremely disrespectful.

I always cleaned my bedroom, in case our conversations overran and Hassan wanted somewhere private to pray. And I would hide any signs that I was living with a female housemate, making sure her laundry wasn't out drying and putting her toiletries away in a drawer. Hassan, of course, never demanded any of these modifications to my environment, nor would he have mentioned it had matters in my house been otherwise (although he did admonish me for smoking on a few occasions). But I felt better knowing that the differences in our lifestyles and our views would be less pronounced and that he would feel more comfortable around me. It was a deception of sorts, but one that I felt was necessary to ensure he opened up in our interviews. More than this, as a ghostwriter I felt it was my job to blend into his world. I was there to examine his movements, to record his life from the sidelines. I feared that if I were too active a presence, I'd alter the real Hassan Butt. To stay in the background was to do my job.

From the window of my flat I could see Hassan approach. He was dressed casually: black T-shirt, combats and a baseball cap. His beard was now very, very short – little more than stubble. (I had also shaved, and when Manji turned up her first remark to us was that she had more facial hair than we did.)

After he'd come up and had sat down at my living room table, Hassan took off his cap. I realised that in the last nine months I'd never seen the top of his head before – in my presence he had always worn a hat or a skullcap. The hair at the back and on the sides of his head had never been longer than a quarter of an inch, so I'd presumed that the hair on top would be the same length. But, seeing it for the first time, I was surprised at the contrast. Shiny with a little hair oil, his hair was jet black, long and extremely thick.

Wearing trousers, a short-sleeve sequinned top and a delicate necklace around her neck, Manji brought a little glamour to the table. She also brought along her Italian colleague Roberta. After introducing herself, Roberta stayed fairly quiet; during the meeting, she answered Manji's phone, took messages and made notes. At one point, while we were all talking, Manji dubbed her 'Abdullah, my little manservant'. She meant it humorously, but neither I nor Hassan laughed.

Manji was both effervescent and commanding, and at first it felt like she was talking to an audience of hundreds rather than to the three people sitting around my table. Worried that Hassan might be a little intimidated, I interrupted her by prompting him to start discussing his theological doubts and his reasons for leaving the network.

Hassan told her just how despondent he had been, and at the end of the story he again laughed off the shock of being inspired by her and Rushdie's dialogue. He then began to ask Manji his own questions. He bluntly told her that he didn't see the need for her to advertise being a lesbian; he himself committed plenty of sins, but he didn't think to write about them or advertise them. Hassan explained that his own view was that Islam stated it was wrong to be a homosexual, but that as long as you didn't make it a public issue – that it remained within the confines of your own home – then Islam allowed such matters to remain private. I started to squirm silently, and began to think that arranging the meeting had been a horrible idea.

Replying in a way that suggested she had answered this question a million times before – and no doubt she had – Manji said that if she hadn't declared her homosexuality then she'd be a hypocrite: asking for honesty from Muslims while keeping the fact that she was a lesbian a secret. In the end, she had stated that she was a lesbian but she never willingly broached the topic. For this stance, Manji added, she had been criticised by Muslim gay and lesbian groups.

Hassan then raised a second criticism. He told Manji that if she had instead called her book *The Trouble with Muslims* then he would have read it. How could Islam be the problem? Wasn't it believers who were getting things wrong?

Manji winced, and explained that she had debated this with her publishers for two months because she shared Hassan's view

– it would have been better to focus on the believers and not the religion. But she didn't want to be taken to court. Her publishers had told her that, by suggesting Muslims were at fault, she would be writing off an entire community and could potentially be sued under Canadian race laws. She joked that if she had been sued, it would have been great for sales. I then pushed Hassan to start talking about his own ideas. While I'd been writing the book, he and I had been discussing whether he would name his former colleagues who weren't in prison or hadn't already been killed. In a sense it was a false question – any publisher would be unlikely to print actual names because of the threat of libel action. However, I still wanted to know where he stood on this. Hassan had explained that if he named people, he would be branded a traitor. The network would no longer engage with the substance of his argument and they would focus solely on his betrayal.

'My aim isn't to get people arrested,' he'd said; 'my aim is to destroy their ideology.' But until that conversation in my living room, he hadn't actually said nor done anything to demonstrate this desire to 'destroy their ideology'. Perhaps it was Manji's presence, or just the occasion of meeting someone new, that made him take the first leap. Bluntly, he stated, 'All suicide bombing is haram – including suicide bombing in Palestine.'

Manji's eyes lit up.

During the interview process for the book, Hassan had started to think that his doubts about Islamist ideology may have been awakened even before the consulate bombing. He told me about a time in late 2001, when he had gone to the offices of a Pakistani newspaper to do an interview. The paper's editor asked Hassan what the main export of Pakistan was. Hassan didn't know. The editor replied that if he didn't know this, how did he expect to run an economy, or an entire country for that matter? Hassan soon realised that even though he'd spent years of his life fighting for an Islamic revolution, no one in al-Muhajiroun – or indeed any of the jihadis he'd met – had any real idea of how to actually run a country. If they really did manage to take over the government one day, how would the people get fed? When Hassan had put that question to Siraj, he was told that the people might starve but 'at least they would be starving for Allah'.

During a long phone conversation together, while Hassan was in the throes of his depression, I remembered the story about the newspaper editor and asked: 'If the jihadis had taken you into a room with loads of advisers and shelves with tons of books and plans for a whole state and said, "Here is the master plan for setting up an Islamic state" – what would you have done?'

'I would have done whatever they would have told me to do. Whatever. Even if they had asked me to do a suicide mission I probably would have done it. Anything. Because I would have realised that whatever I was giving my life for was worthwhile. I don't want to kill people for the sake of killing people, only to realise that you've got nothing planned at the end of it.'

'So if someone asked now, "What do you think about suicide bombing?", what are you going to say?' I asked him.

'Now? I say suicide bombing is wrong because bombing, for me, means that it's not the last option. You can plant a bomb in different places or use a bomb in different ways without having to kill yourself. The principal is that ... '

Hassan paused before continuing. He wanted to give me an example.

'Let's say that you are trapped by the enemy, right, and you're, I don't know, on a cliff or a mountain and you know that by getting caught you're going to endanger more Muslims. It's permitted for you to actually commit suicide in that act.

'That is an opinion. It's not the only opinion. But there is a valid Islamic opinion that it is permitted to commit suicide in this example.

'Suicide bombing on the other hand – or a suicide mission – is only permitted if you have no other viable option. The mere fact that the 7/7 guys had the ability to build bombs … for me, then, that does not give them the right to attach the bombs to themselves. It's completely haram. It's another issue about who they are targeting at this moment in time. I don't know where I stand on that. I'm still trying to get around who is innocent and who is not. But if it had happened in the council estate down the road, I know I would be able to say that this was haram because these people don't know nothing. And probably the same would be said of the majority of the guys who died in London. But I don't know why I can't say it yet [that suicide bombings are haram]. I really don't know where that block is coming from, stopping me from saying this publicly.'

'Was it because 7/7 was carried out by someone you'd met?'

At this, Hassan became even more contemplative.

'Possibly, possibly. And I know Mohammad was a nice guy, I mean he was an Islamic-minded guy, but what I'm trying to get at is that I could have been that person quite easily. Maybe the only difference between me and him is that he was more convinced than I was of what he was doing. He really thought that giving his life would change something. I think that I would need to make sure that there's a plan there.'

I asked Hassan if he thought there were any other differences between him and Mohammad Sidique Khan.

'There's a spiritual aspect to it; you really do want to go back to Allah.' There were times, he said, where he was fed up of the world, fed up of the way everyone behaved. 'And honestly, if an opportunity arose on those days … '

He paused again, longer this time, before carrying on.

'I always said that I did have that ability to do it until I really thought about the fact that people are always saying suicide missions are allowed if there is no other viable option.' He then discussed the opinions of the so called moderate Egyptian sheikh Yusuf al-Qaradawi, who'd pronounced that suicide bombings were allowed only in Palestine because the Palestinians didn't have any other option. But, Hassan argued, they had weapons, they had other means. 'I don't want to say it – oh my God! – Palestinian suicide bombings may be haram, but I'm actually getting to that point.' All the evidence he said that the jihadis could quote to legitimise suicide bombing no longer made sense to him, he said. This applied to 7/7.

'So, 7/7 … was it haram? I'm ninety per cent sure it was, or ninety-five per cent sure it was haram. And I guess the only reason that I'm not a hundred per cent is – yeah, you're probably right – because I knew Mohammad and it's difficult for me. Because you've got to understand, by saying it's haram what I'm ultimately saying is that these guys aren't in Paradise – they're in Hell. And I'm not ready to do that to any Muslim.'

Manji suggested that, to keep Hassan active and occupied, he should get involved in a number of projects she was working on. She mentioned many things: writing articles, a web forum, introductions to various people including book agents and publishers. But the two ideas that seemed most concrete were for Hassan to be interviewed for a film she was producing, to be screened the following year, and the promise to work on a joint documentary with CBS's *60 Minutes*, the pre-eminent US current affairs show. The hope was that they would run a feature about Hassan's ideological transformation – and that this would get him noticed across the world.

The rest of the summer passed quickly, and little was achieved in terms of moving the book closer towards publication. This made Hassan nervous, irritated, and at times angry – even more so when he thought about the steps Manji was achieving to elevate his profile. He would text me to chivvy me about extracting a decent advance from publishers, since if the book was going to cause him problems he'd need the money. (He said he was already having dreams about the problems he would face.) Besides, he said, he didn't 'have a penny left'.

In late August, Manji got involved and sent me a concerned note by email. She wanted to be filled in on what was happening. 'On a related note,' she said that if they could get herself and Hassan on *60 Minutes* sooner rather than later, we'd likely be 'flooded' with publishing offers. Then she added, 'I'm meeting with *60 Minutes* on Monday. They're very interested in my work and how it has affected Hassan.'

By October, one publisher had offered for the book, and their advance – a healthy five-figure sum – was considerable enough for Hassan to think about, as he said, 'putting my life on the line'. During a thirty-minute conversation, I implored him to take the offer – though the money was decent, accepting the offer would mean the work would be published, which I reminded him was the main goal.

Hassan turned to Manji for counsel. She advised Hassan that we should reject the advance because he'd get much better sums from American publishers once the interview with CBS hit the airwaves. He said that he hadn't made up his mind, but I knew that now Manji had put it into his head he was worth significantly more, he'd never take the deal.

A few days later, Hassan phoned to tell me how excited he was. The night before he'd had a dream and now he was adamant that things were going to change for the best – he'd seen it in his vision. 'It was the first time I had a dream with you in it!' he added.

Throughout his life, Hassan had regarded his dreams – and the dreams of others – as godly messages. Now, Hassan told me that even after Manji's counsel he had been minded to take the deal. But this dream had changed his mind. In his vision, we were standing in a grand room with high ceilings. It was the launch party for the book. For months, perhaps even years, we had been faced with much adversity, but we'd finally come through it and got a big advance and now everyone – family and friends, as well as various journalists, authors and political types – were gathered to congratulate us. When Hassan awoke, he knew what had to happen. Although he understood that I wasn't religious, he told me that because of his dream he now believed that we both had to square up to hardship. Because of his dream, he was now sure that turning down the existing offer would be the route to our success. He couldn't put his name to this contract.

I was livid – we'd both spent many months working on the proposal and first chapters. Here was a chance to finally make something of all our efforts. I tried pleading with him. I told him that the advance was just the start of what could be gained in monetary terms, and I reminded him of my own sacrifices: I'd already turned down numerous offers to work on investigations in order to give myself the time I needed to work on the book. We were both partners in this project, and I'd be losing a lot by refusing this offer on the basis of his vision in the small hours of the morning.

But I knew him well enough now to know he wasn't going to budge. To him, his dreams were divine. I thought it all ridiculous and irrational and came to the conclusion that this was far more about massaging his ego than about listening to God.

More importantly, I began to worry that not taking the offer would damage our relationship – the closeness between us, cultivated for the sake of the book but something that I now cherished, might be lost altogether. What made this thought even more painful was that I could see he was on the verge of the most exciting transformation. One of the country's most publicly reviled radicals might just turn the tables on his fellow jihadis. I wanted to remain close to him as he made this journey, not just to document every detail but to be a part of something that was potentially world-changing.

Manji was clearly coming between us. I was concerned about her motives for getting close to Hassan. She was a brilliant operator and probably knew how well it reflected on her to have a reformed jihadi by her side. On Hassan's part, I was starting to see how he wanted to be adored by her. She was quickly becoming one of those paternal replacements – like Nadeem, Sheikh Bakri and Amjad Farooqi – that he'd longed for all his life. And like his relationships with those characters, I could sense he'd be left more damaged at the end of it all. Even though it had seemed so fortuitous, I could only blame myself for introducing them.

I buried this thought. To voice it would only make me appear jealous. And in some ways, I was; I had to admit Manji had something I didn't. Though there was much that bonded me and Hassan – our cultural background, our age, our fathers who had both spent time in prison – there was one obvious division. However much I understood about Islam, however much Hassan praised me for knowing about this or that element of his faith, I wasn't a Muslim myself. I was brought up a Hindu and was now a confirmed atheist. I'd never faced east to pray or recited the Quran. I didn't even believe in God. Not only could Manji connect with him through their shared beliefs, she'd also been through the wars. She knew what it was to lose a community of friends and family, and confront her co-religionists on a public stage.

And, deep down, I felt Hassan was right – his story deserved a bigger reward. I was letting him down as a writer. Though he never doubted that I was investing enough time, the awkward reality was that, despite my best efforts, our proposal was mediocre. I was, I realised, too much of a rookie; a more experienced and adept author would surely have landed him the six-figure deal he wanted. Perhaps for his sake it might be better if Manji took over my role entirely.

I kept all these thoughts to myself. After a short and frustrating conversation, I told Hassan that I had no choice but to work on the book part-time until I had saved up some more money. Hassan replied that he would be busy working full-time with Manji, helping her to spread the idea of Islamic reformation.

For the next few months we fell out of daily contact, speaking perhaps once a week, and then only when we had an obvious reason to do so.

15

Around the same time as Hassan rejected the book offer, Manji's attempts to get Hassan and herself a feature on *60 Minutes* were starting to get results. I was visited by two journalists from CBS's London bureau who wanted to know what Hassan was about. At first I judged that Michael Gavshon, a South African émigré, and his colleague Drew Magratten, a newly married American who had just moved to London from New York, were hardworking but simple people. It was an easy mistake to make. With his polite and gentle manner, the mass of brown curls atop his head and his casual woollen jumper/brown loafers/khaki trouser get-up, Magratten struck me as the archetypal nice guy, someone who had never uttered a profanity in his life and always rang his mother when he should. Though quicker in conversation, with more of a worldly air about him, Gavshon was often the quieter of the two. Both asked me the same questions about Hassan over and over again. First Magratten, and then Gavshon, and then Magratten again – each time rephrasing the questions in a slightly different manner. I assumed that they never really understood what I was trying to say, especially when it came to explaining the generational factors that had driven many young Muslims to become radicals and terrorists. They also took a vast quantity of written material from me. At Hassan's request,

I gave Gavshon and Magratten all of the interview transcripts, the early drafts of the book, all the press clippings that I had found on Hassan's past, and a copy of the entire bibliography on extremism that I'd collected over the years.

I also explained why I believed Hassan was who he said he was. I told them about his links with Yassir al-Sirri, Hassan's emir, and explained that many of the people who Hassan had spoken about had later been arrested on charges of terrorism.

Sajeel was one of the first to be arrested, at the start of 2004 in Pakistan. He was held in prison for three months until his family helped to secure his release. Despite American calls for him to be deported to the US, he was sent back to Britain and banned from Pakistan. A few months later, the Crawley gang were arrested in Britain for trying to make a fertiliser bomb; a few weeks after that, Junaid Babar was arrested in New York. As part of a plea bargain, Junaid told the US authorities everything he knew. His testimony spanned some two thousand pages. I managed to obtain a copy of part of Junaid's statement, and Hassan's name was mentioned at least a dozen times. Junaid talked about the camp he'd been trying to set up, and other people whom Hassan had talked about – such as Sajeel, Tipu and Zaheer – were also mentioned in some detail.

One of the last to be arrested was Tipu. He was caught in an undercover sting as he attempted to buy rocket launchers, machine guns, hand guns and three thousand rounds of ammunition from the boot of a car at a motorway service station in Hertfordshire.

Zaheer was one of the few people not to have been imprisoned by the authorities. I'd gone to visit him in Colindale, London, where he still lived. I found that Hassan's descriptions of both Zaheer and his house matched the reality. Zaheer also confirmed a little of what Hassan had told me about al-Muhajiroun in Pakistan. But, beyond that, Zaheer wasn't willing to talk. For the sake of his kids, he had put that all behind him.

Despite this wealth of information, Gavshon and Magratten still insisted on repeating their questions again and again. But I soon came to realise that this was not a symptom of a lack of intelligence but instead a passionate dedication to surgical thoroughness. They combed over every word, every recollection looking for inconsistencies and contradictions. In the end, they put in six months of work to produce eleven minutes of film.

When they turned to interviewing Hassan, they asked him questions that I myself had asked Hassan a dozen times. Each time, Hassan would answer in a slightly different way – sometimes adding another anecdote, sometimes cracking a joke, or more usually by giving a briefer, punchier answer than the one he had given me. When Magratten asked why Hassan had left the network, Hassan replied, 'They've just turned into killers.' For the time constraints of TV, it was a terrific answer. The pair also asked many questions I hadn't braved asking Hassan so directly. In one interview Magratten was particularly determined to make absolutely sure he knew the substance of what had happened in Pakistan. As Magratten pushed for more detail than I had, it seemed that Hassan became more worried about what he had done. The more worried he was, the less he remembered.

Hassan suddenly sounded hesitant and unwilling to piece together what little he could recall. He seemed unable to explain exactly where and how the consulate bomb had gone off and began flailing for bits of information. He became increasingly flustered at the rapidity of the questions being lobbed at him from all three of us. Astonishingly, he stopped mid-sentence and asked, 'The consulate bombing did happen in 2002, didn't it?'

Magratten and I kept giving each other quizzical looks, wondering exactly what was going on, but Hassan explained his lack of memory – for years he had tried to blank the whole thing out, to erase the episode from his mind, partly out of fear of being arrested and partly due to the burden of guilt he felt.

Along with Magratten, I tried to suggest a possible sequence of events, to help him piece together a timeline. When Magratten and I read him the newspaper clippings and told him that eleven civilians had died that day outside the US consulate, he became very uneasy. Hassan told us that he didn't want to know how many people he had helped to kill. For years, he had avoided reading reports about the incident, and until now he hadn't known just how high the death toll was.

The agreed format for the documentary was a dialogue between Manji and Hassan. This would help to demonstrate how Manji's ideas of *ijtihad* – the principle of Islamic questioning – had affected Hassan to such an extent that he left the network. The crowning moment would be an event in January at the Cambridge University Union, where Hassan would appear publicly for the first time and Manji would interview him about the change in his views.

Manji was also pushing Hassan to continue working on a novel he was writing. Hassan had started typing a few hundred words everyday to keep himself occupied. It soon developed into a full-length narrative of more than 130,000 words, which he provisionally entitled *War Games Proper*.

The novel – about a British terrorist called Khalid who organises a bombing in the US and then tries to start a war between Pakistan and India while being hunted down by a former schoolfriend turned MI5 agent – was written in the style of an airport thriller. The pace of the narrative made up for the hackneyed sentences. Hassan understood how to weave separate subplots together and hold his reader's attention with cliffhangers.

With each chapter, Hassan's list of characters became ever more colourful; there were ex-drug-dealer terrorists, white converts, a pregnant accomplice wife. Surprisingly, considering Hassan's background, the most well-written character was the MI5 agent, Sean Slater, whose empathy for his (more one-dimensional) childhood friend – the terrorist mastermind Khalid – was at times poignant.

The small details needed to fill out a thriller were also there: comprehensive explanations of the type of hotel rooms needed for a terrorist hideout, secret meetings in the toilets of fast food joints, and coded exchanges between conspirators who replaced 'plot' and 'explosives' with 'wedding' and 'presents'.

When Hassan gave a draft of the book to Manji, she encouraged him to continue writing, and Hassan believed that she would help him in getting this book published as well. But for Hassan, Manji's most important role was helping him to organise his security. She had put him in touch with a lawyer to advise him on his legal status in the US. She had also drawn up a plan to protect Hassan once the CBS interview had aired. She told Hassan that, since she had gone through the same thing, it would be easy for her to arrange.

During those winter months, Manji was helping to counsel Hassan and steady his emotional state. She had personal experience of what it was like to lose your entire social network; like Hassan, she had become a pariah in her own community because of her views.

Manji's ability to comfort Hassan was never better than when Hassan's family found out just how far he had moved away from being a jihadi. One evening, Hassan had left his laptop unattended, and one of his brothers had read through all of the email exchanges between Hassan, Manji and myself. Hassan sent me an email when he realised what had happened. He said he was in trouble: 'I need u to contact me urgently,' he wrote.

At the time, I was not only working on the book but also a long piece on the 7/7 bombings, and I had cut myself off for a few weeks to get as much done as possible. So when Hassan asked me to contact him because he needed my help, his email remained unread. When I got in contact a week later, Manji had already managed to pull him through the worst of the trauma of being disowned by his family. Hassan told me that he was feeling 'much better' now but it was a significant moment. He'd needed and asked for my help and I hadn't been there for him. Once again, Manji had stepped into the breach. After that incident, Hassan and I hardly spoke at all. Then he fell out of contact with everyone while he concentrated on a new project: recruiting people out of the network.

As Christmas was closing in, Hassan's lack of communication worried me and I began to think that something had happened to him. Then at noon on Christmas day, he sent an email to Manji, Gavshon and myself. He had good news, he said. For the past ten days he had been with three other jihadis, talking and questioning them about their beliefs. He'd taken them to the Lake District to get them out of their normal environment. It was a tactic he'd used when recruiting for the network. 'Why not use it now!' he exclaimed.

> After about four days there these guys had asked me every question they could think of, and by the Grace of God, I was able to answer them. After that it was my turn to point out weaknesses in their arguments. On the sixth day, one of the brothers decided, that he had had enough. I didn't pressure him to stay, but I just asked him, had he had enough of me, or enough of not being able to answer my questions? When I said that to him, he decided to stay ...
> After a week, they came to the conclusion that I might be right.

'Cutting a long story short,' he said, that weekend they all met again and 'by God's grace, two of them there and then decided to leave the network.' The third guy 'needed more time'.

Hassan was over the moon. Even with his limited resources he said, he had just recruited three people to his way of thinking. 'This is just the beginning.' Together they had already started to flesh out what a counter organisation to the network would look like.

> Irshad, Shiv, Michael u wanted to know where the alternative voice to radical Islam would come from, I firmly believe that it will come from within the movement to begin with, and with the right type of support and exposure I want to create an aggressive, fast paced movement, that will go to the places only the network goes, to compete with them, and God willing take over.

He said that all this was still in the 'conception stage' but he felt that this was the 'nucleus of a new movement'.

Am so happy and so excited, and I know this time next year, I am going to be kicking butts in the network ...

Take care and sleep well

Hassan

The two recruits who had left the network – Mohammed (Mo) and Atif – had been jihadi sympathisers who were once close to Hassan. This was a remarkable turning point. While the fact that he'd addressed the email to Manji confirmed that my usefulness in this new phase of Hassan's life was diminished, I was eager to speak to Atif and Mo. And I would, when they arrived for Hassan's first public appearance in Cambridge on 31 January 2007. The occasion was just a few days shy of the first anniversary of Hassan's departure from the network.

16

The audience gathered at the Cambridge Union were expecting nothing more than a talk from Manji on 'Confessions of a Muslim Dissident'. Because of fears for Hassan's safety – just after *60 Minutes* had filmed Hassan at a pool hall in Manchester, an anonymous caller had rung him to say, 'I'm gonna take your head off your shoulders' – his presence at the event had been kept secret. No one in the audience had any clue that they would be the first members of the public to witness 'an insider' talk openly about the British jihadi network.

With its blood-red leather stalls and vaulted wooden Tudor ceiling, the interior of the Union was a little reminiscent of the House of Lords. On the back wall were paintings and photographs of past Union presidents. Overhead, a gallery ran right around the circumference of the room, and each supporting buttress was decorated with a college's coat of arms.

The gallery was where the *60 Minutes* film crew had set up their cameras, and it was where Gavshon stood for most of the evening. Meanwhile Magratten – who had grown a bushy moustache over the Christmas holidays – traversed between the gallery and the pit, checking sound levels and camera angles. Apart from a few more almond-coloured flecks in her spiky brown hair, Manji had changed little during the six months since I'd seen her.

She had come to the Union dressed casually: blue jeans, red zip-up top, black loafers, and small gold hoops in her ears.

With a takeout coffee in her right hand and a wedge of papers under her left arm, Manji greeted people she knew with her warm, open smile. The TV crew's lighting, which was focused on two wooden chairs in the centre of the room, reflected well off her high cheekbones and flawless teeth.

Hassan and I greeted each other with a long hug. It had been some time since we'd spoken properly, and the embrace felt like a way of apologising to each other. He had brought Atif and Mo, and I got to meet them for the first time. They said little, but when they did speak I noticed that, unlike Hassan, both of them had heavy Manchester accents. They were there in part to help Hassan with security. Atif – a tall, tubby guy – sat in one corner of the room looking up at the balcony, wrapped up in a duffle coat for most of the evening. Mo – taller, slimmer, with a weak chin – was the better dressed of the two. His baby-blue scarf was carefully arranged and his new jeans were slim cut. He sat next to me, beside the entrance to the chamber.

Hassan himself wore a woollen cream jumper, which he took off as he got hotter and more nervous. Underneath that was a light-brown, almost olive *salwar kameez*, and a pair of khaki combat trousers. On his head was a chocolate-brown knitted skullcap, and on his feet a pair of beige Caterpillar boots. I also noticed that he had dabbed *attar* – a non-alcoholic musk – over himself, and that he had grown out his beard a little.

The audience – which numbered about 150 by the time the talk started – were mainly white and there seemed to be many regulars who made it a habit to attend all of the Union's debates and events. Friends gossiped, while other students did some last-minute reading for lectures – one was even reading *The Satanic Verses*, perhaps in preparation for Manji's talk. As the time drew near, Hassan became disengaged and nervous. He was worried about his safety, periodically looking at the entrance then up at the balcony, and then into space, wondering how he'd perform.

About ten minutes past the official start time, the president of the Union got up and introduced Manji, who immediately told the audience that they would soon be 'treated to a surprise'. She was an artful, inspiring speaker, managing to craft a fine balance between performing and communicating, between garnering attention and discussing heavy, intellectual matters.

'Salaam, shalom, and to the Christians in the audience ... how the hell are yer!?' she began. 'I want to take the next few minutes to focus on an idea that's big enough to change your future as well as mine. And that idea is known as "itjihad". This is Islam's own tradition of critical thinking and independent reasoning.' Someone sneezed, taking the edge off Manji's flow. Retorting spontaneously, Manji said, 'God bless you, whichever God we're talking about.'

Sitting to my left, Hassan was too busy thinking about his own introduction to laugh. He had now put on his oval, black-rimmed reading glasses, which hid his long eyelashes. He had also started chewing gum and was wiping his nose with a tissue at increasingly regular intervals.

As Manji was finishing her introduction the balcony door opened, so when Manji said, 'Please welcome Hassan', and the room burst into applause, Hassan missed his cue to stand up and move to the seat next to Manji because he was still looking upstairs. It was an awkward moment, and for a second I thought Hassan might go completely dead with fear.

Manji managed to fill in, and Hassan eventually made it to the front. For the first twenty minutes of the interview, Hassan stumbled and stuttered, peppering his talk with self-deprecating remarks such as: 'Please bear with me, I'm a bit nervous tonight as you can see.' When he described where he lived in Manchester as a poor area where people didn't have access to a good education, he added: 'As you can see from me – I'm not very good with words.'

As he talked, Hassan grew in confidence and found his old fervour for public speaking and debate. 'I don't want to be controversial, because I absolutely despise being controversial,' he told the audience, 'but this idea that Islam is peace, I have an absolute problem with that. That slogan is incorrect. Because if Islam is peace, what is everything else? Does it make it war? Does it make it not peaceful? … Islam isn't peace – it's a religion. That's all it is. It's a religion that has violence and has non-violence.'

When it came to answering questions from the audience he became assertive, and almost stirring in his defiance. When a woman in hijab asked him why he was trying to change her religion Hassan replied: 'As Muslims … we should be able to discuss anything and everything about Islam, right down to "Is the Quran the word of God?" because if you ultimately believe it is perfect then why not debate it? But to say that we believe that it's perfect but we can't talk about it or it's wrong to question it, then it actually shows that you're afraid to be challenged in the first place.'

In response to a man who quoted Martin Luther King – 'those who love peace must learn to organise as effectively as those who love war' – Hassan refined the sentiment with his own direct challenge: 'Every Muslim in this room, ask yourself the question: how many hours a day are you willing to spend on promoting this idea that Islam needs free thought, free ideas? That's when you're gonna win this battle ... Hand on heart, are you willing to go to those places that all of society is afraid to go to, and pass on that message?'

At the end of more than two hours, the talk came to an official close, but for the next forty minutes Hassan continued to tackle questions from various people: a group of women in hijab, officials from the Cambridge Islamic Society, non-Muslims wanting to know what they could do to help. Circling the crowd was the *60 Minutes* cameraman, who'd been instructed not to miss a thing. At the centre of this scrum, Hassan was dynamic, flirtatious and totally buoyed – so much so that when Atif, wary of the long journey back to Manchester, told Hassan that they should be setting off, Hassan replied that he would just have to wait.

Gavshon was pleased with how it all looked and told me how impressed he'd been with Hassan's ability to hold the attention of such a large audience over a long period of time. Magratten said that 'he'd done great'. As for me, I was sincerely proud. Hassan had needed this moment to prove to himself he was capable of the fight ahead. His start had been rocky, but once he was in the swing of things, no one could doubt that he was persuasive. After months of isolation he seemed refreshed, newly energised by the interest of the outside world. When Hassan returned to Manchester later that night, he sent a very long text thanking everyone; it was effusive with praise for his 'sis' Manji, and his 'older brothers' from *60 Minutes*. To me he wrote, 'u know what u mean 2 me and I don't have 2 say n e thing with u. I just one day wish I cud repay u 4 everything u have and continue 2 do.'

The message was deeply touching. In his moment of triumph he'd thanked me with a simple line of gratitude, recognition of the primary bond between us. I felt embarrassed about my feelings towards his relationship with Manji. It was childish to think of us in competition with each other for his trust and affection. Hassan was putting himself in jeopardy for the higher good of battling radical Islam, and I shouldn't have been thinking of anything more than helping him achieve that goal. Manji was right – once *60 Minutes* aired on Sunday 25 March 2007, the offers for a book deal would flood in. And everything on the CBS front appeared to be going perfectly until three days before it went to air, when Manji was informed of a big last-minute editorial decision.

During the week leading up to the CBS broadcast Hassan was unable to focus on what was about to happen to him. He seemed distracted and unengaged, despite the fact that millions of people around the globe would soon know his story and, more importantly, that the network would know that he was speaking out quite emphatically. On Wednesday morning, when some kids broke his window, he spent the whole day trying to get it fixed and refused to pick up the phone because he was 'too busy'. So when I came to hear about what Manji had done, I thought Hassan would finally become focused on the task ahead.

It was Gavshon and Magratten who gave me the lowdown. On Thursday evening, the editors at *60 Minutes*'s head office in New York had decided to cut Manji from the broadcast – it wasn't doing anything for the story and they wanted to focus on Hassan. As a concession, they had left a long interview with her on their website. Stung, Manji had called Hassan and instructed him to contact Gavshon to explain that he didn't want the programme aired unless they stuck to the format everyone had originally agreed to.

Gavshon told Hassan that it was no longer in his hands, and that's when Manji allegedly laid it out bare. Hassan's security had been organised on the basis that she and Hassan were a team. Now the interview wasn't going to go out as agreed, they were no longer a team and she wouldn't be helping.

That night Hassan pleaded with Gavshon and Magratten to find a solution, before finally sending a text to Gavshon saying: 'Am a dead man walking. I haven't got [any] more options.'

For a time, this whole episode only seemed to worsen Hassan's lack of concentration. When I asked him how he was, he replied that inside he was a complete mix of emotions and that 'everything seems to cancel each other out so I can't feel anything'. The closer we got to broadcast, the more Hassan seemed to blank out his problems. I became deeply worried when, on the Friday, he suddenly asked me if I could give the latest draft of his novel a read-through.

Later that night, the press release for the interview came out and it read: 'FORMER JIHADI REVEALS ALL'. It was only then that Hassan began to articulate himself. Mo told him the news was all over Islamic web forums. He became agitated and fretful, worried about what 'they' were going to do to him.

Hassan found out that his family had heard about the interview. They had sent a message through one of his friends – even though the family home was only ten minutes down the road. He said it was the first bit of communication from them in six months. I asked him what they had said. '"You're a sell-out" and whatnot,' he replied. His three Islamist-supporting brothers weren't taking kindly to the idea that Hassan was going public with his criticism of fellow Muslims, especially those who were at the forefront of 'fighting for the cause'. 'I wasn't expecting anything else. That's life really.'

Hassan tried to be upbeat about it, suggesting it was a blessing in disguise that his brother found his emails; it meant that his family could prove to the network they had kicked him out and had nothing to do with Hassan anymore. 'So there's no pressure on them. In that sense it's a big relief to know that no one's going to try to get to me through them.'

When I asked him how he felt about Manji he told me: 'I don't want to fall out ... but the thing is I'm getting hammered for being with Irshad and so the most frustrating thing is that Irshad doesn't want to know about it now.'

Manji's email explained that she was entering a busy period on her documentary and next book and that she'd be stepping back from Project Ijtihad personally and handing it off to someone else. She wrote that she cared for Hassan and the mission and that's why she'd to continue to pitch him to media. But it seemed that's all she had time for. 'And if/when I hear back re: security funding, I'll of course let u know.'

Hassan reflected, 'I got this feeling that I was a trophy for her ... I'm not going to hold grudges. At the end of the day if anyone asks me about Irshad I'm going to speak highly of her even though I feel that she has abandoned me.'

In my notebook I scribbled down my own reactions to the news:

Everything is in a mess. All of this should have planned out months ago and I thought that he had a security plan but he doesn't. He doesn't know what he's going to do and it's looking really, really risky.

By Saturday morning, Hassan had packed up and was already on the road.

I rang to ask him why he didn't leave the country and go abroad. He told me he felt safe in Britain. Having been arrested by the anti-terrorist squad on a number of occasions, he said he was accustomed to the British police and their methods. Abroad, he couldn't be sure what might happen – especially, he said, if American security officials got involved.

I then asked him why he was risking his life at all. Why not just keep his head down? 'Because for me personally, my faith is everything – my love for Islam, my love for Allah and my love for the messenger, peace be upon Him – and I was willing to risk life and limb for my belief in terrorism. Now I don't believe in that, but I should stay true to giving my life and limb for what I believe in now.'

He said he was scared of dying at that moment in time because he hadn't created a counter to the network. He felt that Islam had been completely taken over by people who were misguiding other Muslims. He acknowledged there were certainly people that he'd misguided as well: 'So I have to do this now. It's the only way of salvation for me in the afterlife and salvation in the sense of doing something that's good for humanity, I guess.'

On Sunday 25 March, at 7.00 pm Eastern Standard Time, *60 Minutes* aired across America. Hassan sounded articulate and looked firm in his newfound convictions. 'Killing in the name of Islam for the sake of killing,' he said, 'is a cancer in the Muslim world.' He said that there was much denial in mainstream Muslim society and compared it to an alcoholic's denial. 'As long as we, as Muslims, do not acknowledge that there is a violent streak in Islam,' he said to Bob Simon on screen, 'then we are always going to lose the battle to the militants.'

Right at the end of the eleven-minute film, Simon asked Hassan about the 'bad work' he had done as a terrorist in Pakistan. Hassan said that he would describe his past actions as 'evil, wicked work' but that they were things he didn't want to talk about. Simon then asked how he would atone for what he'd done. Hassan replied: 'Well, hopefully by the work that I intend to start now. Whatever it costs I'm willing to see this through to the end.'

When Hassan watched the interview, his only criticism was that CBS hadn't added more theological content into the piece, especially since such content had taken up so much of the unedited film. But other than that, he didn't seem all that bothered. What was consuming him was Manji. He was start-ing to become bitter, and his previously charitable stance was turning into anger. (When he was irate, he'd slip into using his Manchester accent.)

'It's unethical and very, very cruel to say I can't do nothing for you, because it's all *60 Minutes*' fault,' he told me. A few days later he told me: 'You know the network, yeah, it has got poli-tics but they're more bloody united, no wonder they're winning this war.'

Over the next few days, as I fielded the numerous introductory calls that were coming in from American and British publishers, Hassan calmed down. He was still on the road, staying at bed and breakfasts when he could, paid for with money borrowed from a friend Yassir, he said. Other nights he would stay at safe houses or with Yassir's relatives. I'd met Yassir for a few hours when he travelled down to London with Mo and Atif to watch

Hassan record the *60 Minutes* interview. My impression was that he was smarter and quicker on his feet than Mo and Atif. So it was a comfort to know that Yassir was the one helping Hassan.

Over the phone Hassan and I talked almost every day about theology, and his anger over what had happened appeared to subside. By the first week of April, he started to feel safer – safe enough to return home. It was a bank holiday weekend and Yassir, Atif and Mo would be off work, so there would be people to look out for him, he told me. Despite this, I advised against it. Surely it would still be hazardous? His house was such an obvious target. But Hassan reminded me of something he'd said many times before: 'I don't want to live like a prisoner.'

That Tuesday following the bank holiday, Hassan was still in Manchester. The next day we had a meeting with a respected publisher. He'd been impressed with the *60 Minutes* interview and wanted to meet Hassan in person. I should have been excited. Instead, I was nervous. Something felt off. Hassan had been unresponsive earlier in the day, and when I texted him that evening to check he was prepared for the trip, I didn't get a reply. A second text and a number of phone calls later, I was starting to fret. By nine o'clock that evening, I was worrying that something had gone wrong. Then I got a text from Mo:

Hi Shiv. Hassan was attacked at 6pm, he has just regained consciousness. He is in a private hospital. Will get back to us asap.

17

That night Mo was furious. He'd been angered by Manji's actions and now he blamed Gavshon and Magratten for having left Hassan out to dry. When I rang Mo, he wouldn't pick up the phone. Desperately worried, I sent him a text saying that I would be coming up to Manchester the very next day. After an hour he replied:

> Just finished with Hassan. He doesn't want ANY1 to come over at all. He will contact u he said himself. He wants u to go to the publisher as arranged. Do as he says that's what am advising you. We don't want any1 here. He said he will call you 2mrow.

A third text from Mo explained what had taken place:

> He gt battered and stabbed outside his house! At the moment hes out of danger bt critical! So dnt worry shiv! He will contact u 2mrow himself

Disregarding Mo's advice, I cancelled the meeting with the publisher and drove up to Manchester the next morning. Since Mo wasn't picking up his phone, I didn't know where Hassan was being treated so I waited outside his house in Cheetham Hill.

I noticed other people there: large, heavily built Asian men in expensive cars; strangers who would periodically swing by and peer through the front window, and then leave.

After a few hours, I decided that the only thing I could do was to try and figure out which hospital Hassan was in. I travelled to every infirmary in central Manchester that I could find and asked if they had admitted someone by the name of Hassan Butt. None of the staff knew anything. I rang Mo, but his phone was off. I then rang Atif, but he told me that he wasn't allowed to say anything. When I pressed him about what exactly had happened to Hassan, where he had been stabbed and how it had happened, Atif hung up. I couldn't for the life of me understand why they were both being so evasive. By the evening I was in a panic. Perhaps, I thought, this was some sort of plot on Hassan's life? Then at 7.45 pm, I got a text from Hassan's phone saying that I shouldn't worry and that he was moving from hospital. He wasn't in as bad shape as the guys thought but he warned me to stay away from his house as it was too risky.

> Yaar, just to prove to u tht am ok, am watching the Liverpool match. Injured or not I won't miss this match! I'll call soon bro, u have my word. Also head out of m'cr [Manchester] its safer. Plz respect me.

I waited for his call, and ten minutes later it came. 'Thankfully, I didn't lose that much blood but Yassir says I look as pale as the bed sheets,' he told me. He said he was recuperating in a private ward and he seemed much more upbeat than I expected. At the time I put that down to the fact that Liverpool had just won themselves a place in the semi-finals of the Champions League, but I also thought that it might have something to do with the painkillers and I wondered what would happen once they wore off.

As I had breakfast at my hotel the next morning, I spoke to Magratten on the phone. Like Mo, he was angry. How was *60 Minutes* supposed to help Hassan with his security if he was going to hang out at his house? Magratten said that Hassan had a propensity for playing fast and loose with his safety. The month before, when Magratten had requested to be taken somewhere that gave some insight into Hassan's past, he'd been taken to a pool hall located off a back alley in the rougher end of Manchester. Dimly lit by the coloured lights from a row of old arcade machines, the rundown hall was where Hassan used to hang out and recruit new members for the jihadi network.

When Magratten got there, he wasn't comfortable with the location. 'This place was way out of the way. Even if you had a map you wouldn't be able to find it.' He suggested to Hassan that they would be better off somewhere safer. Hassan assured Magratten that there was nothing to worry about – he could handle the situation. So while a group of Pakistani youths lingered in the background, the cameraman got a few shots of Hassan breaking a rack of balls. It was the next day that Hassan got the anonymous phone call informing him that he would be decapitated.

In the afternoon I received another text from Hassan:

Sorry Yaar, Just got up. We moved early in the morning. I am just exhausted. I have good news though. My family want 2 spk 2 me after they heard wht has happened. I havent responded yet. Will give time b4 I do.

An hour later, Hassan called, and I asked if I could visit him. He was still tired, he said. Yassir had moved him to a safe house in Durham – over a hundred miles away – in the early hours of the morning, and he didn't think he could handle any visitors. I asked him about going to the police and he replied that he'd just discussed that with Yassir. He didn't want to tell the police because he didn't want to be seen as a traitor. He wanted to maintain a middle ground. 'But then,' he added, 'if they just want to kill me then why shouldn't I go and tell the police everything?'

I started to press him and told him I was coming to Durham because I needed to see him. People like the publisher, whose meeting I'd cancelled, would want to know how he was and I had to be able to give them an accurate picture. Hassan said to tell them that he was fine and that he just needed some time alone. If I wanted, he said, I could take whatever deal the publisher was offering. I was surprised – Hassan had never relinquished this much control to me.

I told him that there were other reasons for my visit. I needed to record his thoughts and feelings for the book. But he told me he didn't want this episode of his life to be in the book. 'If people know how hard it is, then no one will ever leave.'

I paused and then told him that it was my first opportunity to witness a very important event in his life first-hand. What I didn't say was that I'd pretty much taken what he'd told me about his life on trust. Sure, I'd done background checks, read through press archives and spoken to as many sources as I could. But I hadn't interviewed anyone who'd directly been able to confirm the full extent of his life in Pakistan or someone who had been close to him when he was growing up in Manchester. That wasn't really my job – I wasn't his biographer, I was his ghostwriter. It was his story to tell and to stand by. Even so, this was my moment to affirm Hassan's credibility.

Not wanting to voice my doubts in his hour of desperation, I told him that I needed details for the book: the coat with the stab holes, the shape of the bruises on his face, the patterns of the bloodstains on his clothes. I needed to see this all with my own eyes. But Hassan told me to get lost. Enraged, he said he was sick of being an object of curiosity to be constantly documented and observed at arm's length. Then, for the first time in the year and a half I'd known him, he put the phone down on me.

A few hours later Hassan sent a text to Gavshon to say he didn't want to meet and that he needed space to get his thoughts sorted. Gavshon rang him and Hassan told Gavshon that he didn't know what to do. He was drowning in a welter of emotion. The need for revenge was burning him up, but wasn't he supposed to have renounced violence? He then told Gavshon that his mother had just heard about the stabbing. After six and a half months of silence, she had picked up the phone to talk to her son. The conversation hadn't lasted long, but just listening to her voice finally made it clear to him just how alone he was.

Hassan started crying, and through his tears he told Gavshon that he didn't know what to do anymore. Gavshon told him that we'd give him the space he needed. I stopped chasing him and headed back to London.

A day or two later, with some money that I had split with him after being reimbursed expenses by *60 Minutes*, Hassan went abroad. I wasn't sure where he'd gone, but I didn't hear from him for three weeks.

18

During this time Hassan's phone remained off. I tried to contact every one of Hassan's immediate family and his associates but I soon realised that no one was going to talk. Their unanimous silence seemed utterly bizarre to me. Hassan may have had a strained relationship with his family, but his friends – Atif, Mo and Yassir, whom he had spent so long helping to break out of the network and whom I'd met on several occasions – were supposed to care about him. And yet they abjectly refused to speak to me or even pick up the phone. This wasn't normal. I couldn't understand why they didn't want to take my calls. Perhaps Hassan had told them how I'd treated him and they'd decided to cut me out?

As I searched for who was responsible for what had taken place, I wondered whether Hassan was to blame for his own fate. He'd refused to leave Manchester because he had wanted to stick it out. 'I don't want to hide anymore and I don't want to look like I'm running away,' he'd said. I could understand that he didn't want to be a pariah any longer and that, after living on his own resources in a non-existent middle ground between Islamic extremism and the rest of the world, he had become too tired and depressed to stay on the road – and too proud to stay away from home. But while he'd told me how he was putting his life on the line for this new endeavour, wasn't it just as true that Hassan enjoyed the public's gaze? At Cambridge he'd said 'I despise being controversial', but in fact Hassan had spent his whole life choosing to stand out and create conflict: getting himself noticed to the point of exclusion at school, college and university; becoming al-Muhajiroun's media messenger; the numerous speeches and talks; tramping through the markets of Pakistan handing out flyers. Even his support for Liverpool FC had been a means of sticking two fingers up at his friends. Then there was the fact that he was writing a book about his life in order to avoid falling into anonymity. Hassan did all of this to be prominent, to provoke, so if he had been stabbed, it wasn't Manji's or Gavshon's or Magratten's fault – it was because he couldn't keep out of the limelight.

From a person who was supposed to be his friend, these were cruel thoughts. I knew from our interviews Hassan had the unenviable trait of sometimes inflating his sense of importance. In fact, I'd read him being described in early news clipping as an outright liar and a fantasist. I was starting to think those warnings could be right. Maybe, just maybe, the stabbing hadn't really happened, and that's why Hassan was so adamant that I not visit him. Wasn't it more likely that Atif hung up on me because Hassan hadn't actually been attacked, and Atif didn't know how to perpetuate the lie when I'd asked him a few detailed questions? And what sort of 'private' hospital ward could Hassan have been admitted to?

But then why lie in the first place? After well over a year trying to get a book out, why fake a stabbing when he had a major meeting with a potential publisher lined up?

*

Desperate for answers, this got me thinking about the oddities of Hassan's relationship with law enforcement. Why hadn't he been charged with a single crime when so many others around him – people who had *tried* to keep themselves off the radar – had been locked up for life? He said he fled Pakistan in 2002 after the bombing of the US consulate; he was soon arrested in Manchester and taken down to the high-security Paddington Green police station in London. But after ten days of questioning and a visit from the spooks, which he said little about, he was released without charge.

A horrible feeling came over me that somehow this could all be some sort of ruse. Jim Booth had once hypothesised that Hassan was an agent for MI5; that his job had been to supply stories to journalists, keeping them informed and controlled. But even if that wild theory was true, it didn't make sense of the stabbing – whether it had actually happened or not.

Wasn't it most likely that Hassan's reaction was akin to that of someone who *had* been viciously attacked? A beaten man, hiding away and cutting off all contact with those around him because he was overwhelmed by a feeling of inadequacy in the face of such intimidation. Hassan, so used to training each day in the gym, readying himself for the battlefield, had been unable to defend himself when the moment actually arrived. And his failure meant that he'd broken his father's first rule: to 'beat the other guy', to fight back and win.

As the weeks went by and the silence continued, I feared that this was the end of the book and of Hassan's emergence as a vociferous challenger to those in the network. But after almost a year and a half spent working on the project, there was no way I was going to give up without at least attempting to get to the bottom of what had happened. So on 25 April I sent Hassan a long email outlining every possible theory to explain his disappearance. Even though it hardly made any sense, I thought I'd include the speculation about him working as an intelligence agent. Partly I thought it would help to provoke him into getting back to me, but I also wanted to see how he'd react to the allegation.

Dear Hassan

I don't know where you are or what you are doing and so in a way I'm not even sure if there is much point in writing this email to you. None of your friends are talking to me and I even rang your family – they really do seem unconcerned. Ali and Bashar were of no help whatsoever. They've even changed the house [phone] number. Like most Muslims involved or touched by the jihadi network, no one wants to talk – especially to anyone who might be a journalist.

So here are five possible reasons for your disappearance:

1. You were stabbed as you said and you are currently having a minor mental breakdown as to your life's purpose.
2. You never left the network and you've been working with the jihadi network all along.
3. You are working for MI5.
4. You are a complete fantasist.
5. You've been killed.

I think that I can dismiss two and four pretty quickly. Your efforts to speak out against the network would seem to be a bizarre way for the network to act in its own interests.

I doubt very much that you are a fantasist, i.e. that you have created your entire life story. You don't seem to have got much out of this last year in terms of money or public face. Also, many of the things you talk about are true. You were undoubtedly in HT and Al Muj. You were also in Pakistan and I guess you were working alongside Yassir al-Sirri. Many parts of your life story check out so I just don't think that you are a fantasist.

If you are dead then obviously there is little point writing this email to you and hence why I will be meeting with the police to report you as a missing person. I would have done it much sooner but for the fact that I believe scenario '1' to be quite likely.

Yes, '1' remains the most plausible situation. Contradictions are raging around your head and you don't want to talk to anyone at all. Being a social being, it must be hard to find that the only way you can reassert control over your life is to send everyone away. As you said to Michael, you just don't know how to respond in a non-violent manner. And maybe you have chosen to retaliate and don't want to get anyone else involved.

However the fact that I never saw the stab wounds or that your friends don't seem to want to talk to me at all, which seems bizarre and strange given that we are on the same side, and that they also don't know where you were stabbed even though they are supposed to have visited you, leads me to believe that you might in fact be working for MI5. If this was the case, then maybe you started working for them in 2002 after your arrest ... and that was why you were released from custody. I guess your task might have been to attract journalists and draw them away from real sources of information. In fact you may have been stabbed and working for MI5 as well, but now want to quit because you find it too risky.

Anyway, the theories continue but what I was writing to say is that if I don't get a reply in the next day then I will report you as missing to the police. I figure that it would be my duty to do so.

I hope the ether sends me a reply.

Shiv

I received a reply the same day:

Dear Shiv,

I am sorry for not contacting u earlier. In fact i have not con-tacted any1, including Mohammed or Atif. I dont want to speak to them right now. Am not having a mental breakdown at all, and in no way do I work for MI5. But yes I dont know how to react without being violent. I have needed time to find myself, and i used the remaining money u gave, for which i am eternally grateful, to do this. Am ok so far, and will contact u shortly. I will be in touch as soon as i can yaar.

Ur comrade

Hassan

By the start of May, Hassan had returned to Britain and I trav-elled to Manchester to interview him about what had happened. I was apprehensive about the meeting. On the one hand, I was there to repair a relationship with a friend. He'd been stabbed and I had treated him like he was just another news story. I'd even written to him accusing him of being a liar during his time of need. And yet on the other hand I still needed to know for certain what had taken place. I needed to grill him about exactly how everything had unfolded, because I needed to find out if he had been telling the truth all this time. My two aims were almost wholly opposed to each other. But there was another issue that was knotting up my insides. What if, as I talked to him, it became clear that he had been lying about being stabbed?

What if he had made the whole thing up? How on earth would I deal with it?

We met in my hotel room in central Manchester, and when he turned up he still looked shaken. It didn't take long before he showed me a thick red mark on his shoulder. Through his beard his right cheek looked bruised. To begin with, the interview was awkward, but as he began to settle down Hassan explained exactly what had happened to him the night he was attacked:

I was coming back home. I took the metro up to the Woodlands stop. When I got off, I noticed these two guys. Obviously with everything that had gone on, I'm on edge. Anyway, I don't feel like … it just didn't feel right. I'm walking, and from my house to the metro link station it's a fifteen-minute walk … I'm noticing these guys are following me and I'm feeling a bit uncomfortable. They weren't from Cheetham Hill. I know most of the people from Cheetham Hill, even the muggers, and I've never seen these guys in my life. So I decide to take a different route, like a route that it only makes sense for me to take. You get me? Why would anybody be taking that route unless … So, walking, walking, walking, and eventually when we get quite close to my house, I've come out of this little alleyway, near the masjid – there's a mosque quite close to my house – and a guy approaches me. And he's dark-skinned. Tamil kind of dark. He comes ahead of me, so there's one ahead and one behind and he goes, 'Have you got a light?' And straight away like that they attack me. One of them pulls my hood, because I had that thick coat on that day. You've seen that duffle coat I wear innit? And he pulls it over my head and they start dragging me down. The guy in front of me, I remember, I hit quite cleanly and then the guy behind me ... well, suddenly I feel two very quick jabs – to my arm and between my shoulders, and I fell down.

Hassan told me that, in a blind and violent fury, he had lashed out in every direction. He thought that his fists had caught both guys, but by then it was too late. Pushing him to the floor they began to kick him, first in the jaw and then in the ribs. Hassan thought that it was all over, and if it hadn't been for a man – an Iranian – screeching his car to a halt alongside Hassan and scaring off the assailants, Hassan believed he would have been murdered.

Hassan then went on to explain what had been going on in his head for the last three weeks. He had been wondering whether there was space in society for people who had changed. Would people genuinely want to help?

In one way, you know what happened with Irshad, I'll be honest with you, even now I feel very betrayed by her. I'm not going to lie. I was inspired by her, I was inspired by what Salman Rushdie said to her because I thought the idea was so perfect, was so right.

As a result of her actions, he said, the promises he'd made to the jihadis he'd converted out of the network could no longer be kept. 'They're like, "You've got nothing again. It would have been better for you to have worked as a taxi driver for the last year. You could have started setting something up by now rather than doing nothing at all."' That hurt him the most, he said.

I swear by Allah, for the last two weeks I was thinking in my head: the jihadi world and this world, it's exactly the same. Full of contradictions, full of lies, and no one's really interested in solving this problem. And I kept thinking: Why am I interested in it? ... Is there any real reason as to why I'm putting my neck on the line if in reality everyone just seems to be out for themselves?

I know for a fact that in [the] jihadi world there is no principle. It's just whatever goes, goes. And it seems like it's exactly like that on the other side.

I feel really bad about what I did to Mohammed and Atif because they feel like I strung them along ... And you remember me saying that if there's nothing for people to leave for, they're not going to leave. Well, I feel like there's nothing there for people.

I asked Hassan why he had been so unwilling to have visitors on the night of the attack and he told me: 'I didn't want anyone to see me. I felt embarrassed, if I'm honest. I've never been beaten that severely.'

Then he admitted how he worried that violence was somehow bred into him. 'You know the problem is this: it's in my blood.'

'Maybe,' he said, 'I need to see a psychologist, someone who understands the human brain.' He pondered over whether the violence inflicted on him as a child had something to do with why he couldn't resolve himself to the fact he'd been beaten up now. 'It plays with my mind ... [that] I haven't done anything in return ... I feel so embarrassed. "Embarrassed" is not the right word, this is like I feel ashamed of myself that I allowed it to happen.'

And then there was the bigger picture. He was supposed to be a reformed character and yet all he could think about was 'revenge'.

The whole point of my story and whatnot is that I've turned my back on violence but have I just turned my back on a certain aspect of violence, and that's what scares me now ... I really feel like I want to meet these guys so I can kill them, so I can show them that I'm prepared to go further than they are, and I wouldn't have stopped if a car had pulled up. And that goes through my mind a lot. The rage is there.

If you defend yourself that's a different issue, but I want to go back and get revenge. That's what is frustrating me. That is what's worrying me. And I don't know how to get those voices out of my head. I want them out if possible and if not, I want them at the back of my head. And so I'm worried about my own psyche because I'm thinking have I turned my back on violence or have I just turned my back on people who are degrading Islam?

After the interview, I came to the conclusion that I had been wrong. Not only could Hassan show me physical evidence of his assault, the thick red mark on his shoulder and the bruising to his jaw, he appeared to be undergoing just the kind of emotional turmoil that the victim of an attack would be battling with: embarrassment, humiliation, shame, and anger. I had to admit that it was a mistake not to have trusted him. And this conclusion – the only one available given the evidence at hand – brought me a sense of relief. After living in Hassan's orbit for so long, I'd been suddenly scared of losing all this energy and time. I was frightened of coming to terms with the prospect that I'd spent more than a year of my life with a man who had the propensity to make things up out of thin air. Alongside that, I still believed Hassan could be something. If he could control his ego, not get waylaid by his uglier side, his drive for personal reward, he might just be able to do something great. But in order to put the book project back on track I knew I'd have to rein him in and get him to take a publishing deal, whatever the advance, however much he thought such an offer might be beneath him.

After our meeting in Manchester, I told Hassan that I would continue to work with him on the condition that he take the next contract that was presented to us, however much it was worth. His acceptance of my demand helped repair the loss of trust between us. And though I never overtly apologised for not believing he'd been the victim of a terrible attack, he knew I'd regretted doubting him and neither of us spoke about it until a year later.

A few weeks after that, we signed with an independent publishing house for a small advance. I also advised him that now he had publicly renounced jihadism on *60 Minutes*, he should write down his thoughts about Islamic theology – the discussions that had been cut from the broadcast – in a column I'd try to get published around the time of the second anniversary of the 7/7 bombings.

Hassan sent me a first draft of his thoughts, and I noticed that his writing was getting much better. I sent back a version I thought would be more suitable, and eventually we had a finished piece that the editor was happy with. The piece began by trying to settle an old debate over the causes of radicalism:

When I was still a member of what is probably best termed the British jihadi network – a series of semi-autonomous British

Muslim terrorist groups linked by a single ideology – I remember how we used to laugh in celebration whenever people on TV proclaimed that the sole cause for Islamic acts of terror like 9/11, the Madrid Bombings and 7/7 was western foreign policy.

By blaming the government for our actions, those who pushed the 'Blair's bombs' line did our propaganda work for us. More importantly they also helped to draw away any critical examination from the real engine of our violence: Islamic theology.

It continued with the lessons that Hassan had been taught from his time as a radical: that since there is no Islamic state – Dar al-Islam (the Land of Islam) – in existence, the whole world must be Dar al-Kufir (the Land of Unbelief); and therefore Islam must declare war upon the whole world. He explained that the main reason radicals had managed to increase their following was that Islamic institutions in Britain just don't want to talk about this complex, difficult side of Islamist theology, focusing instead on the empty slogan 'Islam is Peace'. He went on to explain his outline for a new theological concept: the Land of Co-existence, which would more accurately describe the actuality of Muslim life in the west:

> It isn't enough for Muslims to say that because they feel at home in Britain they can simply ignore those passages of the Quran which instruct on violence and killing unbelievers …
>
> If our country is going to take on radicals and violent extremists, Muslim scholars must go back to the books and come forward with a refashioned set of rules and a revised understanding of the rights and responsibilities of Muslims

whose homes and souls are firmly planted in what I'd like to term the Land of Coexistence.

When this new theological territory is opened up, western Muslims will be able to liberate themselves from defunct models of the world, re-write the rules of interaction and perhaps we will discover that the concept of killing in the name of Islam is no more than an outdated anachronism.

Perhaps the most important line in the article was the one that said moderate British Muslims could not 'simply ignore those passages of the Quran which instruct on violence and killing unbelievers'. For too long, as Hassan had explained on various occasions, Muslim leaders had trotted out the line that 'Islam was peace'. This was not true, he argued. Muslims could certainly be peaceful, but the religion itself had been spread using some of the most awful violence mankind has ever known. As the founder of the faith, the Prophet Muhammad had been in command of an army of believers who killed for their god. There was just no getting around that. To ignore it was not just a sin of omission; it was a complete and utter denial of the problem at hand. This is why Hassan believed that fighting the radicals had to be done with theology – it was the only way to defeat their ideas, their purpose and, ultimately, the terror they sought to bring to the streets of cities around the world.

As the article was about to go to print a doctor and an engineering student no older than Hassan drove a jeep filled with petrol and gas canisters through the doors of Glasgow airport. The frenzy of the attacks created an unusually large amount of interest in what Hassan had written, and the article was reprinted internationally.

For the following few weeks, Hassan received hundreds of emails — CBC in Canada, *Der Spiegel* in Germany, CNN in the US, *Il Foglio* in Italy, and Al Jazeera in Qatar — asking him to comment on his transformation. Letters from readers came pouring in to editorial departments. A few were critical, but the vast majority of them praised Hassan's bravery in admitting his past mistakes and standing up to the radical threat. It seemed that Hassan's new message was bringing him as much attention as his old message had brought him infamy. And all this pleased him.

Following this, and an article I had written on Mohammad Siddique Khan, I was invited to a number of meetings, the most interesting of which was with the Home Office Counter-Terrorism Minister, Tony McNulty. I suggested that Hassan also attend. The Minister's staff agreed to this and after the requisite security checks were made, a date was set in late June.

McNulty was not an expert in counter-terrorism by any means, but neither was he just a political appointment. I had met him once before and noted his enthusiasm and robustness. He had vigorously studied the contours of the problem he had been charged with solving, and was always eager to get to the point in the most courteous way possible.

Surprisingly, it was Hassan who did most of the talking for the next hour. I hadn't been sure what he was going to say, but he ended up telling the minister everything: about his upbringing, joining HT and al-Muhajiroun, and the events that he had been involved with in Pakistan, including funding and his experiences inside a training camp. McNulty was surprised that Hassan was being so frank, and so was I – if a legal confession for law-enforcement purposes had been required, one couldn't have asked for more.

Hassan then explained how he was getting people out of the network and what he believed still needed to be done – that the de-radicalisation process needed to be kept separate from government funding and programming so as not to be tainted by accusations that Hassan was a sell-out, but that officials could support this work by choosing not to prosecute those who left. At this point the minister said, 'Something along the lines of an underground railway?' The metaphor was perhaps a little flawed – a reference to African American slaves fleeing the Deep South in the nineteenth century – but the meaning was understood, and everyone nodded in agreement.

Hassan left the meeting buoyed by the response he'd got. As we were about to head to the lifts, he was approached by one of the civil servants. He said that there was money available under the budget for preventing extremism, which Hassan should consider applying for. He promised to send the forms to us, and urged Hassan to apply.

Hassan thanked him, and again explained the problem of taking government money, even if it was done indirectly. He said that he just wanted their support.

In itself, the meeting had been enough to convince Hassan that the Home Office was endorsing his departure from the network and would not seek to arrest him or deter his work. But the offer of funding was clear encouragement. It seemed that as long as Hassan's de-radicalisation work continued, his past offences – for which he'd never been prosecuted – would be forgiven.

As he was getting out of the cab at Euston station, Hassan said something to me that had a profound effect. I'd asked him how Mo and Atif were keeping and he replied, 'Yeah they're fine, I spoke to Mo last night.' Then he paused. Mo, he said, had asked him a disturbing question: what would happen if he couldn't get rid of the violence within Islam? What if, because of the Prophet's deeds, violence in Islam was inevitable?

'I just brushed him off,' Hassan said. 'What I didn't want to say, but what I was thinking was — if that was the case, I'd have to stop being a Muslim.'

19

In other religions, the deeds of the holy and wise have been obscured by the passage of time. To modern eyes, these stories have become myths or parables. The 'trouble' with Islam is that historians recorded too much of the life of Muhammad. In so doing, they replaced myths with facts, and facts are inescapable.

The first forty years of the Prophet's existence were of little note. He was a merchant from a clan of pacifists in the small town of Mecca, in the desert of Arabia. Then, while meditating on the twenty-seventh night of Ramadan, he said he heard a terrible voice commanding him to 'read', and the illiterate Muhammad began to recite the first verses of the Quran.

At first the Prophet spread this new gospel peacefully. His small band of followers were ridiculed, then threatened, and then forced to flee. After that the Prophet turned violent, and by the end of his life he had waged sixty-five wars, destroyed the Persian Empire and most of the eastern Roman Empire, and massacred or enslaved tens of thousands of his fellow human beings. When jihadis say they are living the example of the Prophet, it is usually this more violent period of Muhammad's life they are referring to.

The new task of somehow finding a way to extricate violence from the texts of Islam took up all of Hassan's time, but there was one historical incident that particularly tested him: the death of the Jewish poet Ka'b bin Ashraf. He was one of the first people to be killed on the direct orders of Muhammad after writing a poem that the Prophet felt had insulted him. The story as recorded is as follows:

> The Messenger of Allah (may peace be upon him) said: 'Who will kill Ka'b bin Ashraf? He has maligned Allah, the Exalted, and His Messenger.'
>
> Muhammad son of Maslama said: 'Messenger of Allah, do you wish that I should kill him?'
>
> 'Yes.'
>
> 'Permit me to talk to him in the way I deem fit.'
>
> 'Talk as you like,' said the Prophet.

Muhammad bin Maslama then went to the poet's home with two co-conspirators and, using the ruse of asking Ka'b bin Ashraf for a loan, killed him.

Hassan explained to me that this was the reason why devout Muslims had called for the deaths of those who had insulted the Prophet after the Danish cartoons were published. It was not because these Muslims were bloodthirsty or quick to take offence – the cartoons were just drawings after all. It was because death was the required punishment for insulting the Prophet as set down by the Prophet himself. That was what they *had* to do.

Surely, I asked Hassan, there was a way of reconciling this story with modern values? Couldn't the story be dismissed as untrue or a myth? Hassan explained that this was quite impossible. After the death of the Prophet, his sayings and lessons – the Hadiths – had been collected by scholars and ranked as to their veracity. At the top were those that were absolutely true, supported by many trustworthy witnesses. The story of Ka'b was considered by all scholars to be of this ranking. So too was the way in which Muslims prayed. The Quran – the word of God – set out the times of prayer but the Prophet himself had explained the way to pray: washing, bowing, the words, and so on. So to doubt the story of Ka'b was also to doubt the way in which over a billion Muslims prayed – you couldn't pick and choose.

Was there not, I asked, some technical loophole in the insult? Since the Prophet was dead, surely you couldn't actually insult him anymore. Hassan replied that the Prophet's message must be eternal, otherwise it would have become meaningless after his death, so insulting him now would be the same as insulting him during his lifetime.

'What do the liberal scholars say about Ka'b?' I asked. Hassan said that they had a better answer. They looked between the text and the historical context.

'Well, the scholars have Ka'b's poem, so they have studied it and they say that the poem slanders Muslim women.' (The poem states that Muslim women have large buttocks, and when Hassan told me this I laughed – all this over big butts.)

'They also say that the last verse is treasonous.' In the poem, Ka'b calls for the recently defeated armies to rise up and save him from the tyranny of Muhammad. 'So the liberals say that because there was a war going on, Ka'b committed treason.'

'No that's not right,' Hassan said, trying to remember the right word. Then he remembered it: 'Sedition!' At this point we both laughed at the incongruity of exclaiming sedition with such joy.

Sedition – the act of rousing people to revolt against the state – seemed a more reasonable interpretation. During times of war, most countries had laws against sedition – even if the punishment wasn't death. That might easily explain why Ka'b would have been killed.

But Hassan said this was only one interpretation of the historical incident. Most scholars (certainly the radical ones) preferred the more obvious, literal meaning. Sedition or not, if you insult the Prophet, you'll be assassinated.

Furthermore, the jihadis' interpretation is that Muslims are at war and, since there is no Islamic state, anyone has the right to claim the insult and carry out the punishment. The killings of the Dutch film-maker Theo van Gogh in Amsterdam and the Japanese translator of Salman Rushdie's *The Satanic Verses* in the 1990s were two such punishments.

Perhaps there was another way, I suggested. 'Instead of trying to find fault with the interpretation, couldn't you just say that the Prophet was wrong, that he made mistakes? Maybe God's Messenger shouldn't have ordered the death of Ka'b bin Ashraf?'

This time, Hassan laughed alone.

'Oh yaar, you're going to get me into so much trouble.'

A few weeks later Hassan found a story that he thought might help to demonstrate that the Prophet could have made mistakes in his life. It was called 'The Camel's Tail'.

One day, the story went, a farmer was pollinating his date trees with a brush made from a camel's tail when the Prophet passed by. The Prophet asked the farmer what he was doing and, when the farmer explained, the Prophet told him that using a camel's tail like this did not please him. The farmer replied, 'Since you are the Prophet I will do as you say.'

When harvest came, the farmer returned to the Prophet. 'I did what you said and now my crops have failed,' the farmer cried.

The Prophet replied that although he was the Messenger of God, he was not an expert on all matters – his advice to the farmer had been given in his capacity as an ordinary man and not as the Prophet of God.

And so there it was: by his own admission, the Prophet could get things wrong – he was fallible. And maybe you could therefore argue that the violence he had initiated was also a mistake – the orders of a mere man.

I believed that this nascent idea – that the Prophet Muhammad had made mistakes – was how Hassan's memoir should close. It would be a fitting end to a long narrative arc, from Hassan's adherence to the logic of Islam in his youth to his eventual questioning of its very foundations in adulthood.

It felt to me like he'd reached the apex of his journey to leave al-Qaeda. This would show more than just a departure or a break. I imagined that he could turn to face his former brothers in faith and take apart their system of beliefs. I saw him fighting pure literalism with a deeper, more complex literalism. If we ended the book in this way, it would show that he was willing to test the piety of ordinary Muslims and radicals alike – a brave thing even to contemplate, let alone carry out. I wrote a few draft paragraphs of the things we'd been discussing and sent them to Hassan:

As the words in the Quran state, the Prophet is the most perfect example of humankind. Yet why do we infer from this that he is perfect? This status belongs to God alone. The Prophet is perfect as a man and a man only and therefore he is fallible. In no way does this suggest that the Prophet may have committed any kind of sin. But is there not a difference between sin and making a mistake, an error of judgement?

Though I didn't discuss it with Hassan, I realised that I was dangerously overstepping in my role as a ghostwriter. I was practically putting words into his mouth, shaping his character in the book, willing him to become something he yet wasn't.

Although Hassan felt my paragraphs articulated his thinking, he wasn't ready to say publicly that the Prophet was fallible. To reform the image of the Prophet in the eyes of Muslims, to make him just a man who had perhaps been mistaken in ordering the killing and immiseration of ordinary civilians, could cause many problems for him; criticising the Prophet or even critiquing his legacy was such dangerous ground. But what made it so dangerous – the fact that it was a statement that had the capacity to challenge so much – also made it exhilarating. I knew Hassan felt this, and despite my fears over my role, I thought it wouldn't be long before I could persuade him to come out with it openly.

Of course there was still the question of whether Hassan could be the person to carry such an argument. But, given the story about his past that he was about to tell the world, he undoubtedly had the credentials. He still felt that he'd been let down by Manji's promises and now believed he could control his drive to be recognised (the 'whispers of Shaytan', as he described it). The stabbing had forced him to confront his inner aggression, he said. In our interview afterwards, he'd shown a capacity for self-reflection that would surprise those who only knew him as a terrorist thug. I believed that his recent experiences had made him mentally stronger. And that was the important thing.

It was at this moment that I put all of our past tribulations, including the loss of trust and amity following the stabbing, behind us. We had a fascinating story to tell the world, and a new line of argument to use in the battle against his foes. We were on the verge of a very exciting moment and both of us were eager to see how much change it could effect. I was not only grateful that I'd stuck by Hassan, I was ready to support him whatever the trial.

It would not take long to arrive. On Wednesday, 19 March 2008, the police arrived at my home.

ORDER

20

At 7.50 am there was a firm knock on the door to my flat. Half-dressed, I answered it to find three police officers – a woman and two men – outside. The one in front, Detective Sergeant Graham Smith, asked if he could come in.

I asked what it was about.

'We'd rather not say in front of your neighbours,' he replied.

He had a Lancashire accent and as he spoke he accentuated the vowels. The lilt lent a certain tone of gentility to what he was saying.

I couldn't see anyone else in the hallway.

'That's okay,' I replied. 'I know my neighbours well enough.'

Smith told me that they were from the Greater Manchester Police's Counter-Terrorism Unit. They wanted to have a chat, but inside the house, where it would be 'more private'. He was confident in what he was saying – there was no shyness about it – and pleasant, almost.

'Sorry, I don't understand – what is it about?'

'It's about a book that you're writing.'

I worried about inviting them inside and giving them greater right to search the property. I looked at Smith a little longer. Although he was muscular, he was certainly not young, and most men would have let themselves go at his age. This physique on an older man gave a toughness to his appearance. I decided against letting them inside.

I asked if they could return in two hours, pointing out that I wasn't even dressed yet. I suggested a cafe around the corner where they could wait. They hadn't yet eaten, so I recommended the Israeli breakfast: scrambled eggs, bagel, cream cheese, chopped cucumber and tomato. And off they went.

Two hours was just enough time to prepare for what I knew was coming. I gathered together all my notes and tapes on terrorism – everything I could lay my hands on – and put them in a bag. Then my flatmate took the bag from the house and delivered it to a friend who was leaving for Paris that evening. I knew the owner of a bookshop there who would be able to keep the tapes safe. I called Hassan but he didn't pick up, which was not unusual, as he often slept in until a little after ten. I then called a mentor of mine for advice, and he recommended a lawyer.

When the police returned, I was ready.

'How were the eggs?' I asked as we sat down in my living room. 'Just great, thanks.' I served them tea and then fretted about it – was there enough milk, sugar, biscuits? They replied that everything was fine. I told Smith that I would be recording the meeting – 'journalist's habit' – and he didn't object.

He began by saying, 'Your liberty is not at risk today.' Then he quickly corrected himself: 'I'm saying that today, I don't mean that it might be in the future.' He paused and then stumbled into a lot of jargon and it was hard to follow exactly what he meant.

'We're going through a procedure to try and access documentation which you may have possession of. And there is process for doing that. There is court, which we will explore if necessary. However, before we do that we have to ask you if you're ready to hand over that documentation.'

I was confused. He handed me a letter.

'It is a very serious matter and we don't want to rush any-thing. We don't want people to make mistakes. We've dedicated two days to making sure that if you want to speak to us, we're here...' Then, working up a friendly-looking half-smile, he added: 'The police are at your disposal.'

The letter was from the Greater Manchester Police's head law-yer, and I took my time reading it:

Mr Shiv Malik
BY HAND

Wednesday, 19 March 2008

Dear Mr Malik,

Leaving Al-Qaeda – Inside the Life and Mind of a British Jihadist by Hassan Butt with Shiv Malik

I am instructed by [the] GMP Counter-Terrorism Unit who are currently investigating Hassan Butt (DOB 12.12.76) for his involvement in terrorism activities. For several years Hassan Butt has been known as a self-proclaimed radical Islamist and has actively sought the television, radio and newspaper media providing interviews extolling violent jihad ... I understand that the book is due for release in April 2008.

Consequently you will hold material which is likely to be of substantial value to this terrorism investigation since there are reasonable grounds for believing that it will:

- Provide evidence of Hassan Butt's ability to facilitate train-ing for Al Qaeda sympathizers;

- Demonstrate Hassan Butt's association with convicted terrorists/criminals/suspects and his influence amongst this group;
- Demonstrate Hassan Butt's role and activities in facilitating support for individuals fighting coalition forces in Afghanistan.

Furthermore, there is an ongoing prosecution of a close associate of Hassan Butt, namely Habib Ahmed, who is charged with offences under the [Counter-]Terrorism Act 2000. This case is scheduled to come to trial later this year. Within this matter a defence statement has been served which contends that Hassan Butt is the instigator of certain actions and that Ahmed's actions have been in order to facilitate media reports/ productions ...

We would be grateful if you could provide the material within the next 24 hours. However, in order to protect the integrity of the terrorist investigation relating to Hassan Butt and the ongoing prosecution of Habib Ahmed and to safeguard your journalistic independence, we intend to apply for a production order under Schedule 5 of the [Counter-]Terrorism Act 2000.

I sincerely hope that this matter can be resolved by consent and accordingly I attach a copy of the draft production order.

I asked Smith what Habib Ahmed had been charged with – at the time I could not recall who he was, as Hassan had only vaguely referred to him as an old friend called 'Ahmed'. Smith explained that all he could say was that Habib Ahmed had been arrested for aiding terrorism, and one of the charges related to making a documentary. In his defence statement, Habib had said that there was nothing sinister about the documentary – he had been ordered by Hassan to go to a camp and get interviews about the 7/7 bombers. Was this the same documentary I'd helped Hassan pursue three years prior?

The rest of the conversation was short. I knew what they wanted me to do: hand them my notes and tapes so they could prosecute Hassan. If I didn't comply, they would go to a judge the following Tuesday and force me – using their powers under the Counter-Terrorism Act – to give them what they wanted.

Smith then handed me the draft production order. It was an exhaustive list of everything I might possibly have: tapes, videos, recordings, notes, phone messages, financial records, and much more. This wasn't just a demand for materials related to Hassan's book. It would mean handing them almost everything I had ever worked on as a journalist writing about terrorism.

I told Smith that there was some mistake. Didn't he know that Hassan had met with the counter-terrorism minister; that the Home Office had offered him funds to continue with his de-radicalisation work? To prosecute him now would make a mockery of government actions. Smith was not aware of this, and asked for the details of the meeting. I duly obliged.

The letter inferred that Hassan was still a terrorist, so I asked whether this investigation into Hassan's offences related to his past or something more – something post-2006, after he'd left the network. Smith told me that he wasn't at liberty to say. I told him that it would make all the difference. Again, Smith replied that he wasn't able to say. I figured that this was because they didn't have anything recent on Hassan, and I became more confident. As the three officers got up to leave I told Smith, 'You know, if you prosecute Hassan now, no one will ever leave the jihadi network.' He shrugged and told me that I had twenty-four hours to make my decision.

Every reporter knows the first rule of journalism: never betray your source. If the Greater Manchester Police wanted everything I had ever worked on then I would be betraying people who, for their own reasons and despite my encouragement, had been too afraid to go to the police. Not terrorists, but ordinary people who had happened to watch their peers, colleagues and family members become radicalised. Only by spending many long weeks gaining their trust had I been able to encourage them to tell me their stories. The thought of having to break that trust was reason enough to go to court and fight the production order.

However, Hassan wasn't a source in the classic sense. I was writing for him, he was known, and by the book's very genre – autobiography – it was obvious that he *wanted* to be known. If he consented to handing over the tapes, or just a draft of the book, then maybe Smith's superiors would be placated and I wouldn't have to hand over everything.

Later that morning, the police also turned up at the publishers and demanded to see the manuscript of the book. The publishers were hoping to avoid a costly legal battle; they said they wanted to 'work behind the scenes instead of in front of them'. I reminded them that Hassan had trusted them – they had a duty to him. The publishers told me they would hold off from handing anything over.

After Smith and his colleagues had left, I got hold of Hassan. He was shocked that the police had come to my house without any warning and confused as to why they hadn't come to arrest him instead. When I explained that the publishers had wanted to hand over their copy of the manuscript, Hassan became angry. If the police got hold of the book before it was published, they would start raiding everyone's homes: Zaheer, Mo, Atif ... 'Not even because they think they'll find something but just to put pressure on me. It's what they're doing with Habib.' He thought they'd also go through it line by line and twist words and sentences to suit their purposes.

I asked Hassan about what had happened with Habib. Hassan said that Habib was his closest friend. They had met at Bury College and Habib had then followed him to Wolverhampton University and joined al-Muhajiroun after hearing Omar Bakri speak. Habib was also the person in the dream that had sent Hassan to Pakistan and, because of that, Hassan had persuaded Habib to fly out there with him in July 2001. Hassan felt responsible in a way, because he had asked Habib to carry on working on the documentary – 'the one I wanted to do with you' – and in late 2006 the police had arrested Habib 'on a bloody trumped-up charge'.

'Excuse my language but this is bloody ridiculous. Honestly, Shiv, the Manchester Police really hate me. I embarrassed them because they could never charge me with anything and now they want to ruin my life by getting at the people around me.'

Hassan said he would ring the officers in charge and try to cooperate with them. I gave him the numbers of Detective Sergeant Levi and Detective Inspector Richardson, whose contact details were on the letter. Then Hassan remembered that Yassir al-Sirri's name was in the book as well. (We'd been debating whether to change it or not, but for the sake of convenience I had used his real name in the early drafts.)

'Oh God, yaar, if Yassir finds out his name is in there, I'm a dead man.'

'So you want me to go to court to fight this?'

'Yes. Definitely.'

Upon reflection, I should have thought more about why Habib had been arrested. I took the evidence I knew at face value – both Hassan and the GMP had said that Habib was being put on trial for trying to make a documentary. I'd remembered of course that Hassan had wanted to make a film around the time we'd first met. I also remembered thinking that he would per-haps keep on trying to get it commissioned.

The reason the film had never been commissioned was that going to a training camp to talk to terrorists was a risky business both ethically and legally. Hassan had been foolish in sending Habib to do his work but I could see how a misunderstand-ing could have arisen, especially if the Manchester police were 'after' Hassan. From what I knew, the charges could well be trumped-up. (I noted that on the letter they'd given me, they had got Hassan's date of birth wrong, making him four years older than he actually was, and this only added to the impression that the police were liable to be mistaken on details.)

And yet I didn't question why Hassan hadn't told me about Habib's arrest. The arrest of his closest friend was a very serious matter. As his ghostwriter, didn't I have a right to know some-thing as important as this? He should have told me. (I only came to this conclusion when I had been given much more informa-tion about what Habib had been getting up to.)

I suppose I let these questions fall by the wayside because I had crossed a line with Hassan. I was willing to give him the benefit of the doubt and willing to take his word for things, because I thought he was being courageous and I marvelled at what he was doing. He wasn't just a source – he'd become my friend, and in his hour of need I would stand behind him.

No one expected much from the hearing at Manchester Crown Court. The main line of defence was that the police's demand for my material was an unnecessary infringement of a journalist's rights since Hassan Butt was willing to cooperate. Mention was also made of the Home Office meeting and that funds had been offered to him, and it was put to the judge that the left hand of the state didn't know what the right hand was doing.

The defence lawyers also presented a legal catch-22. One of the most established legal rights is the right not to be forced to incriminate one's self – in other words, the right to silence. However, the amended Counter-Terrorism Act in 2000 had made it illegal not to tell the police about any matter that might be useful in a terrorist investigation, something that I had worried about during my first face-to-face conversation with Hassan. Given that the Manchester police now wanted my notes for just such an investigation, if the judge granted the order I could potentially be handing over documents that the police could use against me. They could say that I hadn't disclosed vital information and that the proof was in the tapes and my interviews with Hassan. In effect, any judgement could force me to incriminate myself – therefore stripping me of my right to silence – unless the police gave assurances that I wouldn't be prosecuted. And that was something the police wouldn't do.

After a week, the judge gave his ruling. We had lost, and so the next day we lodged our appeal at the Royal Courts of Justice on the Strand.

*

Alongside the legal battle, a campaign had been mounted to raise funds and garner support. The staff at Index on Censorship and the writers' charity PEN helped organise media backing: columnists from left and right were asked to champion my cause; a letter criticising the actions of the GMP was signed by journalists, editors and the heads of human rights organisations, and was published in *The Times*; the *Guardian* wrote a leader urging the judges to see sense; politicians lent their support and contacts; and the case was given sympathetic coverage on television and radio, in newspapers both in the UK and US, and all over the Internet. I'd now become the centre of a story which had not even been told.

The debate was framed not just as a battle between the police and a journalist protecting his sources. Questions were raised about why Hassan had not been arrested before the police came to my house, and why he was being pursued by the police only now, after he'd come out against extremism. The line that was repeated was that if Hassan was prosecuted, no one would ever leave the network to come out against extremism. One columnist put it: 'How the jihadis will laugh at the stupidity of a country that can't tell its allies from its enemies.'

Some of these articles also highlighted the geographical divide between London and Manchester – and explored all the prejudices that the divide entailed. The implication was that the Manchester police were oafs who had no understanding of the complex intricacies of policing terrorism. Their actions lacked finesse, and their new independent terrorism unit, set up in the aftermath of 7/7, was inexperienced and quickly becoming inept. The new unit was out of the London loop. In return, I'm sure the Manchester police thought that we were a weak and unprincipled lot, willing to exchange natural justice for political expediency. Worse, they believed we'd been suckered by a sweet-talker who behind the scenes was up to his old extremist ways. They had not been conned; they knew better.

In public, however, the police declined to give any comment.

My initial legal bill was paid for by contributions from friends and family, as well as donations from a number of news organisations for which I had worked over the years. However, once the appeal had been lodged, a much larger sum of money – tens of thousands of pounds – would be needed to pay for a senior barrister to represent the case in the Royal Courts against the GMP. For this I had to ask the National Union of Journalists and the *Sunday Times* to support me. Generously, they stepped in and their assistance allowed the appeal to go forward. But it was not just for my sake that they came to my aid; I had become the first journalist to appeal a decision under the powers of the Counter-Terrorism Act, so defeat could mean that a precedent was set against journalists and the protection of our sources far into the future. It had suddenly become a very serious matter for the rights of the free press.

One of my lawyers, Rhona – a tall, energetic solicitor with a sharp eye – warned me that we had now become pawns in our own game. Once the case had been passed up to the appeals court, the real decisions were going to be made elsewhere. Media executives, police chiefs and senior civil servants were each weighing and determining their own interests in this skirmish between the various branches of the establishment. Soon, their decisions would be handed down to the lawyers, the government representatives, the investigating officers and the editors concerned. Yes, the case was a sincere struggle over the meaning and the interpretation of the law, but because of its importance the court had become a stage on which each of the actors present was no longer his own master. Deference would have to be paid, not just to their Lordships sitting high on their ornately engraved wooden podium, but also to other forces that would probably always remain hidden to us.

Since everything was now on hold, Hassan had become more and more despondent. Once again, affairs in his life had taken an unpredictable turn and the lack of control made him frustrated and disillusioned. His feelings came to a head during a conversation he had with me on 17 April. Although our appeal got the go ahead, the publishers had decided not to defend themselves against the police action, so the judges had granted the police permission to take away the draft manuscript of the book. Hassan felt that this was a blow too far. It was now only a matter of time before the police came for him and he didn't want to be a 'sitting duck' any longer.

'Shiv, I want to tell you something crazy,' he said.

I told him that I already thought everything we were doing was crazy. This made him laugh loudly and freely.

'No, this is really crazy. I want to go to a judge.'

'What?'

'I want to go to a judge and confess everything. I'm not going to testify against anyone. I just want to say to him: "These are the things I've done; do with me what you want to. Exonerate me of everything or send me to prison but do something."' He was fed up, he said. He didn't want to continue to live like this, always waiting for the police to make the next move. He wanted to put them on the back foot, and do something unprecedented by confessing everything.

His sense of sacrifice made a deep impression on me. That he could hold strong to his ideals and purpose despite the threat of prison, that he could lay himself open to judgement, filled me with admiration. Not only had he been willing to question everything – his past, the network, his Prophet – but he'd also been forced to suffer in order to do so. And now, pushed to the limit, he was willing to sacrifice even more. It was a bold and honest plan and I'd never held him in such high esteem as I did in that moment.

I told him how brave he was being and said that I'd speak to my lawyers about how it could be done. Hassan said that he'd speak to a solicitor who had acted on his behalf in the past. The next day, when we spoke again, we found that we had both been given similar advice: under English law there wasn't a procedure for going to a judge and confessing to a crime of this sort. Charges would have to be prepared against him first, or Hassan could go to the police and confess, but that's exactly what he didn't want to do. He said he couldn't trust them to treat him fairly or honestly and he didn't want to give them them the satisfaction of seeing him on the back foot.

I suggested we go public and that he give an interview to the press stating that he wanted to confess, and maybe something would come of this. At the very least, it would act as a record of his intent, which he would have whatever happened in the future. That weekend, the piece appeared in the *Sunday Times*:

A former jihadist from Britain who claims to have renounced violence is willing to go to prison to prove his sincerity.

Hassan Butt, once a member of the extremist group Al-Muhajiroun, is so exasperated at still being the target of police investigations that he is willing to plead guilt to past crimes and take his punishment – if that's what is required to escape his former life.

He claims Greater Manchester police are harassing him over suspicions that he is secretly still a jihadist. Yet he says he now works to woo Muslims away from violence – and that the Home Office encourages his efforts ...

Butt, who believes his attempts to promote moderation are being undermined, said: 'I'm not in denial about anything. I'm not asking for immunity or favours. I just want to be able to get on with my life and undo the work that I did. I've fund-raised for terrorism. I've trained in a training camp and I've sent other people to train. I am willing to plead guilty. I'm not looking to get locked up but if I have to, I have to.'

A few days after the *Sunday Times* article went to press, I attended an event about de-radicalisation that had been organised by an interfaith charity. It was held in a small lecture theatre at London University, and various speakers came to the podium to outline their solutions to the problem of Islamic radicalism on campus.

Halfway through, the civil servant who had offered Hassan funding walked in through the back doors and sat down a few rows in front of me. We had not met since that day at the Home Office, but I had phoned him twice to explain what had happened with the Manchester police. Both times he had thanked me for the information but he was never willing to talk further about the matter. His reticence and senior rank made me wonder how much more he might know.

He had not seen me so at the end of the event, as he passed me on his way to the exit, I stood up and greeted him. He suddenly looked uncomfortable. He nodded at me and then kept going. I followed him outside into the corridor and touched him on the shoulder. He turned.

'I didn't expect to see you here,' he said.

'I wasn't sure whether to come or not,' I replied. 'Look – can I ask you about Hassan? You supported him and now the police are trying to prosecute him. It doesn't make any sense.'

He looked around and then signalled for me to follow him into an alcove a little further down the corridor.

'Is this strictly off the record?'

'Yes,' I said.

'Because I shouldn't be talking to you at all, you understand that.'

'Yes.'

'As you can imagine, you're not privy to certain pieces of information.'

I nodded. I think he wanted to leave it at that, but I waited for more of an answer, so he continued. 'There's a wider context to all of this which you don't know about. That's all I can say.'

'I still don't understand,' I replied.

'That's all I can say. I really have to leave now. Goodbye.'

On 30 April Hassan sent me a message to say that his mother was seriously ill in Pakistan and that he needed to go out there soon.

I was not sure if his mother really was ill, but I had no proof to the contrary and I guessed that this was his way of justifying his departure from the country without looking rash or cowardly. Leaving was perhaps a means of regaining control, or perhaps bringing things to a head. I didn't know which – Hassan had never been the patient type.

Since the police hadn't made a move after the *Sunday Times* article, I didn't think that they would stop him. On the other hand, I fretted because I didn't think that it would look good for the appeal if he left. But he had every right to go, and since the appeal wasn't due to start until 21 May he could make it there and back in good time.

On the morning of Friday 9 May, he texted again to say things had got worse with his mother and that he'd be catching the next available flight to Pakistan at 5.45pm that day. At four o'clock I called his mobile. It went straight to voicemail. The phone had been switched off. Hassan had been arrested.

21

Until then, the investigation into Hassan Butt – 'Operation Quill', as it was officially termed – had not been going well for the Greater Manchester Police. But with Hassan's attempted departure to Lahore, they had a reason to arrest him and take him in for questioning. Afterwards, one of the officers admitted to me that his arrest had come earlier than they had ideally wanted, but with this act they began their fight back, and they did not stop until they had got what they wanted.

That night, news reports were saying that a terrorist suspect had been detained at Manchester airport trying to 'flee' the country – he had bought his ticket a short while before the departure of the flight to Pakistan. Counter-terrorism officers were also searching three properties, and two cars had been removed for 'forensic examination'.

Without publicly confirming his name, the GMP briefed the media that the man they'd arrested was a Home Office adviser. Reporters knew who they meant. The Home Office was forced onto the defensive and responded by saying: 'Ministers meet a range of people as part of government business. It would be remiss for them not to. More broadly, the government has been clear that it will look to work with people who are serious about taking practical steps to counter violent extremism and we will continue to do that.'

The next morning, a Saturday, the GMP also served the BBC, the *Sunday Times* and the London headquarters of CBS with draft production orders demanding that they hand over all their material concerning Hassan Butt. This was perhaps a tactical error because it only served to galvanise the media against the police. They also sent my lawyers some new information: the prosecution's case against Habib Ahmed.

Until now I'd thought that Habib, Hassan's best friend, had essentially been arrested because of a misunderstanding about a documentary. But these new documents made it clear that it was far more serious than that. Habib had been caught with diaries full of the contact details of al-Qaeda's most senior members. These were written in invisible ink and had been given to him in Dubai in December 2005 (a month before Hassan's own trip) to take back to England. During transit from Dubai to Britain, the police had opened his bag, photographed the diaries and then put them back into his luggage. When they arrested him in August 2006, they found the diaries at his house. The evidence against him was pretty open and shut.

The person who had given Habib the diaries was called Rangzieb Ahmed (no relation), a thirty-one-year-old Pakistani from Rochdale who had already served seven years in an Indian prison during the 1990s for suspicious activity in Kashmir. Shortly after Habib's arrest, Rangzieb was arrested in Pakistan, deported to Britain and then charged with being a 'director of terrorism' – the first person in the UK to be charged with such an offence.

Habib's wife Mehreen had also been arrested, for giving money and material support to her husband. She had been let out on bail and was looking after their two young children at their small terraced house, which was located only a few streets away from where Hassan lived in Cheetham Hill.

It had been a very large operation and security services had not only recorded the conversations between Habib and Rangzieb in Manchester, but also in their hotel room – the Hotel Versailles – in Dubai. This meant that both the domestic and foreign security services (MI5 and MI6 respectively) were likely to have been involved in some way.

Hassan and Mo had also been covertly recorded speaking to Habib in his car while driving around Manchester, and the police were alleging their complicity in terrorist activity – the main point being that Habib and Mo had gone to Pakistan together during April and May 2006 to be trained in how to make bombs.

There was now little doubt that Hassan's best friend was involved in some sort of terrorist activity. Yet in some ways, these covert recordings helped support Hassan's story that he had indeed left the network. Before leaving for his meeting in Dubai, Hassan had talked about raising funds for 'the brothers', but a few weeks after his return he was recorded telling Habib that killing was wrong: 'They're targeting people and the thing is, it's not Islamic,' the transcript read. Hassan was also recorded talking about writing a book that would make it clear that Muslims were still in theological denial: 'These people feel guilty that Islam does this, so they deny it.'

This all sounded a lot like what he'd said to me at the time. In fact, it sounded very like what he had written in the outline for his tract, *Radical Islam*. Comparing the dates of the covert recordings and the email he'd sent to me with *Radical Islam* attached, I noted that there were just ten days between them. Reading and re-reading the transcripts from the bug in the vehicle – picking apart each sentence, each choice of words – it seemed clearer to me that Hassan's testimony from the wiretap matched with what he'd told me. He really had wanted to leave the jihadi network; he really had undergone a change of heart. He was telling the truth. Unless, of course, he'd known about the bug all along. If he had, then perhaps he was banking on the fact that it would corroborate his cover story down the line. But that kind of planning would take such foresight, such skill, it seemed beyond the capability of just one person.

I had been trying to get hold of Hassan's solicitor all day but I'd received no answer because he was with Hassan in the police station. Desperate for information, I dialled Detective Sergeant Smith's mobile number. Perhaps it wasn't a wise thing to do considering we were in the middle of a legal dispute, but if I was careful enough I could find out what I needed to know: had Hassan really left al-Qaeda?

Smith confirmed that Hassan had been arrested. I asked if the police would be detaining him for a long time. Smith said that he couldn't inform me about such matters and that I would have to speak to the press office if I wanted to find out anything else. I asked for a few more details about what had already come out in the media, but again Smith referred me to the press office.

I had one final question: whether Hassan was being held in regard to offences carried out post-2006 – after he'd written to me, and after his departure from the network – because I would be 'concerned' if that were the case. Aware of the legal complications that could be thrown up by what I had just said to Smith, I stressed the word 'concerned' and said that nothing in this conversation should prejudice my position in court.

Sensing my lack of confidence, Smith said that if he was asked to testify in court he would give a truthful appraisal of what had just taken place but he reassured me that he understood the sensitive nature of our conversation.

He and I agreed on a form of words to relay to his seniors, that being: 'it would cause me concern if Mr Butt had been involved in offences post-2006'. Again I stressed 'concern', believing that the term would be meaningful in the moment, yet suitably vague under examination at a later date.

Smith rang back just after 1.00 pm. He told me that Hassan was undergoing a staged interview and that they would be 'putting things to him during the week' at Pendleton Police Station. He added that 'it would be unfair to Hassan' if he told me what these matters related to and it would also 'ruin the integrity of the investigation'. But the police, Smith said, felt confident that they would be able to demonstrate 'that Mr Butt has had one over you'.

By Sunday I finally managed to get hold of Hassan's solicitor and ask how Hassan was.

'I don't want to sound dramatic but it's similar to a prisoner-of-war camp,' he said, adding that Hassan was being kept shackled most of the time. Three guards had to walk him, step by step, from his prison cell to the interview room that he could be summoned to at any time of day or night. Hassan had been put on suicide watch, so the lights in his cell were permanently kept on. He was sleep deprived. There were regular strip searches and the solicitor was also thoroughly searched on his way in and out. He had to surrender his shoes, pen and belt each time. 'They say it's for the health and safety of the officers, but … '

Threatened with imminent interrogation, spending night after night in a floodlit cell being shaken awake by police – the thought that Hassan could be held like this for almost a month without the police laying a single charge against him made my stomach churn.

I wanted to know if Hassan had confessed, but I didn't want to ask outright in case the solicitor clammed up and refused to talk. Instead, I asked what the charges were. 'Well I can't discuss that with you but at the moment they're just reading out a pile of statements he gave to the press over the years. Hassan isn't giving any comment.'

'What? They're just reading out news clippings?'

'Yup.'

'Nothing else?'

'No.'

'So that means they don't have anything on him.'

'Well, I guess not.'

'And he's not going to confess to anything if they haven't got any evidence, is he?'

'That I can't discuss.'

On Tuesday 13 May – the fifth day of Hassan's detention – Detective Sergeant Smith called me at 12.43pm. He said he would try to give me a bullet-pointed version of the charges, but before he gave me access to this information he wanted to know if I'd be a witness. Presumably this would be in a case against Hassan, but he also seemed to be suggesting that I give evidence against Habib Ahmed in his trial.

'We need you on side ... We do appreciate your desire to protect your sources and my bosses are keen to help you with this

… You do not need to disclose other material and sources.'

Though it wouldn't have changed any of my decisions, I asked him why this hadn't been offered before. He replied that the production order, with its exhaustive list of demands, had been a 'necessary evil'.

Then, in a reference to a criticism from a columnist in one of the Sunday papers, he said: 'This is not about tick-box policing … It's very hard to go against someone who is held in esteem by the Home Office … We have no problems with what we are doing.'

I knew that if the GMP were asking me to be a witness against Hassan, they must be desperate. I declined the offer; they could force me to hand over my notes, but I wouldn't willingly betray Hassan.

On Thursday 15 May I received another document from the police.

Greater Manchester Police Counter Terrorism Unit is conducting a terrorist investigation in relation to the following individual:

- Hassan Butt (Born 27.04.80)
- Alias: Abdul Ghani
- Home Address: 16 Copthall Lane, Cheetham Hill, Manchester

I noticed that they'd now got his date of birth correct but I was curious about the alias name 'Abdul Ghani'. I didn't think Hassan had ever used an alias. He'd never mentioned one, and because he had been on TV and pictured in the newspapers so often, everyone already knew his real name. What would be the point of using a fake one?

I read on:

> Butt was arrested at 3.55 pm on Friday the 9 May 2008 on the
> pier in Terminal 2 at Manchester Airport. The suspect had just
> booked himself onto a Pakistani International Airways Flight
> to Lahore.
>
> Butt was arrested for the following Terrorism Act 2000
> offences: s.11 Membership of a Proscribed Organisation, s.15
> Fund-raising for Terrorism, s54 Weapons Training and s56
> Directing a Terrorist Organisation.
>
> During the first review by Inspector Walker, Butt stated
> that he did not understand why he was at the police sta-
> tion. Inspector Walker explained the four offences ... Butt
> responded: '*Tell my solicitor now and I will tell you every-
> thing. All that you said is true. Yes I have done that.*' These
> comments were witnessed by two other police officers.

With this remark, it seemed that Hassan would confess. However,
when they started interviewing him in earnest, putting to him
'sixty documentary exhibits' – the press clippings and the manuscript of the book, which they had got from the publishers –
Hassan refused to give comment. Then, a day later, he read out a
statement prepared with his solicitor that 'urged officers to provide full disclosure'. Hassan wanted to know everything that the
police had on him before he talked. The police did not do this, so
Hassan carried on saying 'no comment' until the early evening of
13 May, when something occurred that made him change tack:

> Butt then stated that he now wished to speak and would
> explain events in the following four phases:

- From 0 to 15/16 years of age.
- From 15/16 years to 21 years of age (concluding at the time of the 9/11 attacks).
- From 21 years (post 9/11) to the present day.
- His relationship with the media.

I noted that the first three phases of his life were how I had split up my own interviews with him. The police said that his replies were 'comparable with events in the manuscript', especially regarding the early parts of his life, but there were some 'notable exceptions' in the rest of his story. For example, he said he had never fired a gun or gone to a training camp – this was an elaborate story he had made up. When asked about raising money, Hassan replied, 'Hand on heart I probably knew what was going to happen to the money.' A confession of sorts, but not the direct admission about funding terrorism he had given to so many others, including the Home Office minister.

The document also laid out some of the other evidence against Hassan:

In September 2007 a statement was obtained from Junaid Babar, a convicted terrorist awaiting sentence in the USA ... Babar describes Butt as a person he had a close relationship with, meeting on a daily basis whilst Butt was in Pakistan. He goes on to indicate that Butt was heavily involved in terrorist activities whilst in Pakistan.

The statement from Babar was expected. He'd given the police sworn information on pretty much everyone else he'd met during that time – why would he leave Hassan out?

Having searched Hassan's house they found letters from Habib Ahmed, the head of the Crawley bombers Omar Khayam, and another convicted terrorist. The letters suggested that Hassan had sent money to all of them while they were locked up. They were small amounts: £50 to Habib, £100 to Khayam. Some of these letters were dated just nine months ago.

Then the police outlined their suspicion that Hassan 'is actively raising and laundering funds to be used for terrorist activities. This belief is supported by the unusual financial activity, suspicious benefit claims and intertwined use of addresses and accounts.' They said this dated back to 2003 and concluded by saying: 'Ultimately, the source of Hassan Butt's income cannot be identified at this time.'

While the statement from Junaid Babar was expected, the visits and money to prisoners were not. Although it was not illegal, it did not look good at all for Hassan to be consorting with and financially aiding convicted terrorists. Perhaps this was Hassan's way of opening up the lines of communication with people he was attempting to recruit out of the network.

The police then suggested some possible motives for Hassan's actions:

One consideration within the investigation is that Butt has manipulated his association with Malik for his own ends, and/ or that of furthering his terrorist activities. This may include gaining access to people or places he would otherwise have difficulty in doing so.

Within the manuscript Malik quotes an email sent by BUTT: *I want your help to get a job in a think tank or as a consultant for ppl who are concerned to work towards building bridges into my world.*

An example of this may be the meeting between Butt and the Government Minister Mr McNulty.

I'd included the entirety of Hassan's email from 7 February 2006 in the draft preface that I'd handed to the publishers. It was the moment he'd first told me he'd left the network and didn't know what to do with himself. I'd thought it a useful way of explaining to the reader how the book had come about. Now, the police were quoting it back to me as evidence that I'd been 'manipulated' from the very start. It made me sick to my core to see the book being used against me in this way. And I could now appreciate for myself why Hassan had been so worried about handing over the manuscript before publication.

But at the end of the GMP document was one paragraph that could not be reinterpreted in Hassan's favour. It was about the stabbing. Buried in a section about how Hassan had made repeated visits to Habib in prison was this key paragraph:

One of the occasions that Butt visited [Habib] Ahmed was at 10.45 am on the 11 April 2007, the day after he had been supposedly attacked and stabbed outside Woodlands Road Tram Station. The manuscript refers to Butt's actions this day as: *Recuperating in bed at, he said, a private hospital, Hassan had just finished watching the Liverpool v PSV Eindhoven Champions League Match.*

I stopped reading. If Hassan had been visiting his friend Habib in prison on the morning of 11 April – a fact that was easy enough for the police to verify, and so not one that was likely to be wrong in a submission to the courts – then Hassan's story about the stabbing fell apart. If he'd been visiting Habib in jail, Hassan could not have been on painkillers, recovering from general anaesthetic in a hospital bed. If he'd been talking directly to Habib that very morning, Hassan could not have been fast asleep in a private ward, looking 'as pale as the bed sheets'. If this was true, then Hassan had lied about the attack, and the details about private wards and painkillers were deliberate fabrications to make Gavshon, Magratten and me believe that he had been attacked by his enemies. He would have manufactured the incident, including his tears and Mo's texts, with every intention of deceiving us.

Panic seized me. The questions had suddenly become overwhelmingly numerous. If he had lied about this, then where did his credibility begin or end? What else had he lied about? Who on earth had I spent all these years interviewing, helping and supporting? Who was I now laying myself on the line for?

I needed to talk this through and immediately phoned Gavshon, who patched me into a conference call with Magratten. Drew was angry. He'd known something was wrong all along. Although it had come after the broadcast of *60 Minutes*, he said we should have followed our instincts and tracked Hassan down at the time, instead of backing off because Hassan had 'broken down'. But Gavshon had heard the tears. They had been genuine, he said, as real as any he'd ever heard. As for me, I had seen the stab marks.

Magratten started asking me about the injuries. I described the thick red mark on Hassan's shoulder, the bruise on his cheek and how he had walked into our interview on 3 May with a

slight limp. Throughout our conversation he had found it difficult to sit without shifting continuously because, he said, he was
still sore from the attack.

Could all this have been faked, or were the police just wrong
about Hassan's visit to the prison? And if all three of us had
been manipulated, then for what purpose? To what end?

22

On Saturday 17 May – four days before the appeal – Graham Smith called me at exactly 3.00 pm and read out a statement: 'We need to speak to you about the detention of Hassan Butt. We want to speak to you as a witness, not as a suspect. This is because of what Hassan Butt has said in his interview.'

Smith took his time with each sentence, pausing to give each word gravitas, but the emphasis was in all the wrong places and I missed the subtleties of what he was putting to me: 'It is important that we establish the truth surrounding the content of the book. Hassan has stated that he has lied to you about his terrorist activities and, furthermore, you have embellished his version of events.'

I told Smith that I understood our joint desire to seek the truth. But in order to maintain the integrity of the judicial review that we were involved in, I didn't think that it would be appropriate to talk further.

Going off script, Smith replied that the police were giving me the opportunity to clarify what Hassan had said to me during the writing of the book. My personal integrity with the police, the Home Office and the media was at stake, he warned.

Embellishing his version of events? My personal integrity? It sounded like Smith was trying to scare me into coming on side.

Yes, the details about Hassan's prison visit the day after the 'stabbing' had thoroughly shaken me. But without rock-solid facts, I still didn't know what to make of it all. And writing a book like Hassan's had been complicated. Maybe he had 'embellished' a story here and there. I suspected that for effect Hassan may have gone over the top in relating some of his exploits, but it felt more likely that he'd gotten carried away in flourishes of detail, than that he had made things up completely. This was after all an autobiography, not a drab and exacting court statement.

In any case, with only four days left before the appeal there was no way I could suddenly change my mind about everything and start acting as a witness for the police. The court papers had already been filed, the lawyers had put in weeks of work, the media statements had gone out and the articles of support had been published. Even if I wanted to, I didn't have the power to reverse the whole process – and certainly not on the basis of a few words from a copper.

I told Smith this. He tried to convince me otherwise, but after a minute or so he gave up and we ended our conversation.

The day before the appeal – Hassan's twelfth day in detention – Rhona called and told me to come to her office. The police had sent through a twenty-page fax.

When I got there, she sat me down in one of the small meeting rooms on the ground floor. She was dressed in casual clothes: a red-and-blue fleece top and trainers. She usually wore this outfit around the office, but today it seemed to jar with the seriousness of the tone she was employing. I asked her what the fax was about.

'It's the transcripts from his interviews in police custody,' she said.

I was perplexed. I asked her if it was normal for the police to give out interview transcripts during an investigation. Rhona told me that, in all her years as a solicitor, she'd never seen or heard anything like it. 'I don't know why they've done it. It will ruin the integrity of their case against him.'

I asked Rhona what the transcripts said.

'It's not good.' Rhona tried to think of a gentle way to put it, but then decided to just say it straight: 'Hassan's told the police that he made everything up and that you, well … egged him on to do it.' So this was what Smith had been talking about. Once Rhona had left the room, I read the fax.

According to the interview summary, Hassan was saying that everything he'd told me was a lie, a highly elaborate scam to make money. This habit of his had started when he first became the spokesperson for al-Muhajiroun. The police asked him how he had become the group's spokesperson and his answer did not differ much from the one he had given me for the book: he'd realised it was an opportunity to make money.

Why am I just giving them everything so easily on a plate you know? They're making their money and these lads have got massive budgets. Why not try to make some money out of this? So the first time I tried was with Channel Five, there was a reporter, I don't want to mention his name because I don't want to embarrass him but I asked for 300 dollars. He negotiated down to 200 dollars for an interview with guys that were from Britain.

So a lot of the al-Muhajiroun guys that had come that weren't going out to fight, we were dressing them up as fighters basically. Getting hold of guns in Pakistan, it's like you know a gun a penny ... so we get hold of weapons and start these mock, or these fake type of interviews. So we set up interviews with Sky, Channel Five, BBC, ABC, and the newspapers as well. *The Times*, the *Express* and eventually from 200 dollars it went to 1,500 dollars. So I thought I can actually make my own money.

He then went on to explain how he'd scammed the media with similar interviews, including one that Habib had given dressed up and masked to a reporter from the *Sunday Times* in Manchester. But eventually his scheme was busted when one paper, the *Daily Mirror*, decided to entrap him. With Habib acting as a go-between, they offered Hassan £100,000 to tell his story during his brief return to the UK in December 2001. While Habib attempted to secure the cash, Hassan was photographed lurking behind a pillar in Trafalgar Square. The story ran a few days later with the headline: 'War on Terror: Security Farce: Beyond the Law; Exclusive: We Track Hate Filled Terror Agent The Law Cannot Touch.'

When a television news station tried the same thing a year or so later, it was clear that Hassan had built himself up into such a bogeyman that he had become the target of undercover reporting. That's when, he told the police, he decided to try a different moneymaking scam:

So I think in my head why not try to sell something to the media? [But] if I contact the BBC, Channel 4, ITV, and I'm still portraying myself as jihadi to them ... they don't talk to me.

So I started making closer relationships with people ... who were very senior reporters within the BBC ... giving them hints on how to go forward in documentaries that they were making – building a rapport with them first.

I like this type of fictional world, even the book that I've given in myself, is fictional. I like the idea of making films. I like the idea of engaging in books and things like that – fictional pieces. So I thought, that's another way of advancing my career.

By now, Hassan said, he had already put his jihadi ideology behind him, but when the BBC's Jim Booth asked him if it was alright if I gave him a call, Hassan decided to carry on posing as a radical to get some cash.

The document continued: 'When Malik attended at his address Butt had strategically placed [radical] books about the room and was working out in the gym.' The interviewer had asked if Hassan said he was still involved to maintain my interest, and Hassan replied: 'Yeah, [that] I'm still a jihadi, which was a lie.'

Hassan described what happened next:

[So Shiv asks], 'have you ever met Mohammad Sidique Khan?' And at first I said 'no', and he thought I was lying to him just to cover my back. He said, 'Look Hassan, I'm not working for, you know, the authorities, I mean it's great if you have known him and you know, it shows that you know their mindset' … I didn't say anything at that point.

[Then] I think: well, why don't I just admit that I've met him a couple of times? It's not as though anyone could ever be able to verify what I'm saying. So I said alright, fair enough, let's just say I've met Mohammad Sidique Khan. So eventually you know – I didn't drop it in, in the next meeting – I did it slowly so it looked … it felt natural to him, and looked natural – that

I'm opening up to him. And at the same time I'm pondering upon, you know how I'm going to build a relationship.

The next phase of Hassan's plan was to stage his departure from the network to make it look like he had broken off from the chain of command:

So then this whole elaborate type of thinking comes into place in the sense of we think, or rather I think, coz it was my idea, but obviously I had people who were supporting me in what I was doing, and I said right I've slowly got to tell these guys [in the media] that I've changed.

So I planned this trip to Dubai – which is where I went – I spent three weeks in Dubai, and did nothing, absolutely nothing except for relax. It was a break for me because it was the first time I went abroad in about three years.

With the idea of the book becoming a reality after he'd returned from Dubai, Hassan described his version of our interview process and his confessed involvement in the Karachi bombings:

Well basically ... the more I got to know about Shiv the more I got to realise that he wants me to keep pushing further and further to say things that I'm not basically ... you know at that time I think my reputation had completely exceeded me ... anyway Shiv was trying to get more and more and more.

So I'm sitting there and he goes have you done any more than this terrorism? ... I'm thinking this guy isn't satisfied. It's still not enough for him. He still wants more, and he wants more, and he wants more ... So I sat ... thinking how can

I fit everything into my timeline … I started doing a bit of research on the Internet. I thought let's have a look at what was happening round about May or June … the year I went back to Pakistan, and it just happened round about that time … [I didn't mention] the specifics until I knew more detail and felt that I could actually convince Shiv about [the bombings]. But by then, to be honest with you, anything I would have said, Shiv would have believed. So that's how I slipped it in.

They asked him if he'd ever been involved in a terrorist plot, and he told them: 'No, never … we never got involved in any type of violence with al-Muhajiroun.'

When the interviewing officer asked him about going to a training camp, Hassan replied that this was also a made-up story. He then explained why he had told journalists that he had been to a camp:

It's like, you know, adding spice and flavour to the whole story … I can't say to people you should go out and get trained if I've not said [I've done] it myself, so at this point I say, yeah I've been training hard … and I made up an elaborate story about being privately trained … [But] I've never fired a gun …

So these guys thought: whoa, this is really going to be an explosive story. At the same time I'm thinking in my head that if this book does come out, it would be [read] with a lot more – what's the words I'm looking for? – you know, a lot more than if someone's just had the thoughts, and never gone beyond that … That's how I sold it. Do I feel guilty for sensationalising it? No, I don't, because that's what the media wants and that's what the media got from me.

Then Hassan explained why he was coming clean with the police after years of lying to the media: 'I don't want to go to prison as a result of something that I have never done.'

In the last section of the interview, Hassan was asked about the stabbing:

> God this is embarrassing – sorry. I actually arranged for myself to be stabbed in the shoulder – sorry, in my arm and in my back – because I knew if I said I had been attacked, Shiv was going to ask for some proof so basically I stabbed myself ...
>
> You know it was just part of the whole scam ... it was arranged for me to be stabbed twice and it wasn't done in an attacking way it was actually done inside my house ... with a small penknife ... they were small wounds, the knife was sterilised before being used. I know it sounds crazy ... to a certain degree I was trying to push [Shiv] forwards because he wasn't working as fast on the book as I wanted.

When I finished reading, I called Rhona back to the meeting room and asked if she wanted a cigarette. She didn't usually smoke but she'd have one now. Sitting together on the wall outside the office, Rhona tried to console me but I could see she thought Hassan had betrayed me and that although I probably hadn't 'egged' Hassan on, she was fairly convinced that Hassan's story was a pack of lies and that I'd swallowed it whole.

Despite this she told me, 'You know when you go into court tomorrow you'll still be a journalist trying to protect his sources.' Her words rang a little hollow. The wider moral argument – that source or not Hassan needed defending against those who wanted him punished for life, that the concept of redemption itself needed to be defended – was now in tatters.

Was it really possible that Hassan had lied to me all this time? If this were the case, he would have had to sustain his lies for years. It would have required a massive effort on his behalf – imagining details and then remembering them months, years later when I, and others, asked about them again and again. Surely he would have needed help?

He had alluded to collusion when he said he 'had people who were supporting me in what I was doing'. But who were these people – Mo or Atif? – and why were they helping him with his ruse? If it was money, it hardly seemed worth the effort – Hassan had only made six or seven thousand pounds from the book and the articles we'd done over three years we'd known each other. He had even let me have a larger cut of the book advance than I was entitled to. In fact, he'd offered me all of it, and *I'd* declined.

If he had wanted to make serious money, it would have been better for him to have waited until the book was published. Now he had destroyed any possibility of this by declaring himself a liar.

Perhaps he'd done it for fame, for celebrity? Perhaps he was an attention seeker through and through? This was very possible.

But was it not more likely that he was now lying to the police – destroying his credibility in exchange for his liberty? This seemed like the most obvious answer. Even though he had declared publicly that he would go to prison, when faced with the reality of incarceration he'd caved and tried to save himself.

But what about the stabbing? It was not illegal to *get* stabbed. He could just as well have told the police that he was stabbed – maybe not by jihadis – and it wouldn't have made any difference to his charge sheet. Combined with the visit to Habib in prison it was probably true – though bizarre – that he had in fact stabbed himself with a sterilised penknife. This would explain a lot: Mo and Atif's unwillingness to speak to me, Hassan's evasiveness that day, his begging Gavshon to respect his personal space so we'd back off trying to visit him and his request for me not to write about the incident.

But the implications of this led back in a circle. If Hassan could manufacture an incident like this with the help of alibis, a panoply of verbal details (the directions back from the metro stop; the request for a lighter; the pulling down of his hood; the 'Iranian' man in his car), physical proof in the shape of the wounds themselves, and a theatre of emotions to complete the picture – anger, guilt, shame, circumspection – then what would stop him from creating the rest of his story?

As he had noted himself, he had the ability to invent whole novels, so what was to say that Hassan hadn't imagined an entire existence in Pakistan? If he could fake tears, then he could just as easily fake all those months of depression while 'leaving the network', and all those stories of intimidation and violence – the broken windows, the slashed tyres, the two guys at his nephew's primary school and the nasty phone calls – for which I had taken his word.

But then inventing the stabbing seemed pointless. Hassan had told the police that he'd arranged to have himself stabbed so I would work faster on the book. But if he had stabbed himself, then why not pick another day? Why choose for someone to stab him just before our first meeting with a big publisher in London – a sure way of sabotaging the very thing he professed to want? His explanation didn't make sense. And if he had gone to see

Habib in prison, he couldn't just turn up on a whim. Habib was a suspect in a high-security prison – Hassan would have had to book his visit well in advance. He would have known for a few weeks at least that the two appointments clashed. Did that mean he'd never had any intention of going to meet the publishers?

And why go to see Habib at all? As a visitor he'd be signed in, searched, checked, filmed and monitored, and the records would be kept. It would be obvious that he hadn't been attacked and left for dead the night before, and the police would have easy access to high-quality evidence. He could have stayed low at his house for a few days and no one would have been any wiser – by visiting Habib, it was as if he wanted to be caught.

As for my own position, I wondered whether I'd actually 'egged him on'. It was a horrible thought – could I have pushed him into such massive fabrications? I thought back to how our interviews had progressed. I knew how I'd acted towards him; I knew what he'd really said to me. But thankfully I didn't have to rely on my memory – almost everything between us had been recorded on tape or noted down contemporaneously. I'd even recorded our phone calls. Hassan could say anything he wanted but these were still facts. If needs be, the police and my lawyers – even the public – could hear the whole lot, could listen to the nature of each of my questions and judge my conduct for themselves.

But I began to think that somehow my influence had taken a much subtler form. There were hundreds of times when he'd talked and I'd nodded in encouragement, exclaiming how interesting it all was, asking him to carry on and tell me more. Rather than critically question whether this or that event had actually happened, I'd helped him piece together events – including the consulate bombing in Pakistan. He'd known what I wanted to hear – I'd made it clear that the publishers would like drama, and he knew that as his ghostwriter I would take it all down faithfully, with little interrogation. Whatever the case, I'd certainly spent too long sitting at his feet, listening passively to this inside story of a radical instead of being the reporter I'd always imagined I'd be.

I was overwhelmed then with a desire to rebut his damning allegations by breaking my promise of confidentiality and handing over all my tapes and notes. As his ghostwriter – his shadow through this whole process – didn't he have an obligation to protect me too? Why did he have to plunge the knife into my back, and drag my reputation down with him by portraying me as the commissioner of his lies? And why did I have to save Hassan from the GMP now he was so obviously betraying me? Why not cooperate with the police?

As Rhona had pointed out, the principle of protecting my sources – not just Hassan, but all the other contacts I'd talked to and interviewed over the years – was the only thing I had left in this fight. And with less than a day to go, there was no practicable way of backing out without angering everyone who had put so much effort and money into supporting me. Not without suffering humiliation in front of the court and in the press. I'd just have to brave the appeal hearing.

My only relief was that since the police interviews were part of a confidential investigation, Hassan's statements were unlikely ever to be made public, at least until well after the appeal. That would give me enough time to retrieve my notes and recordings from the bookshop in Paris, listen to every single tape again, sort through my evidence, and piece together with absolute certainty what had really gone on. Then I could prepare to defend myself against Hassan's career-destroying accusations.

23

The Royal Courts of Justice – with its tall gothic spires, cavernous stone atrium, and warren of wood-panelled courtrooms, each packed with dusty books – stand as a testament to English law: a continuous, uninterrupted body of judgement handed down from generation to generation for hundreds of years. As a journalist I'd go on to report many times about the cases being argued and decided upon in those courtrooms. But it is only when you yourself are the subject of a case, staring up at the judges who can order you to act against your own reasoned decisions, that you feel the full weight of that history pressing down upon you.

As the bewigged judges entered Courtroom Three, around forty people rose until they had sat down on their wooden thrones, positioned high above the ground. Sunlight streamed in, glinting off the particles of dust floating around the room and dousing everything in a pale, sepia hue. Behind the three judges – the maximum number for any appeal – was an engraved seal of the Crown. Beneath their dais, the clerks and other court officials were perched at their counters, lit by desk lamps with green porcelain shades. Much lower – so low that the light from the lamps glared directly into their eyes if they gazed up at the judges – were the barristers (all Queen's Counsel) who would be arguing the case in front of their Lordships. Behind them were the junior barristers and then the senior solicitors. Further back still sat the junior solicitors and then, finally, the public. These benches were packed with my family, friends and supporters, including Gavshon and Magratten.

Flanking the room were the press benches, where a handful of reporters sat. Some I knew well, others were strangers to me, sent by agencies. All the benches in the court were straight-backed, like church pews, and the lack of legroom meant that those with bad posture were forced to lean forward to be comfortable – as if in contemplation, prayer or submission.

After my own barrister had given his opening arguments about the protection of sources and the risks of self-incrimination, Andrew Edis, who was representing the GMP, took to the floor. Edis – who would later be known for the phone-hacking trial against the prime minister's former head of communications and the former editor of the *Sun*, Rebekah Brooks – was a large, barrel-chested man whose gravelly voice boomed across the courtroom. As he spoke, solicitors and clerks began tapping on their laptops, creating a staccato chorus like the patter of rain on a window.

It did not take long before Edis began revealing what Hassan had said during his interviews with the police; it was the first of three surprises that day. The sections he read were short – a few sentences here and there about how Hassan had denied having ever met Mohammad Sidique Khan, being involved in a terrorist plot or attending a training camp. In the press gallery, people were busily writing down Edis's words. The knowledge of what else was in those transcripts made my stomach drop. But then Edis stopped.

My lawyers began passing notes to me. They couldn't understand why this was happening. The police interviews were part
of an ongoing investigation, so reading out the transcripts in
public would completely prejudice the case against Hassan.

More than that, disclosing the transcripts seemed to muddy
the police's argument. This was an appeal and not a fresh hearing. The lawyers were supposed to be arguing about the rights
and wrongs of the decision arrived at by the judge in Manchester
('the judge below', as he was called), not new reasons for why an
order should or shouldn't be granted.

And Edis seemed to be arguing two contradictory positions at
the same time. On the one hand, he was saying that his clients,
the Manchester Police, believed Hassan Butt was a terrorist.
They believed he had lied during his time in detention, and if
they had access to my tapes they would have proof of Hassan
confessing to acts of terrorism.

Yet on the other hand, Edis seemed to be saying that the
police believed Hassan was a fantasist, and that the only way to
be sure of this was for me to hand over my tapes; these would
demonstrate he had attempted to swindle the British public.
Edis compared the scenario to the Hitler Diaries hoax of 1983.
But, as was pointed out in court, the police were supposed to be
investigating actual crimes and not imagined ones. So what did
they believe? Was Hassan a terrorist or a fantasist?

An answer of sorts – the second surprise – came towards
the end of the day, when Edis stood up to tell the court that
Hassan Butt had just been released from custody without
charge. He was a free man but, Edis added, 'the investigation
is continuing'. The insinuation was that, without my interview
tapes, they had been unable to charge Hassan. If that was true

it did not say much about the skills of the Manchester Police, but maybe they didn't have enough evidence to charge him. That would explain why they had been so desperate for me to become a witness.

Or perhaps they had let Hassan go through lack of evidence because he simply hadn't committed any crimes. Perhaps he really was a fantasist? Like many others, I left the courtroom that day more confused than ever as to who Hassan Butt really was. Once more, he had managed to evade the law; although he was one of the most well-known radicals in Britain, no one had ever been able to pin anything on him.

I gathered my belongings and made my way outside to the Strand, where the day's third surprise awaited me. As I walked out through the grand concentric arches of the front entrance and into the sunlight of a late spring afternoon, I saw a reporter holding a microphone. Beside him was his cameraman. They were from *Channel 4 News*.

I knew the reporter well. He had been the first journalist to interview Hassan about his past and his subsequent departure from the network. The interview had been conducted in a blacked-out hotel room in Kings Cross. But it was never used. Hassan had asked the reporter to keep his identity secret because at that time, June 2006, Hassan felt that it was still 'too dangerous' for him to denounce the network in public. The reporter had told Hassan that he could not guarantee his anonymity if the police came knocking, and the interview had been left on the shelf, much to the journalist's frustration.

We hadn't spoken to each other since then but it seemed like a long time ago, so I went over and asked him how he was. He asked if he could put a few questions to me. I told him that my lawyers had advised me not to say anything, but that I'd try and give him some answers.

What I didn't know was that, a few hours before, the Manchester police had given him a copy of Hassan's interview transcripts – far, far more than had been read out in court – including the parts about the stabbing and Hassan's attempt to hoax the media. He'd seen almost everything I'd been faxed the previous day.

He turned to the cameraman to check that everything was running and then, pointing the microphone towards me, he began with his first question: 'Can I ask you whether what's emerged today means the book is a sham?'

I was not expecting that question and I stalled, trying to search for some sort of answer. He was right: it was a sham there was no denying it. But instead of answering, I spouted something about legal restrictions. It was a poor reply – hesitant and full of pauses.

Then he followed with a second question: 'He's shafted you, hasn't he?'

My eyes widened. The question was so blunt that I hesitated once more. There was so much I wanted to explain but without being able to tell him everything – going over the whole story from beginning to end – I found I couldn't say anything. So I repeated my first response and added, 'we will see'. The reporter smiled and thanked me. I'd been given my right of reply and I'd come up with nonsense dressed to look like restraint. Then, with his cameraman in tow, he left to file his report. In a few hours, everyone would know I'd been taken for a fool. My naivety would become a matter of public record.

It would be a month before the judges handed down their verdict, so with Hassan released I went to see him in Manchester to get some answers. I arranged the meeting with a few short emails and texts, not wanting to say anything more in case I became angry and he decided to call it off.

The morning before our meeting, at 1.52 am, he texted me to tell me not to come. He said his house had been broken into and he was 'too stressed'. I lost my cool and I texted him back, saying 'Hey, you've fucked my career, so make time. I don't give a shit if you're "stressed". Don't piss me off … ' I followed this up with a phone call and during our conversation I started swearing at him – I didn't want to hear any more fabrications. I also insinuated that if he didn't make time I would hand over the tapes to the police. Hassan conceded, but only, he said, because he felt 'personally obligated' to do so.

I told him to pick me up from the station. In hindsight this was a mistake. It gave the wrong signal – that we were still friends and that I still trusted him and didn't mind depending on him. The reality was that our relationship was over. I only needed him so I could find out the truth.

When I got into Manchester at 2.10 pm, Hassan was waiting for me in a compact red Nissan – not the usual Audi or Jag he'd 'borrowed' from one of his older brothers. He was wearing a flak jacket over a *salwar kameez* and a pair of sandals with solid heels, the type used for trekking. The hair on the top of his head, which had once been a thick mass, was clipped right down to the skin and his beard was patchy, and longer than I'd ever seen it. His physical transformation into a jihadi appeared complete.

In the car I didn't know what to say, so I asked after his family. Hassan said that the car was bugged, or at least he assumed that it was, and he didn't want to say anything. We passed the rest of the journey in silence.

He drove me to a park next to his childhood home. The park was more of a muddy field, a little larger than a football pitch, surrounded by a few trees. In one corner there was a little fenced area that was tarmacked over, and inside the fence was a round-about, a swing and a climbing frame. Looking for somewhere to sit, we headed for the swings.

Before we sat down Hassan told me that he would have to search me. He needed to check if I was recording him, and that was why he was wearing sandals – so I could search him as well. He patted me down thoroughly, then asked me to take off my boots. I handed them to him and he looked inside. While he did this he apologised – 'I'm really sorry yaar'. When he finished he asked if I wanted to check him. I declined and we sat on the swings.

He asked me what I wanted to talk about. I had prepared a list of questions, which I'd committed to memory because I knew that Hassan would not allow our meeting to be recorded on paper or on tape. Memorising the order and the wording of the questions would help me remember the structure of what was said and would make it easier to document his replies on the train home. The first question on the list was something neutral: something I thought that he would answer easily; something that would get him talking: 'What was it like inside the police station?'

He seemed a little thrown. 'Why does that matter?'

'I just want to know what it was like … the conditions.'

'Why does it matter?'

'I don't know why. I guess I'm still in the habit of keeping notes.'

'I don't understand why it matters,' he reiterated.

I told him that I wasn't sure that the book was over. I might try to salvage something from what had been written.

He changed the topic. 'What did you mean when you said that I've fucked your career?'

I explained that I'd spent almost three years writing this book with him and had stood by him when it counted. Now he'd made a fool out of me and everyone else who'd put their faith in his cause.

Hassan didn't seem to understand. 'But how have I fucked your career? You can still carry on with the book. And what did you mean about being dangerous to me?'

I explained that I and all the other journalists who'd been landed with production orders would now want to defend their own credibility and hand over any material to the police. 'It's in everyone's interest to see you prosecuted and convicted, Hassan, otherwise all these stories have been lies. And the thing is, you've done stuff.'

'What stuff?' Hassan snapped back angrily.

'I don't think anyone's been *that* gullible,' I said, and I went through some of the evidence about Junaid Babar, what had gone on in Pakistan, the fact that people like Zaheer, Tipu and Sajeel were real. Whatever he'd told the police, he hadn't invented his entire life and a complete cast of characters in Pakistan. Some of these things had really happened.

Hassan was quiet for a few seconds, then decided to answer my first question about the conditions in the police cell. He told me that he wasn't able to say why he'd changed his stance in custody, but everything he'd said was the result of the legal advice he'd been given.

At this point, an old man and a small child came into the playground and went over to the climbing frame, twenty metres away. Hassan suddenly became nervous, looking around the park, then looking at the kid, then the park again.

'It's just a kid and his grandddad,' I said.

'You'd be surprised who the security services get to do their work for them,' he replied.

I told him if it was bothering him we could get up and walk around the field. He agreed to do this. The ground underfoot was soft and wet. I tried to keep the conversation going.

'So, after the fifth day you decided to tell them that everything was a lie, but the bit I don't understand is … getting stabbed isn't a crime. Why did you tell the police that that was a lie?'

'It was a lie.'

'You're really telling me that you stabbed yourself?'

'Everything that I told the police is true.'

'So you were visiting Habib?'

'No.' Hassan stopped walking. Then he stammered 'Yes'. Then changed his answer again. 'No … Don't believe everything the police tell you.'

'Okay, so where were you?'

He told me that he couldn't say. But after a minute he said that he had been visiting Habib. He hadn't been attacked. Then he backtracked again.

'It doesn't matter if I was stabbed or not. The question is: if you didn't believe me, why did you report it? I even told you not to report it.'

I had confirmed the incident to a journalist after they'd rung me, but I was incredulous that he was trying to shift the blame. Hassan didn't look at me as he continued talking. 'I told you what you wanted to hear. This is what you wanted: a good story. And I gave it to you.'

I wanted to lunge at him. Break his nose. Smash his face. Instead I breathed, paused and returned to the running order of my questions.

'Okay ... so if you stabbed yourself, then why do it the night before the meeting with the publishers? Why not choose another day? Didn't you want to go? Didn't you want the book to be published?'

Hassan remained quiet for an entire minute. During this silence we reached one end of the park. We turned back on ourselves and, as we did, he looked at me and started speaking again. This time, his voice was less animated and his tone less combative.

'What did you expect me to do? Come on yaar. I wasn't going to do forty years. They were telling me I was going to serve forty years in prison if I pleaded guilty. Maybe, *maybe* I'd get a reduced sentence, but only if I testified against twelve – no, fourteen guys. I wasn't going to do that. Fourteen guys? These people were my friends. And you tell me, yeah, whatever the police were saying, about me still being a jihadi, I actually said those things on *60 Minutes*, I wrote that article in the newspaper about leaving. If I went to prison, where was I going to fit in? Tell me that. Where did I belong between the racists and the jihadis? For forty years? No way. I wasn't going to do that. Seven years I'd thought, or maybe ten. But forty?

'And who was there to help me? Everyone got their story out of me and then left. What did I get out of this? Only my mother was there for me [over the phone] saying, "Do what you have to do to get out of there."'

Suddenly we came to a stop. On the ground in front of us, protruding from the short, dewy grass, was a dead hedgehog. Hassan tilted his head down, and for a second I thought he was going to pick it up. But he just stared at it intensely. 'Poor thing,' he muttered.

The child and the granddad had moved away from the playground so we sat down on the swings again. I asked him about the statement from Junaid. Had he seen it? And, if he had, didn't it mean that the police had evidence against him? Hassan just laughed and shrugged his shoulders.

What about this alias that the police said he was using: Abdul Ghani? It had been mentioned in one of the documents they'd sent me.

'Oh that. I don't why they told you that, 'cos it's nothing, it's just a fake name I used when we were with HT to, like, book rooms and avoid car insurance and stuff.'

Then I asked him about his confession to the police, just after his arrest at the airport. This angered him.

'What confession?' he shot back.

I reminded him of what he had said: 'Tell my solicitor now and I will tell you everything. All that you said is true. Yes I have done that.'

'No. No. No. I didn't say that at all.'

'Well, two police officers heard you say it.'

'No, they're wrong. I said, "Tell my solicitor now and I will tell you everything that *is* true and all that I have done."'

Hassan had an answer for everything, and I was becoming increasingly exasperated. Off at the far end of the field, beside the trees, a middle-aged man appeared with his dog, but this did not seem to bother Hassan as much as the kid and the old man had done. Above us, the sky was overcast. It looked like it might start to rain. I looked at Hassan, and he was staring straight ahead. Then, without turning to me, he said, 'I don't know who I am anymore.'

Maybe it was right to say that at this point – given that his responses to questions were so varied – the lies had wound him up into a tight ball of confusion. At least, this is what I wrote in my notes afterwards. I had no more patience left for my list of questions and so I resorted to an expression of emotion. 'You know I liked you. I regarded you as a friend.'

'Don't say that,' he said.

'Why?'

'It makes it so much harder.'

'Makes what harder?' I wanted to ask, but I didn't. Instead, I threatened him – half in jest – 'You know I can still give the notes and the tapes to the police.'

In a tired but slightly self-satisfied way he replied, 'I've dealt with everything. It's okay.'

I laughed. 'How is any of this okay? You know if you'd gone to prison, stuck to everything you said you'd do, people would have saved you in the end. They would have respected your integrity. But now you've burned all your bridges. What you did might have looked like a good option at the time, and I don't know what pressure you were under inside the police station but now ... now you've lost the wider game.'

'The west is never gonna win this war if it keeps locking people – '

'No Hassan,' I interrupted, 'I'm not fucking talking about that. I'm talking about *you*. No one can ever trust anything you say.'

Hassan paused. Then he said, 'Yeah, well, I had to do it for Habib.' At first I didn't understand what he was saying, but then I realised he was suggesting that by telling the police he was a charlatan, Habib's attempts to 'make a documentary' about a training camp would seem wrongheaded, but not illegal. His suggestion made me laugh again.

'You're never going to able to save Habib now.'

I was bemused that a man who was supposed to have made a career out of lying to the media hadn't learned the first principle of duplicity: it's not the facts that matter, but what people will believe.

'Hassan, in court the arbiter of truth is not some impartial investigator, it's twelve members of a jury. When you get on that stand no one's going to believe you because the first thing the lawyer's going to say is: "Hassan Butt is a liar". And what are you going to say? "Yes"?'

Hassan let his head drop into his hands. He remained like that for a while and I started readying myself to leave – retying my shoelaces and zipping up my coat.

Then, with his face still in his hands, he said, 'You know Shiv, if I could tell you everything, you would understand … ' He slid his hands away from his face and looked up at me. 'But it's just not in my interest to tell anyone who the real Hassan Butt is.'

With that, I told him not to bother dropping me back to the station – I'd catch a taxi instead.

24

Complex lying takes many different forms. One of the least well-diagnosed conditions is what psychiatrists and psychologists refer to as pseudologia fantastica (PF). Whether it is a disorder in itself or just a symptom of a larger malaise – grouped with other 'lying' illnesses, known as 'factitious disorders' – is still disputed, but what all experts agree on is that when talking to compulsive liars, it is very hard to discover the truth. These people weave fact and fiction together in such an intricate matrix that the two are 'virtually indistinguishable' to the listener.

The earliest English-language definition of PF comes from William and Mary Healy, an American couple who studied adolescent criminals at the start of the twentieth century:

> Pathological lying is falsification entirely disproportionate to any discernible end in view, engaged in by a person who, at the time of observation, cannot definitely be declared insane, feeble-minded or epileptic. Such lying rarely, if ever, centres about a single event; although exhibited in very occasional cases for a short time, it manifests itself most frequently by far over a period of years or even a life time ... Extensive, very complicated fabrications may be evolved. This has led to the synonyms:— mythomania; pseudologia phantastica.

As a disorder, PF is thought to be rare – the Healys believed that only one per cent of the adolescent criminal population they studied suffered from it – but within the literature there are numerous cases of this type of lying: the long-serving Alabama judge who said that he was the first herpetologist (amphibian expert) at the city zoo and was interned in a Chinese prison camp during the Korean War (which is why he refused to eat in Chinese restaurants and also why doctors diagnosed him with post-traumatic stress disorder), though he had never been posted to Korea nor worked in a zoo; the man who carried on an email correspondence for three years with a stranger he'd met in a bar, pretending to be numerous different people – even a female love interest – then declaring he had cancer, although all of this was fake; the patient who awed doctors and nurses with her stories about freedom fighting for Israel in the 1948 Arab–Israeli war and her good works for the UN, going so far as to concoct paperwork to prove her story when she was challenged. Even Baron Munchausen, after whom Munchausen syndrome (the disorder where people travel from hospital to hospital presenting with faked illnesses in the hope of receiving medical attention) was named, was made famous because the Baron's tall stories were popular all over Europe.

People with PF are different from delusional or psychotic patients (for example a woman proclaiming she is Joan of Arc) because, as the psychiatrists Mark Feldman and Charles Ford write:

As intense and outlandish as PF is, these stories don't cross the line into the realm of delusions because the tellers of these tales understand the difference between fact and fiction and know when they are lying. They believe their own lies only to the extent necessary to be totally convincing and upon confrontation they will acknowledge at least in part what they have lied about.

However, as Ford warns, 'In their explanations of the discrepancies, they may – convincingly – provide new fabrications. Attempting to determine the "truth" from these persons is like trying to catch a greased pig.'

Working around the same time as the Healys, Dr Ernest Dupré listed a number of criteria to determine whether a patient was a pseudologue (a pathological liar): their stories must be probable and maintain a connection to reality; however fanciful the adventures, they must not strike the audience as ridiculous; and while the stories may vary in content, 'the distinctive role of the hero, heroine, or victim is almost always reserved for the storyteller'.

In many ways, pseudologues are more akin to swindlers or silky-tongued con-artists, as they can be likeable and charming, often presenting an easy, self-assured manner that commands success. They sound so believable that otherwise-discerning people are quickly drawn into their web of lies.

The way they lie also helps them deceive others. Unlike 'normal' liars, who supply very few details and must concentrate hard to avoid discovery, the pseudologue creates his or her stories in a dream state almost subconsciously. Anton Delbrück, the German doctor who coined the term 'pseudologia fantastica' in 1891, suggested that this state was similar to self-hypnosis. Like the hypnotised patient, compulsive liars are both aware and not aware of what they are doing.

Other traits manifested include frequent career or job changes, vanity, an average or above average intelligence with a high verbal IQ, an overactive imagination, and a low tolerance for frustration, irritability, emotionality and laziness.

The bemusing aspect of this condition is the pseudologue's motive. Most 'normal' lies are told for external reasons, for example to avoid punishment – 'No, I did not eat all the biscuits' – or to avoid offence or awkwardness – 'Yes, of course you look great in those trousers, darling'. In some cases, people lie for economic gain. But pathological lies seem out of proportion to any perceived external benefits. Most psychiatrists agree that disastrous consequences are often inflicted upon the pseudologue once their deceit is discovered: relationships, careers and even lives are destroyed. When the lies of the Alabama judge were uncovered, for example, he committed suicide. Therefore, the main motive for such behaviour is believed to be internal, driven by the needs of the ego.

For each pseudologue the internal motive is different (and often hard to determine because of the obvious difficulty of ascertaining an honest family history). But psychiatrists have put forward a number of ideas. Fantasies, it is thought, can be created to protect people from memories of abuse or 'family set-ups leading to inferiority situations'. In this way, a pathological liar's behaviour can be a reaction 'against deeply felt pain' and is a 'psychic substitution for endurance'.

Another motive is the gratification of having people listen to them. Like the novelist reading aloud, the imaginative stories of the pseudologue induce real responses from their audience and this can give them an enhanced sense of power and well-being. As Dr Helene Deutsch wrote in the 1920s: 'Whereas a lie is usually goal-directed and for a reason, pseudology, like poetry, can be a gratification in itself.'

But most experts believe that PF is essentially a complicated form of attention-seeking. Fantasies are a mechanism that relieves compulsive liars of the feeling of 'social inferiority'. The Healys put it most bluntly: 'All pathological liars have a purpose – to decorate their own persons, to tell something interesting, and an ego motive is always present. They all lie about something they wish to possess or be.'

Hassan's character was consistent with many of the pseudologue's traits. He was certainly verbose, of above average intelligence and he had an overactive imagination, amply demonstrated by the novel he had written. He'd never had a real job in his life, only temporary ones that had each lasted a few months, and there was little doubt he had a low tolerance for frustration. During the writing of the book, he constantly phoned and texted me to ask if I was done, or how the commissioning was going, and he would often become angry if things weren't turning out the way he wanted. And, if what he had told the police was true, he'd stabbed himself to make me go faster.

But at the same time, he was charming and had fostered an easy, 'likeable' manner; he was willing to pay for meals, eager to drop and pick me up, forever attempting to be helpful to those around him. He was even prepared to put his professed beliefs to one side in order to be more likeable – shaking hands with women and making friends with homosexuals. In this way he was like a mirror, reflecting other people's needs – whether those needs were the desire for a rational theological discussion or just a good quote – in order to reap admiration. Maybe even his critique of his religion was itself just a mechanism for winning approval from western liberals like myself?

The manner in which he had lied was also consistent with PF. His stories had an imaginative fluency. If Hassan was a liar, then he was clearly able to invent hundreds, even thousands of details without prompting – always offering ('Oh, did I tell you?'), always flowing without pause or hesitation, as if his stories came from deep within his memory. His description of Amjad Farooqi, for example, was a wellspring of poetic description referencing past figures, drawing on emotions, noting little habits and details to paint a full and rounded picture:

> He was a very quiet man. He would only speak when spoken to. He wasn't Omar Bakri, he wasn't in your face. You knew you were speaking to someone special, or he made you feel that way. And there was an intense look about him when he looked at you, like he was looking right into your heart basically. It made me very close to him, and I felt inspired. No – 'inspired' is the wrong word. I felt in awe of him.

And then there was the fact that he always placed himself at the centre of his stories. It was somewhat understandable, given that it was his autobiography, but he always had to be the hero/victim in all circumstances – whether it was leading the fight against the white racists at school, battling on behalf of his own community for the true Islam, standing against the west as a jihadi, or speaking out as the lone man against the network.

But, perhaps most convincingly, if Hassan were a pseudologue it would explain why he went to such lengths for so little obvious gain. If he had lied for money then his efforts over the last three years were out of all proportion to any 'discernible end in view'. Moreover, Hassan knew that he could be put in prison for admitting the crimes he'd professed to having been involved in. If Hassan had wanted to swindle money, he would have been better off doing something else … anything else.

The idea that his lies were motivated by internal reasons made far more sense. As he had written in his email from Dubai, he didn't want a normal nine-to-five job. He didn't want to 'fade away'. He enjoyed the attention of being known. It gave him a 'buzz'; he liked being famous. But if attention-seeking was just a mechanism for relief, what was the underlying cause? Why did he wish to be something he was not – a terrorist – and then spend years trying to convince the British public and everyone else around him that that's what he was?

Could he have been using his fantasies of terrorism to escape childhood trauma? If Hassan had wanted, he could have presented this abuse as further evidence of his victimhood, but he had always downplayed his father's 'harshness'. At the time, I believed he'd dismissed these episodes as unimportant because he was either being honest, or he hadn't felt emotionally intimidated any longer. However, another reason now seemed possible. Hassan had downplayed the abuse because he couldn't bring himself to denounce his father – to do so would be a form of rejection.

This theme of rejection (and subsequent failure) was prevalent in Hassan's life. He was always getting thrown out of institutions and social groups: school, college, Hizb ut-Tahrir, university. Usually this was because of his behaviour – his inability to pipe down, behave and conform. He'd also been cruelly rejected by the people he'd looked up to or most loved in his life: his father, Rabia, Omar Bakri, Irshad Manji and (if leaving the network hadn't been a ruse) most of his family and friends.

The rejection from Manji was something I had been able to witness. She had been quick to give praise, encouragement and support, and Hassan had attached himself to her very readily, looking up to her as both friend and mentor. It may have been no coincidence that a few weeks after her withdrawal – and also after the high of the *60 Minutes* broadcast had died down – Hassan had decided to 'stab' himself. The 'stabbing' was a way to reassert his victim status and soak up the attention that came from that. It would boost his ego but, more importantly, it also shielded him from the pain of Manji's rejection. The only flaw was that he hadn't reckoned on Gavshon, Magratten and myself wanting to see proof. I'd never asked to see the slashed tyres or broken windows he'd reported to me earlier. Why would he have thought this time would be different?

Perhaps all of Hassan's fantasies had been a way of shielding himself from his past failures. His stories and the attention he received in the media (whether positive or negative) created a sense of belonging and achievement. In an age of celebrity, where fame denoted social status, Hassan's dramatic tales were his passport in. Jihadi or ex-jihadi, his imagination allowed him to inhabit the world of television, radio, books, newspapers and public debates. Every time his stories became more extravagant, he received even more attention. The more famous he became, the less he had to confront his past rejections; by the end, Hassan was willing to tell people whatever he thought they wanted to hear.

It seemed like a solid theory – I, and many others, had been completely fooled by an attention-seeking fantasist. Yet there was one problem. If Hassan was a fantasist, then the parallels between the facts of his life and the story he had told were improbably coincidental.

25

The judges from the Royal Courts of Justice delivered a mixed ruling. They allowed me to retain most of my notes on terrorism, including notes from other sources whom I'd interviewed during my research on the causes of terrorism. In itself that was a victory. However, they also stated that I would have to hand over any materials that had been created by my direct interaction with Hassan: interview tapes, notes, texts and manuscripts. They invited the police to grant me immunity from prosecution – a welcome and supportive move – but they also believed that these problems could have been resolved through negotiation rather than going through the appeals process. I felt that with Hassan's and my own credibility shot through, there was no way I could continue with the case to the House of Lords. I had protected my stock of information from other sources. What would I be fighting for? The recordings of a self-confessed serial liar, already well known to the police? I conceded, and accepted the judgement.

This led to an awkward series of meetings with the police. The main handover of materials took place in my lawyers' offices, but it was not just a case of giving them a package. Every tape and notebook had to be evidenced and sealed individually; I was made to hand over my possessions against my will to people who regarded me as hostile. This took half a day, which made the process even more painful. They also extracted text messages from my mobile phone, which required technical procedures that had to take place on police property around London. It was here – away from the lawyers – that I managed to glean more information about Hassan.

The police believed that for the majority of his adult life, Hassan Butt had been a terrorist. He had been on the 'periphery of every major terrorist investigation in Greater Manchester' and after his return from Pakistan, a million pounds had gone through various bank accounts that belonged to him. This is what the GMP had meant by 'unusual financial activity'. For a man without a job, a million pounds was a huge sum of money.

Convicting Hassan had become the personal aim of some of the most senior staff on the investigating team, who believed that he had gotten away with crime after crime under their very noses. One of the senior officers had described his frustration to another journalist: 'Imagine rape wasn't illegal and you knew someone who was raping people every day. Then, suddenly, the day they change the law and make rape illegal, he stops raping and there's nothing you can do about it.' This analogy about the law changing was likely to have been a reference to the 2004 and 2006 Terrorism Acts that had made many actions, such as verbal support for terrorism, illegal.

I also learned that, after Hassan's arrest, the police had put together a file that included Junaid Babar's statement and sent it to the Crown Prosecution Service. But the government lawyers had returned the file, saying that it didn't contain enough evidence to lay charges and go to trial. So the police had been forced to let him go.

*

One reason the Manchester police did not have enough evidence to charge Hassan was because – I was told – the security services in London were not cooperating with them. When asked for Hassan's dossier, the spooks had refused to hand over anything substantial. Moreover, the GMP could not explain the provenance of certain pieces of information they had been given by the security services during their investigation of Habib and others who knew Hassan. These tip-offs proved crucial to their investigations, but when they tried to work out where MI5 had got the information from, the only explanation they could come up with was that it was from Hassan himself. But if that were correct, it would mean that Hassan was working for MI5.

In a meeting in a police evidence facility near Crystal Palace in south London, I was told why the Manchester cops had publicly released the transcripts, despite the fact that it would jeopardise their investigation. Effectively, if they couldn't prosecute Hassan because of a lack of evidence, then they damn well weren't going to let him publish a book about his exploits. So they released the transcripts to the media knowing that what he'd said in their interviews with him would totally destroy his credibility, the book and any possible future as a public figure.

So what could be known beyond reasonable doubt? Hassan had been part of a network of real people: Sajeel Shahid, Kazi Rahman ('Tipu'), Junaid Babar and the Crawley gang. These people, along with other members of al-Muhajiroun, had all been arrested or convicted at one point or another with terrorism-related offences.

By 2003 this group of British radicals had a functioning training camp up in the mountains of Pakistan and were preparing acts of terrorism. This camp was where the Crawley gang, and the lead 7/7 plotter, Mohammad Sidique Khan, learned how to fire weapons. Junaid Babar had talked about bomb-making and the camp in some detail, describing how they crushed up chemicals with a mortar and pestle, fired machine guns, and how smuggling aluminium powder through airport customs had proved fairly easy. He said the person who had provided the explosives training had been from Sipah-e-Sahaba, Amjad Farooqi's terrorist organisation.

No one could deny that Hassan had been at al-Muhajiroun's Pakistan office during the formative stages of this network in 2001 and 2002 – there were dozens of reels of video footage to prove it. Babar had stated that while in Britain, Hassan had continued his fundraising efforts to get the training camp started. He also said that on Hassan's return to the UK in 2002 he had stayed at his house in Manchester on several occasions. Babar had even invited Hassan to his wedding.

If Hassan wasn't actively supporting jihad, why would any of these people have fraternised with him? And, more importantly, while everyone else at the Pakistani office of al-Muhajiroun had become involved in terrorism in some form or another, would Hassan have been the only person to have stayed out of the fray?

And what about Hassan's emir, Yassir al-Sirri? I had a certifiable connection between Hassan and al-Sirri. There was also the evidence of a documentary film-maker who had witnessed a meeting between Hassan, al-Sirri and other senior British radicals – including Abu Qatada – off the Edgware Road in London, just after 7 July. The film-maker hadn't been allowed into the room, but he'd seen Hassan and the others go in together and then leave again.

Abu Qatada was as serious and dangerous as they came. The British government had spent nearly a decade battling through the courts to deport him. On one of the few occasions he was free from either effective house arrest or police custody, Abu Qatada had been photographed walking beside al-Sirri.

Al-Sirri was also a serious radical. In 1994, he'd been sentenced to death in absentia for his alleged involvement in the assassination attempt on the former Egyptian prime minister, Atef Sedki. Sedki survived the car bomb, but in the explosion a twelve-year-old girl was peppered with shrapnel and killed. The attack was carried out by Islamic Jihad, an Egyptian terrorist organisation headed by Dr Ayman al-Zawahiri, who took over command of al-Qaeda after Osama Bin Laden's death.

After the attack, al-Sirri left Egypt for Britain. On the grounds that he was facing persecution from a military dictatorship, the British government granted him asylum. Perhaps predictably, seeking refuge in Britain didn't appear to stop his involvement in radicalism. On 23 October 2001, the Metropolitan Police arrested al-Sirri for circulating al-Qaeda propaganda. But after his arrest, al-Sirri was charged with a much more serious offence: being the spark that destroyed the Twin Towers.

On September 9 2001 two journalists had gone to visit Ahmad Shah Massoud – the leader of the Northern Alliance, an anti-Taliban group – at his base in northern Afghanistan. They were making a documentary entitled *Afghanistan: Past, Present and Future* and wanted him to feature in it. In fact, the journalists were al-Qaeda operatives and their video camera was a bomb that they detonated during the interview, killing Massoud instantly.

For al-Qaeda, the assassination acted as both a tactical manoeuvre – without their leader, the Northern League eventually dissolved into factionalism – and the signal to begin the attack on the US.

Massoud's bodyguards had trusted these two journalists because they were accredited as part of a media company based in London: the Islamic Observation Centre. But if they had delved a little further, they would have found that the IOC had been founded by Yassir al-Sirri, the comrade of al-Qaeda's future leader, and they might have taken a little more care in protecting Massoud's life. When al-Sirri was brought to court in the UK for this offence, the judge said that he had been an 'unwitting' cog in a complex terrorist machine and let him leave a free man.

Abu Qatada and al-Sirri's al-Qaeda credentials only begged the question: if Hassan wasn't the real thing, why did two such dangerous – and well-connected – terrorists allow a fantasist into their private meetings?

Then there were Hassan's links to Habib Ahmed and Habib's co-defendant, Rangzieb. From the trial to come, I would learn that Hassan had introduced the two at his home in Cheetham Hill in 2003. He also admitted paying for Habib's flight out to Dubai to visit Rangzieb. It was in Dubai that Habib had taken receipt of the diaries containing the details of the highest-ranking terrorists in al-Qaeda. Almost every element of the diaries' movement had been covertly monitored by Dubai's security services and police, all the way to their eventual recovery in Habib's house. Perhaps it was strange that Habib had kept them at home, especially since Hassan's house – half a mile up the road – was continually being raided by the police, but these were the stated facts.

Though he had lived in Pakistan most of his life, Rangzieb Ahmed was from the Greater Manchester area and often came back to visit family. He had a serious record. He was a member of the Kashmiri-based terror group Harkut-ul-Mujahideen and had numerous links to both Pakistani and British terrorists, the most interesting of which was to Yasin Omar, the head of the suicide cell whose bombs had failed to go off on the London Underground on 21 July 2005.

Then there were Hassan's professed encounters with Omar Sheikh and Mohammad Sidique Khan. There was no way to prove the latter one way or the other – I couldn't trust Hassan, Junaid was in prison in the US and not permitted to speak to the media, and Khan had blown himself up – but it was known that Junaid and Khan had known each other, as Junaid had taken Khan to the training camp he'd set up in Pakistan.

As for Hassan's association with Omar Sheikh, this too was impossible to prove but not an outlandish connection. Omar Sheikh was a fellow Brit in Pakistan and, again, there was public testimony that a number of people in al-Muhajiroun, including Tipu, had made direct contact with Sheikh just before his arrest in February 2002. It was possible that Sheikh and Hassan had met at Tipu's house while he was recovering from his operation. But there were other links between Hassan and Sheikh that made the encounter more probable. For example, Rangzieb Ahmed and Sheikh knew each other – while Rangzieb had been in prison in India during the 1990s, he'd had some money deposited in his account for prison comforts. The person who had sent him this money was Omar Sheikh.

The last major connection was with Amjad Farooqi. Unlike the brief encounter with Omar Sheikh, this association was far more central to Hassan's story. Could Hassan have known a man like this? It was possible that he had made the whole thing up. Interestingly, Omar Sheikh and Amjad Farooqi did know each other. In fact, Omar Sheikh owed Amjad Farooqi his freedom.

Incarcerated in an Indian jail, Sheikh was only released by authorities in 1999 after the Air India plane hijacking, when militants had threatened to kill all the passengers. The lead hijacker was understood to be one Amjad Farooqi. Sheikh and Farooqi were subsequently connected with the kidnapping and murder of Daniel Pearl. Farooqi was also named as the major suspect in the deaths of the French engineers and the bombing of the US consulate in Karachi. Of course it was entirely possible that Hassan had made the whole thing up by intelligently piecing together enough information from the Internet. There was nothing else to substantiate the claim after Amjad Farooqi was meant to have been killed in a firefight with Pakistani police in late 2004.

Last of all, there was Hassan's trip to Dubai. I'd seen his arrival stamp in his passport, the police had documented his travel and, moreover, he hadn't denied going there. So what had he been up to? While security services had recorded Habib's and Rangzieb's movements, it seemed that they hadn't done the same with Hassan, or if they had then this information had not been handed over to the Manchester police.

But perhaps the most obvious evidence of Hassan's involvement in terrorism was in plain sight. There was no doubt he had been part of a network of committed jihadis. Most of them were awaiting trial, or had been locked up or killed at some point. Establishing whether Hassan himself had fired a gun or been part of a bomb plot seemed secondary to the fact that there were deeds on record that undeniably emanated from him.

Whether uttered by a genuine terrorist or not, Hassan's interviews with journalists throughout those years had created an effect. His words had produced anxiety in the British population. He could argue, as he had done during police interviews, that he'd been doing it for the money. But the outcome was the same – Hassan had acted as a messenger for his fanatical associates, delivering words of hate and terror. And those words had instilled fear in the minds of those listening. When he'd said, 'For every one British Muslim killed, there are a dozen waiting to take their place and become martyrs as well', or when he called on young British Muslims to 'strike at the heart of the enemy', or when he told the *Sunday Times* that around fifty prospective suicide bombers were 'waiting for the right time', or when he said that he envied the Madrid bombers and wanted to emulate their actions, all these statements travelled around the world – each creating their own headlines and filling pages of print, reams of text on websites, and hours of footage on TV stations – and all these words manufactured fear. With or without intent – whether he was acting apart or even, as the Manchester police began to believe, operating with the knowledge of some MI5 desk officer – Hassan appeared plausible enough to make the public scared of 'the terrorists': al-Qaeda, jihadis, or often just Muslims in general. In that way he was culpable. In that way, his words were part of what we label 'terrorism'. In that way, Hassan Butt was as real a terrorist as any other.

26

The trial of Habib Ahmed was held in Courtroom Two at Manchester Crown Court. Situated off the modernist main atrium, the courtroom was protected by armed police guards at all times. During the times of most interest in the case, the line to gain entry was very long, as each person had to be checked and searched individually.

The room was spacious and illuminated mainly with the natural light that streamed in from a large skylight. The central focus of the courtroom was the dock: a large, solid cube that sprung from the bowels of the building – where the holding cells were – and rose high above the floor as if it were a rock formation at the Giant's Causeway. Each side of the cube was opaque except for the front, which was made of thick plate glass so that the judge, the jury and the press could stare straight at them, but the accused could not see not their family and friends in the public gallery because it was situated directly behind the dock.

For three months, Habib Ahmed sat there as the prosecution laid out the evidence of his criminality and tried to persuade the jury to convict him. Alongside Habib sat his wife, Mehreen Haji, and his co-conspirator, Rangzieb Ahmed.

Rangzieb had been charged with many offences but the gravest was the allegation that he was a director of terrorism. In court, he wore a suit and reading glasses and had a rather professorial manner about him, sometimes choosing to consult papers, or sometimes the translator who had been supplied to him in case he made any mistakes with his English.

Mehreen was petite and mousy-looking. She always wore a hijab that covered not just her hair but also the sides and back of her head and neck. She had a certain sweetness and docility that might make her attractive to a more dominating type of man.

Her husband Habib was well-built with broad shoulders. He was beginning to bald at the crown and this made him appear more like the young father he was. Comparing him to the pictures taken at the time of his arrest, it was clear that he had lost weight in prison. He had also gotten rid of his beard, and he looked better for it. Sometimes he wore a polo shirt; at other times, a button-down shirt with a brown cardigan over the top. Unlike Rangzieb, he never dressed formally, even when he was in the witness box.

Day after day, Habib and his wife sat next to each other, sometimes laughing or smiling during the proceedings, but usually just staring out at the courtroom. They never touched, but even without physical displays of affection it was plain to see that they were comfortable in each other's company. When the court recessed for the day, a look of anxiety would appear on Mehreen's face. Habib would be led down to the cells first, and only when all the bolts and locks had been secured again was she allowed out of the dock. She would gather her belongings from one of the small anterooms and make her way back home, where their two young children were waiting.

The jury was made up of five men and seven women. Three of the women were black, the rest of the jury were Caucasian, and their ages varied from early twenties to mid-sixties. It was to these twelve people that the prosecution – led by the commanding Andrew Edis, the same barrister from my hearings – laid out the key accusations.

Rangzieb was in the dock because he had been planning attacks and coordinating other cells in Britain. Habib was there because he'd taken receipt of the diaries that contained the contact details of al-Qaeda's top people, written in invisible ink. Habib's wife was in the dock because it was alleged that she'd known what had taken place in Dubai and had given money to her husband for the purposes of terrorism. All this had occurred between December 2005 and July 2006 – just as I was starting to form my relationship with Hassan.

It took over a month for the prosecution to list its articles of evidence – the details of the secret probes in Dubai and Manchester, the diaries, the posters and radical literature found at Habib's house, travel documentation, computer records, photos, videos, newspaper clippings – and to present all the witness statements from police officers and technical experts.

Since Hassan was being called as a witness for Habib's defence, the prosecution also presented evidence about their relationship and their radical pasts. They revealed how Habib and Hassan had been arrested for defacing traffic lights with al-Muhajiroun stickers. They showed the court that in early 2001 Hassan had been one of the signatories on Habib and Mehreen's marriage certificate, a marriage conducted by Omar Bakri. They told the jury that Habib and Hassan had flown out together to Pakistan on 16 July 2001 and then they presented a poster recovered from Habib's house that it seemed he had kept as a memento. It was an advert for a talk called 'Jihad in Manchester' and it had taken place after Hassan had fled Pakistan in 2002. The speakers were Omar Bakri, the hook-handed Abu Hamza and, of course, Hassan.

After the prosecution's case had been presented, Habib came to the witness box to defend himself. He had a strong Manchester accent and his answers were brief and inarticulate. Under cross-examination he often agreed with whatever the prosecution put to him, unable to spot the linguistic traps that were being set. When Edis questioned him about the secretly recorded conversations with Rangzieb in their hotel room in Dubai, and the language that was used – they referred to 'managers', 'companies', 'business', 'workers', 'directors' and 'uncles' – Habib responded that he couldn't remember what they'd been talking about and that he didn't know why he had used these words; it was not as if Rangzieb and Habib were working for any known company.

Edis enjoyed picking over the words and phrases that had been used in these conversations – he asserted that they were all code for elements of al-Qaeda – especially in one instance where it seemed that Habib and Rangzieb had confused themselves. The transcripts of the bugged conversations read like an am-dram version of *The Wire*, and Habib floundered under the pressure of Edis's persistence for several days.

On 20 November Hassan took his seat in the witness box. It was this moment that attracted the most press attention. On the first day he wore a thick navy jumper over beige *salwar kameez*. His beard was still long, and because of the mounds of documents he had to read he kept his glasses on throughout most of his four days on the stand.

After Hassan had taken his oath on the Quran, the judge warned him about incriminating himself. Hassan said that he understood this and then Habib's lawyer began putting his questions to Hassan which helped explain to the court how Hassan and Habib knew each other and how their lives had been intertwined; where did they go to school; how he had joined HT; how he had met Mehreen; how he had suggested they get married; his meeting with Omar Bakri at Wolverhampton University; his work for al-Muhajiroun in Pakistan. Finally Habib's lawyer asked Hassan the reasons why he thought Habib had been wrongly accused.

Hassan's replies were dense, long, and delivered with an air of defiance. On at least a dozen occasions, the judge had to tell Hassan to slow down for the sake of the stenographer or to cut his answer short, complaining of 'information overload'. Hassan would try to shorten what he was saying, but whenever he spotted an opening he would turn his body to address the jury directly and give another long-winded answer.

In the afternoon, it was Edis's turn to cross-examine Hassan. Those on the press bench flicked to a fresh page in their notebooks and awaited the contest.

Edis began: 'Mr Butt, would you agree with me if I were to suggest to you that you are a liar?'

'In regards to?' Hassan replied.

'Just as a characteristic of yours. You're a liar?'

'Not as a characteristic, no, but I would lie to make money from the press – yes, I would.'

'So you're a professional liar?'

'I would to make money, yes.'

'You don't just lie for fun, you lie for money?'

'Absolutely, yes.'

'And if the money's right, you'll say absolutely anything?'

'Absolutely anything, yes. That's correct.'

'However scandalous?'

'However scandalous, yes.'

'However frightening?'

'However frightening, yes.'

'However much it damages community relations?'

'Absolutely, yeah.'

'However much it causes trouble for your fellow Muslims?'

'Yes.'

'You have absolutely no morals at all, do you?'

'I wouldn't agree with the last part.'

'You don't agree with that?'

'No, I don't, no. You see, the press are going to print things anyway, and they were printing things before I was saying things. And basically, if I wasn't going to cash up on it, somebody else was going to.'

'Actually, what you're doing here in that witness box today is lying in just the same way.'

'No, sir.'

'You will tell any story anybody wants you to tell if they have a good enough lever on you.'

'No, sir. That's not true.'

'Money, perhaps. Loyalty, perhaps, your adherence to the same cause, but as long as they've got a decent lever, you will say absolutely anything.'

'No, sir, that's not true.'

'And you're pretty good at it, aren't you? Lying, I mean. You're pretty good at it.'

'No, sir.'

'Well, you have managed to fool quite a lot of people.'

'I fooled the press because they wanted to be fooled.'

For the next thirty minutes, Edis questioned Hassan about the various interviews he had given in the media. Hassan replied that they were all lies to make money, or lies to keep up the impression that he was a jihadi. Then Edis asked Hassan about the name 'Abdul Ghani' and why he had used it. Hassan replied in the same way he had with me, that the name was used during his time in HT to book rooms and cover his tracks with car insurance.

Unsatisfied, Edis asked about the name again, going on to enquire about one occasion Hassan had used the alias to purchase mobile phones. As the exchange continued, Hassan's replies caused bewilderment amongst the press and the jury, and serious consternation amongst the lawyers, the Greater Manchester detectives and the judge's bench. Because of this, Edis hurriedly wrapped up and requested that the judge close the court to everyone, including the defendants. Justice Saunders granted the request and the court was cleared. Only a few of the lawyers, and a single police officer, were allowed to remain to discuss what had taken place.

The next day, a Friday, the court remained unexpectedly closed for further discussion; on Monday the questioning began again, except this time Hassan interrupted his own answers by telling the jury that he could not speak about certain things because Justice Saunders had put a restriction on him. This continued throughout the whole day until, somewhat exasperated, the judge was finally forced to explain to the jury why this was happening:

'Mr Butt has on several occasions now said he can't answer a question because I put a restriction on what he said. I hope that very soon everything will become apparent to you, about what that is all about.

'Can I just assure you that I will make sure that you hear anything which is relevant and important to you to hear in your considerations. I am not setting out to keep things from you. I hope you will take my word for that. That's what I wanted to say, because I didn't want you to go away speculating. Please do not speculate about that at all, don't even think about it. Hopefully it will all be resolved by tomorrow.'

Tomorrow came, but before Hassan made it back onto the stand, Edis made a formal application in court:

'My Lord, this is an application for part of the evidence given by the witness Hassan Butt to be heard in camera; that is to say, with the press and public excluded.

'The application is made in the interests of national security and to avoid identification of a witness or any other person. It will be supported by evidence, which we will invite the court to consider not in open court. It relates to evidence which he has given in open court so far, but which hitherto cannot be reported – and which we will submit ought not to be reported hereafter, but that is a matter which we'll take up at a more convenient time in relation to his evidence that he had an association with the security services, which he has said in open court.'

Justice Saunders decided to grant the order and, for the next few hours, the court remained closed to the public while Hassan gave the rest of his evidence.

*

It took the jury three days to find Habib and Rangzieb guilty of several of the charges. Rangzieb was convicted of being a director of terrorism for al-Qaeda and for possessing an article useful to terrorism (the invisible-ink diaries). Habib was found guilty of being a member of al-Qaeda, and of possessing the diaries and an article on bomb-making that was considered useful for terrorism. He was found not guilty on the count of attending a training camp for terrorist purposes. Mehreen was acquitted on all charges and released.

The next day, the court was packed for the sentencing. Upstairs in the public gallery sat fifty men. They were there for Habib. Amongst them were Mo, Atif, Yassir, and Hassan himself. The women – Habib's mother and his wife and a few others – sat downstairs.

The judge read out his statement. About Rangzieb he said: 'You were a not insignificant member of al-Qaeda, a terror group that is prepared to kill and maim innocent people indiscriminately to achieve their aims.

'I am satisfied you are dedicated to the cause of Islamic terrorism. You are an intelligent, capable and superficially reasonable man who is involved in terrorism. That makes you an extremely dangerous man.' He sentenced him to forty years in prison.

Then he turned his attention to Habib. 'You joined Rangzieb Ahmed in Dubai when he was on a terrorist mission and assisted him by bringing back materials to this country which were extremely important.

'They may not have contained the details of how to make bombs but they were in my view just as important to al-Qaeda. Without them Rangzieb Ahmed would not have been able to carry on organising terrorism.

'You were a committed member of al-Qaeda and prepared, I'm satisfied, to take part in a suicide attack.' He then sentenced Habib to a total of ten years in prison.

With this, the chant went up from the gallery of upstairs: 'Takbir!' and the response, from all fifty men, 'Allahu Akhbar.' This was repeated twice more. The chorus was deafeningly loud. When it stopped, all that filled the air was the sound of Habib's mother emitting a piercing scream.

27

After the trial, I stopped by Hassan's house in Cheetham Hill, the place where we had first met all those years ago. By all appearances, the place looked abandoned. The front door, which had been broken down during the police raid, had been replaced by chipboard. On it someone had scrawled the number of the house in thick black marker pen, as if it were a warning to others that some deadly disease was festering inside.

Around the back, the lawn had been left to grow over and the flagstones were being overtaken by long strands of grass. Through the back window I could see that all of his gym equipment had been removed. The living room had also been emptied of everything except the sofa and the bookshelf.

Suddenly, a man appeared at the first floor window. He was a young Asian male, around Hassan's age. He stared down at me and asked what I wanted. I told him I was looking for Hassan. He said he didn't know who that was. He told me to go away, so I left.

Not long after, a full order was made concerning the evidence Hassan had given in court:

IT IS ORDERED UNDER SECTION 11 of the CONTEMPT OF COURT ACT 1981 and in pursuance of the existing *in camera order* that:

The court having ordered that the press and public be excluded from part of these proceedings for the due administration of justice, no report is to be published or mention made by anyone of the answers given by a defence witness, Hassan Butt, when asked by prosecution counsel whether he had purchased mobile phones in aliases, including in the name 'Abdul Ghani' and why he had done so. The evidence in respect of which this order is made was heard on 20th November 2008 …

This order to remain until further order.

There had been just enough said in open court to piece together an ending for Hassan's story and finally untangle sufficient fact from fiction in order to bring it to a conclusion. At least for my own sanity, I needed to finish this. But when the order was issued I fell into despair. It stopped me from explaining what had gone on that day and, without being able to draw upon what Hassan had told the jury, I had no ending and no way of settling anything.

What I needed to do now was go back to regular work to earn some money. After spending so many months fighting my own court case and then following Habib's prosecution in Manchester, I was broke. The publishers had naturally called time on the book contract – I was just grateful they hadn't asked for the advance back. But having not been able to focus on anything else for at least nine months, I had no stories to pitch, no way to get back into the swing of reporting.

Various desk editors were willing to offer the odd shift writing about the weather and rehashing bits of newswire copy, but I felt they were partly doing so out of pity. I took what I could, but then I started to feel too embarrassed to show my face in a newsroom. Conversing with other reporters was too painful. When they would commiserate about how I'd been hoodwinked by a real-life Walter Mitty, I'd start running through some of the reasons as to why that wasn't the case. Hassan wasn't an out-and-out fantasist, I'd exclaim. But without being able to tell the whole story, without being able to communicate its complexity and its ending, I sounded even more naive. It was far better not to talk about it at all.

Feeling exhausted and humiliated, I decided to quit journalism and went to work for my father, managing his corner shop on the outskirts of London. For a year, the humdrum of standing at the till – making runs to the cash-and-carry to fill up on stock, bartering with the bank, and dealing with the drug addicts pushing their stolen goods – kept me occupied and gave me enough income to tick over. But not a day passed without me thinking about who Hassan Butt really was and why events had turned out the way they had. When I wasn't serving customers, I was ruminating over counterfactual scenarios: what if I'd cooperated with the police, what if I hadn't backed off the day of the stabbing, what if I'd never started the book in the first place and just let Hassan find his own way? I also wondered why he'd picked me, and not some more established or renowned author to write his autobiography. I feared it was because, as a wide-eyed twenty-something, I was easier to manipulate.

I spent my free time reading over my notes, going through police documents and searching through our interview transcripts, looking for extra clues or new angles to pursue. Anything that might help the story to a conclusion.

On a few occasions I even went up to Manchester to try and speak to people. But no one would talk. It was like Beeston all over again. Mo and Atif refused to pick up the phone. Hassan's brothers wouldn't say a word. I even approached Habib's wife, but like everyone else she declined to be interviewed. Out of Hassan's associates from his time in al-Muhajiroun that weren't in prison, I could only track down Sajeel and Zaheer. Sajeel, who was running a private primary school in east London, told me everything Hassan had said was a lie but refused to explain anything more. Zaheer would have nothing to do with me.

I eventually travelled to the US to pursue Junaid. Amazingly, he had been released after spending just four and a half years in prison. Even though he'd confessed to trying to assassinate the president of Pakistan, amongst many other things, the judge had given him bail and then time served as reward for turning state's witness and testifying against his former terrorist colleagues.

I managed to find his address and his mother was happy enough to sit with me on her porch in Queens, but she had little to say. Her eldest son, she told me, had disappeared. His wife Fatima and his daughter Leila had been living at her home for a few years while Junaid was in jail. Then one day, she came home to find that the wife had packed up and left with Leila, without a goodbye or even a note.

Famously, Junaid had told the world's media that he was fighting for the jihadi cause even though his mother had almost died on 9/11. I asked her what had happened that day. She confirmed that she had indeed worked in the Twin Towers, in the collections department for the Bank of America on the ninth floor. She had managed to escape by the stairs.

'What was Junaid's reaction [that day]?' I asked.

'He didn't care ... My son-in-law, he called him and asked, "Where's your mother?" and he said, "I have no idea." And when I came home, it was three o'clock, he was there, and he didn't say anything like, "Thanks God."' She said he had continued to sit on the sofa, watching TV.

'He didn't give you a hug?' I asked.

'No,' she replied. 'He was selfish. He cared only about his own self. That's it. I can't tell you. Sometimes, you know, you raise the kids but you don't know them.'

I eventually tracked down Rabia. Having not known whether she was real or if Hassan had simply invented the whole love affair to spice up the book, I was surprised to discover that she was a counsellor with a PhD, married (or re-married?) with children and doing well for herself. I called her up, but as soon as I mentioned Hassan she became extremely hostile and refused to speak to me any further, adding that I could write whatever I wanted about her – she didn't care. After a few weeks, she rang back to ask if I could change her name, which I did, but when I asked her if any of his story was true – if they had actually gotten married – she said she'd love to tell me everything but she couldn't. She never explained what was stopping her from talking about it.

I also approached Manji in case she knew anything more. She wanted nothing to do with Hassan. He'd repeatedly lied and even threatened her, she said, adding: 'I realised that he cannot be trusted. That's all I have to say. I want nothing more to do with Hassan or his "story", however it gets told.' She never replied to any of my further emails.

Desperate, I rang a few of the Manchester detectives, including Graham Smith, to ask them to give me the inside track on what they'd found, but they rebuffed me in the strongest possible terms and referred me straight to the press office. When I

asked the media team whether they believed Hassan was a terrorist or a fantasist, they emailed me a statement that resembled
the 'rape' analogy I'd heard sometime before:

> Butt has espoused extremist views and violently extremist views in
> the past. That conduct tapered off when new terrorism legislation
> was enacted in parliament ...
>
> Simply because an individual associates with people who subse-
> quently commit offences against terrorism legislation does not per
> se mean that they themselves are terrorists. However, his associa-
> tion with people subsequently convicted of terrorism offences and
> his previously well-publicised views on violent extremism may be
> indicative of his mindset at any given time.

Reluctantly, I eventually contacted Hassan. He was living in
his mum's house, and had taken up helping defence solicitors
research their terrorism cases. After that he had started selling
knitwear on eBay, even making a bit of cash doing so. He'd gone
into the textile business, like his father. Initially Hassan said he
was minded to help because he owed me that much at least.
When I asked, he confirmed that he'd worked with security services. But I reminded him he was a self-certified liar; without
documentary evidence I couldn't use anything he said. Hassan
told me he had a number of conversations with his MI5 handler
on tape. However, when he refused to share the recordings – he
needed them as 'insurance' – I let my temper get the better of
me. Years had passed since the trial, but his betrayal still stung
because I found it impossible to admit to myself that a man I'd
allowed myself to admire had sold me out so treacherously.

Some time later, when I informed Hassan a book would be
published, he became quite worried about what might happen

to him once the story was out. He asked if he could see the draft manuscript and so I sent him a copy. After he'd read it, he told me he'd much prefer that the book wasn't published, because he did not want to be thrust into the spotlight after all these years of quietly getting on with his life. But if I was going ahead, he wanted me to make known what his current views were on a number of key matters including his involvement with the security services and Yassir al-Sirri. He sent me an email with the points listed in order:

1. The Prophet Muhammed (peace be upon him) is the best of creation free, from any sins and mistakes. I do NOT believe that Prophet Muhammed (p.b.u.h.) did anything wrong whatsoever especially in regards to the assassination of K'ab bin Ashraf.
2. Jihad (fighting in the way of Allah) is a vital part of Islam and anyone who denies this is not a Muslim.
3. People like Manji and Rushdie have nothing to do with Islam and I do not support any of their works or ideas and never have.
4. Yassir al Sirri was never my emir and I have never been his student.
5. I have never worked for the MI5 nor have I ever received any payment for them. Neither as an informant nor official worker. I have however met with officials from MI5 on many occasions in my days with Al Muhajiroun. I would advise that no Muslim should EVER work or sit with MI5. This is a potential act that could lead a Muslim becoming an apostate.

Still referring to MI5 he then added, 'The many things I did, were done for a reason I can't disclose, but those brothers who know the truth can testify on my behalf.'

*

Although the last line was fairly cryptic, few of the points he emailed me squared with what he'd told me beforehand, what I'd witnessed or what I had found out. It was also a shame to see him disavow his ideas about his Islamic reformation. But his email reaffirmed that the only person who'd be able to tell me what had happened to Hassan Butt, was Hassan Butt himself.

I eventually went back to being a journalist. I co-wrote a book about economics and landed a job as a reporter with the *Guardian*. The anger, embarrassment and desperate need for answers eventually subsided. I learned to live with not having anything to show for all those years working with and placing my faith in Hassan. I stopped caring about trying to publicly exonerate myself. The whole sorry saga may have faded entirely if I hadn't bumped into an old contact in a cafe. We got conversing about the years past: the book, my source-protection trial, Hassan. The contact, who worked in criminal law, then suggested there might be a way to help with the ending. Over the next year and a half, I began to pull at the right threads and piece together information on who Hassan Butt really was.

Hassan had been involved in terrorism, and not just in his capacity as the messenger. He had effectively acted as a recruitment agent and helped collect funds for the Taliban. He'd most likely helped fund Amjad Farooqi's operations and had known of the consulate bombing – and more besides, including a failed plot to assassinate the Pakistani president, Pervez Musharraf.

He'd also lied about significant moments in his own life. It was never clear whether he'd ever been beaten by his father. I was told that his story of the training camp was certainly fabricated. He'd been telling the truth when, under interview at the police station, he had said that he'd never learned how to fire a gun or raid a house with his fellow fighters.

The most important piece of information though was that he'd been recruited as an informant for MI5. The sources I spoke to differed on when and how this had happened. One told me they'd understood it had been when he was arrested after leaving Pakistan in 2002. During his ten days inside the high-security Paddington Green police station Hassan had been turned – exchanging his liberty for a life of duplicity. Another source who worked as a civil servant thought that Hassan had been an agent before even journeying out to Pakistan. There was no dream or midnight vision prompting his migration, only an instruction from a handler to get on a plane.

This would not have been unusual. Informants working for special police units had being infiltrating all sorts of politically active groups on the left and right for decades. By 2001, al-Muhajiroun had been so thoroughly infiltrated that a good proportion of its senior leadership were acting as informants for the spooks. Reporting on the very people they were also encouraging to be extreme. The civil servant told me that the young Hassan Butt, with his influence over a dozen Muslim men in the Midlands and north Manchester, and then many more in Lahore and Islamabad, was a powerful source of information. But he was also no ordinary informant.

Whether he was fully aware of what he was doing I do not know, but some time after 9/11 Hassan played an additional role. As well as passing back intelligence, he was encouraged to interact with journalists and take to the airwaves as readily as he could. This was not about keeping his cover. If anything, the more he talked about the jihadi threat, the more his reputation as a serious Islamic radical diminished as public figures questioned why he'd willingly place himself in the spotlight. Hassan carried this job out with great aplomb, successfully managing to play the role of the hardened radical on innumerable occasions between 2001 and 2005. He was also asked to repeat information he'd been specifically fed. One example of this was when he told a Sunday newspaper that 'almost fifty' Brits were willing to become suicide bombers and strike the UK when the time was right.

So what was the aim of such exercises? This was never confirmed to me, but indirectly it was explained that his briefings to journalists served two purposes. First as Jim Booth had once suggested, they drew the media away from active investigations. Hassan would distract reporters with bits of information and analysis to keep them from straying into live investigations and interviewing suspects who were being monitored. This helped the security services to work unhindered and track their targets without journalists inadvertently stepping on their toes. At the same time, Hassan would also keep reporters informed about ongoing threats by giving off-the-record briefings and, most importantly, interviews for broadcast to the wider public.

The reason for this was that, until the Beeston bombers brought home the realities of domestic terrorism on 7 July 2005, MI5 found it could not move the political class into supporting new laws and sacrificing extra resources for the fight against terrorism. MI5 lacked an effective way of communicating the problems it and the country were facing, in particular as genuine British jihadis wanted nothing to do with public appearances. Therefore the security services employed proxies to fill the role of the messenger.

No one was more effective at this than someone like Hassan. While al-Qaeda's Bin Laden and al-Zawahiri represented a distant, almost abstract threat – the foreigner in a cave on the other side of the world – Hassan and others like him were employed to make real the nature of the domestic menace.

Hassan dressed like a westerner, used our mannerisms, spoke our language, and was educated and born in Britain. So when he smiled while explaining he wanted to kill us, the public understood the depth of the problem they faced by battling the enemy within. No number of briefings from articulate men in suits could ever achieve such an effect. As the horror became apparent and fear took hold, the hope was that the public would be more prepared to support the laws and tactics needed to deal with the dozens of genuine terrorists plotting destruction and planning to kill ordinary people on the streets of the UK.

Hassan, I was told, willingly played his assigned role. In fact, nothing flattered his ego more than living the life of an undercover informant. He became immersed in the material he needed to spin his increasingly intricate web of fantasy and duplicity. He could act at being the heroic spy while holding his secret meetings with his handler, but also live the life of a deadly warrior while being interviewed as a jihadi. And he never had to worry about being prosecuted. He would never end up in court on terrorism charges because one thing could be relied upon: MI5 would never disclose their relationship with him.

After 7/7, the game changed. The danger was real, obvious and overt. Nothing explained the need for enhanced security more pointedly than a Yorkshire teenager blowing himself up on a London bus. As his former radical associates were arrested one by one, Hassan's usefulness diminished along with his ability to provide information.

I was never given any specific information on exactly what happened next. I can only suppose that Hassan tried to forge a new career in leading much needed de-radicalisation efforts, perhaps even under the continuing instruction of the security services. What I was told was that the Home Office were genuinely interested in offering him funding to convert others out of the network. They had no one in the north of England who could work to prevent terrorism and they were very eager to get a foothold there. Hassan offered them that possibility and they were ready to take him onboard.

Standing in the way of that plan were the Manchester police. The GMP's new counter-terrorist unit couldn't stand Hassan getting away with his crimes. Every time he appeared on TV or was quoted in the press, it rubbed salt in the wound of their ongoing investigation. When they learned of our book and his 'departure' from the network, and saw his interview on *60 Minutes*, they decided that it was all a step too far. They initiated Operation Quill.

The problem they faced was that they'd been kept out of the London loop. The spooks in Thames House did not trust the detectives from the North, and wouldn't hand over their files on Hassan.

After government lawyers told the GMP they didn't have enough evidence to prosecute their target, they made a deal with Hassan while he was being interviewed in the police cell. Hassan would disavow himself of the book, and in return they'd stop trying to put him behind bars for the crimes he'd confessed to in the manuscript.

*

Jihadi, reformist, informant, fantasist. The matrix of characters Hassan inhabited has left him utterly depleted of any sense of identity. Maybe the only true words he ever spoke were when I saw him for one of the last times, during our walk through the park, and he said, 'I don't know who I am anymore.'

For Hassan, fact and fiction became one and the same. Having lived imagined lives, he is now a man without a reliable history, without identity. How will he describe himself to others when his mind is a repository full of incoherent, made-up stories? How will he form lasting relationships when he had no handle on where he has come from and no appreciation of a life lived truthfully and with integrity? How will he maintain a marriage? How could he ever be a father? The deceptions that he once thrived on cultivating have ended up destroying the rest of his existence.

As to whether he really believed that the route to solving the violence within Islam was to tackle the great theological issues, I was never sure. I don't know whether he truly thought the Prophet could make mistakes and, looking back, I am not sure whether he even believed God existed. But whatever was really going on inside his soul, I always felt – even at the end – that he was right to reason in the way he did. He was right to ask of jihadis, 'When does the killing stop?' – because killing couldn't be their ultimate aim. He was right to say that killing in the name of Islam was a cancer in the Muslim world. He was right to question his religion's most fundamental tenets.

My mistake was being captivated by these statements instead of continuing to question the man who was saying them. I felt that Hassan was saying something profound and true, and I believed that such a message delivered from a genuine reformed jihadi had the ability to change things fundamentally. I believed we had crossed an ideological divide – that the two of us had man-aged to understand each other against all odds and perhaps for the betterment of society. There was no space now for questions about whether he'd ever truly been involved in trying to bomb the US consulate, whether he'd been a spy for British intelligence, whether he'd been seriously involved with al-Qaeda. Or whether he was, as I'd been warned in black and white right at the start of my journey, the kind of person to make things up – a fantasist.

After having spent so long interviewing him, winning his trust, acting as his friend and believing in his cause, I had become complicit in the fantasy. There was a point as I was readying his life story for publication, when I didn't want to interrogate him about seemingly small inconsistencies in times, dates, names and locations, in case the whole tale fell apart. I took his word that he'd been attacked in his home by jihadis or stabbed in the street, even though my instincts told me something wasn't right. I wasn't being sloppy, but I wasn't rigorous, either. I wanted his story to be true because I wanted to believe there was a way out of the mess of terrorism. And, being completely honest, I wanted to be leading the way.

So I guess Hassan was right. He'd told me what I wanted to hear and I'd swallowed it whole. Rather than confronting my doubts, I'd pushed them deep into the recesses of my conscious-ness because I could not admit to myself or the world that I had invested in a rotten messenger. It was only the policeman's knock at my door that stopped me from sealing a terrible fate and perpetuating an awful fiction.

That the messenger was not all that he seemed should shock and appal us. Not because of the act of deceit – after all the security services and people like Hassan Butt are in the deception business – but because of the consequences of that deceit.

Since the 9/11 attacks, fear has been one of the most pervasive characteristics of western societies. We can feel its effect at all times, as it has come to shape every part of our lives. From our commute to work, to our holidays, to picking up the paper or switching on the TV, we are asked to be ever vigilant and yet to remain calm. To carry on with our lives as if nothing has changed and yet remain scared of the imminent threat – a threat that is invisible and dormant but ever poised to strike. This perpetual state of low level fear has not just changed our daily lives, but also our relationship with those who govern us.

The list of what has already been justified because of terrorism is disquieting. It includes secret trials, mass spying on communications of all forms, clandestine global rendition programmes, several methods of torture, the creation of mass databases of information and thousands of criminal laws, increased and even indefinite detention without trial, the contravention and circumvention of international law, and the expansion of the apparatus of the security state.

Should questions ever be raised about the use of such powers – whether they are all necessary, whether they should continue to be maintained – we are told that those not involved in terrorism need not worry: the innocent have nothing to fear.

This statement can be understood in two slightly different ways. The first is more obvious; the innocent have nothing to fear *by this*. Acts of spying, the suspension of normal practice and torture – it is being argued – are not things that the ordinary person should worry about. The innocent will be able to go about their business unaffected. It is only those whom the state

315

finger as suspicious, the 'un-innocent', who will be the ones sub-ject to these tough new measures – rendition, a month's deten-tion without trial. This is meant to reassure us.

This dialectic approach – innocent versus un-innocent – not only serves to shut down dissent (why would anyone question acts of torture, extra-judicial killing or the creation of mass databases unless they were guilty of something?) it is also the moment when those who deploy such an approach attempt to strip citizens of their entitlement. When authority is allowed to determine guilt before due process of the courts, citizens become mere subjects serving under the whim of others rather than standing equal under the law. To accept punitive and intrusive practices on the basis that such things will be reserved for oth-ers, is a sure way of giving up one's own rights.

But the statement – 'the innocent have nothing to fear' – is also a threat. Whilst the innocent may have nothing to fear, the argument is that secret trials, torture or rendition are necessary as part of the government's armoury to scare terrorists into sub-mission. Should such practices be halted, dangerous people will be less fearful of the state. And by implication you, the ordinary member of society, will have to be that little bit more terrified because the state will lose the ability to protect you fully in the manner it would like. In this way, we are asked not to debate the use of such powers, to consider whether it is appropriate say for the government to spy on all of our communications, we are subtly being asked, 'How afraid would you like to be?'.

The threat is an effective one. To hand over extra powers or accept the acts of those who govern in our name is to ask that fear be excised from our lives. Such threats, when spoken by our leaders, become a soothing siren's song. And this is the ultimate cost of terrorism. People aren't called upon to be citizens in a democracy – to think and debate. They are cajoled and frightened into becoming unthinking subjects who give away their liberty so that their life can be a little freer from fear. Such is the age of terror. Our leaders no longer offer us the means to fulfil our dreams but ask us to quietly sacrifice our rights so they may try to end our nightmares. And that fear – the currency that greases all these machinations – is what Hassan Butt and those running him, helped breed and perpetuate. It is because of him, and doubtless others like him, that control and power were able to be purchased off the backs of our fear.

Yet we all have the ability to control our terrors. In our centuries-long battle to impose clear lines of cause and effect upon the complexities of life, we are the ones who force ourselves to succumb to the power of the soothing narrator and his clever acts of deception. We are the ones who trick ourselves in order to feel better.

As a narrator myself, I know how deep these acts of deception can run. I refused to see the complexities of what was before me with Hassan. The archetypal young angry Muslim was no such thing. It was a role he acted brilliantly but underneath, there was an entire world of emotion and contradiction. Nor was Hassan Butt a redeemed radical turned saviour – that was my concoction so that the story of his life, which I spent so long working on, would arc into a perfectly neat conclusion to make my reader feel hopeful about the world they lived in. It was a false hope.

It does not have to be like this. In times of distress we do not have to be dependent on simplistic stories, and vulnerable to the power of those who wield them. Instead of succumbing to our fears, we can elevate ourselves. The incomprehensible needn't be threatening. The messenger does not have to control us with his messages.

Two and a half thousand years ago, when the world was full of horrifying mysteries and the potentiality for terror abounded in ways we cannot comprehend today, there were those who knew the antidote to fear was not bigger armies, greater power for the king or the subjection of a nation's people. They understood the antidote to fear was reason.

In the midst of war, grieving the dead and on the precipice of disaster, Athens's 'first citizen' Pericles did not call upon those gathered to put greater faith in the Oracle or their king. They had no king; they were a democracy. He explained that they would deal with the great terror of war with reason. It was, he reminded each and every man, the responsibility of the citizen to be involved in politics – to debate, to argue each policy. Never was this more true than in times of war and uncertainty. Reason, he argued, would give them fortitude. That way they could understand their enemy and inform themselves of the danger and potential for great tragedy, but also the capacity for reward. In their forum, they would lay bare the full complexity of what they faced.

This was the source of one the city's greatest strengths and what made Athens an education for all Greece, Pericles argued. 'Others are brave out of ignorance; and, when they stop to think, they begin to fear. But the man who can most truly be accounted brave is he who best knows the meaning of what is sweet in life and of what is terrible, and then goes out undeterred to meet what is to come.'

In an age of demagogues who wield fear as a weapon, we'd be wise to pay heed to such ancient wisdom. Terrible things have always existed and will always exist. There will always be shocks, disasters and sudden horrors. In these moments we will be all too eager to accept the story that make us feel the world is certain again. And all too often those stories will be riven with fantastic fictions because they are being delivered by those seeking to manipulate us for their own purposes. But manipulative fictions can never truly make calamity less terrifying. Only cold, careful reason can do this. And when we recognise that our desire to believe in dangerous myths says more about ourselves than those myths can ever tell us about the world, we will be able to act humanely and sanely. The messenger is never all he seems because we will forever try to seek out the easiest path to a life free of fear. Remember that. In that truth lies your freedom.

END NOTE

In 2018, Hassan Butt was found guilty of orchestrating a massive online fraud and sentenced to thirteen years in prison.

ACKNOWLEDGEMENTS

This book's existence is due in very large part to those who gave their support, not just in the writing, but in the unfolding of the events described (as the events described unfolded).

I am indebted to Martin Bright, Richard Watson, Jim Booth, Masood Khan, Nick Cohen, Ian Cobain, Ian Katz, Nicholas Hellen, Mustafa Khalili, Innes Bowen, David Taub, Jan Thompson, Salil Tripathi and the staff at the *New Statesman*, for their sharp journalistic guidance and editorial support; Padraig Reidy for warming the courthouse benches and fighting for source protection; Karrie Fransman for coordinating my fundraiser, and Annabel Schild for her particularly generous contribution; Roy Mincoff, Rhona Friedman, Neil O'May and Alex Balin for battling so hard for me in the courtroom; Sylvia Whitman for always being up for getting entangled; Keith Ibbetson for giving me a space to think in; David Lee, JS Rafaeli, Hilary Drummond, Marina Kemp and Mona Chalabi for reading and even rereading drafts; Becky Hardie for grappling with the earliest incarnations; and the Bonis and my darling sister for doing what families do best. I shall quite literally never be able to repay Jeremy Dear and the NUJ, and Mark Skipworth and the *Sunday Times* for backing my legal battle, and of course English Pen for their campaigning on my behalf.

Special thanks must go to my agent Sophie Lambert, not just for keeping the faith but for putting up with my interminable silences and delays. My editor Laura Hassan, you have been persistent, incredibly brave, and searingly incisive at every turn. Gill Phillips, I am eternally privileged for every minute of your counsel. Ed Howker, you brought me back from despair's edge and kept me in journalism, for which I cannot thank you enough. My mother, you are a rock and always expert at navigating a crisis. My wife – I'm so, so sorry this has hung over every single year of our life together. Thank you for loving me.